To: My great one
Friend.

Dr. _____

Fatal Analysis

Fatal Analysis

A True Story of Professional Privilege and Murder

Dr. Martin Obler
and
Thomas Clavin

New Horizon Press   Far Hills, NJ

Requests for permission should be addressed to:

New Horizon Press

P.O. Box 669

Far Hills, New Jersey 07931

Obler, Martin and Clavin, Thomas

Fatal Analysis: A True Story of Professional Privilege and Serial Murder

Library of Congress Catalog Card Number: Pending

ISBN: 0-88282-152-0

Interior Design: Howard Simpson

New Horizon Press

Manufactured in the U.S.A.

2000   1999   1998   1997 /   5   4   3   2   1

...he was hesitating between two kinds of morality; on the one side, the morality of sympathy, of personal devotion and, on the other side, a morality of a wider scope but of more debatable validity. He had to choose between those two. What could help him to choose? ...Which is the hardest road?...Which is the most useful aim, the general one of fighting in and for the whole community, or the precise aim of helping one person to live? Who can give an answer to that *a priori?* No one.... It is in this world that man has to decide what he is and what others are.

Jean-Paul Sartre
Existentialism and Humanism

Acknowledgments

We would like to thank our wives, Robyn and Nancy, for putting up with us during the intense work on this book, and our children for their help and patience — Gil, Dita, Ricky, Alicia, Kathryn, and Brendan.

Thanks also to Dr. Joan Dunphy for her encouragement and editing, and to colleagues and others who assisted in the preparation of this book who for reasons of confidentiality cannot be mentioned here.

Authors' Note

This book was inspired by and is based on Dr. Martin Obler's real experiences as a therapist. It reflects his perceptions and opinions of the past, present and future. In order to comply with confidentiality as well as to protect the privacy of himself and others, we have changed, added or altered some names, events and locations. The personalities, actions, conversations and events have been reconstructed from Dr. Obler's memory, documents, personal papers and press accounts. In some instances chronology has been altered.

Contents

Prologue

Standing in the shadowed doorway waiting for her to meet me, I felt like a criminal. Funny thing, the person I was waiting for was a cop.

There had been another murder, and Detective Callahan was not happy with me. Furious would be more accurate. She figured I knew how it happened, why, and who did it. She was right. Would I tell her? I wanted to, but I hoped I wouldn't.

If I was really smart, I told myself, I'd take off now and keep walking, fast, and not turn back. Keep going too, out of this cesspool of a city with its victims and psychopaths—and people like me, who existed in the middle and every day faced the risk of becoming one or the other.

As I was about to step out of the doorway, Callahan got out of an unmarked car about two hundred feet up Eighth Avenue. The car turned down a side street and double-parked. As Callahan approached, her wavy red hair bounced and her legs flashed as she walked briskly in the waning winter sunlight. I reminded myself that she was smart and tough, one of the best Homicide had.

I could tell by the look on her face she was angry. Maybe this time she'd follow up on her threat to arrest me. She couldn't get me on murder one, but accessory might stick. If I was on the jury I'd vote to convict me.

Callahan drew closer, her eyes scanning ahead in search of me. I pressed back against the doorway of the abandoned shop. It used to sell magazines, cigarettes, and who knew what else. The owner had been shot to death during a robbery a few weeks ago. It was in all the newspapers but the stories were short: there wasn't much reader interest in such a routine killing on the West Side of New York City.

Not like the murders I was involved in. The headlines screamed those details. It was only a matter of time before the stories included my name, for either concealing the killer or becoming his latest victim.

I was already acting the part of a fugitive. To get to this rendezvous I'd skulked around like someone trying to elude the police, instead of meeting a cop. Surreptitiously, I left my office in Greenwich Village an hour before, took the subway to the Upper West Side, switched to the crosstown bus through Central Park, caught the Lexington line at 86th and took it to Grand Central, then the #7 train to Times Square, and finally walked the last few blocks to this doorway—all the time glancing over my shoulder.

I hadn't seen anyone that looked like him. Of course, that didn't mean much with his predatory behavior and talent for disguise. But I was pretty sure he hadn't followed me. When he was close, I sensed his presence.

The detective was now twenty feet away. Her green

eyes shifted quickly. Was she scared? Probably not. I was. Not just for myself but for the people I loved, especially my children and Rachel. He wouldn't hesitate to go after them. The only thing stopping him was that he realized killing the people I loved would terminate his game. For him, my vulnerability meant his power.

That wasn't the only insurance. He knew the dilemma I was in concerning therapist and patient confidentiality and all that went with it. He was the killer who roamed free and I was the one trapped. I shivered.

Callahan drew nearer. Five more long-legged strides and she stopped. She turned her head halfway, then tilted it, nodding slightly. She knew. She'd been down many more mean streets than I had.

I emerged from the doorway and we walked together, almost sauntering. We turned the corner. When we stood outside a place that sold hot dogs and fruit drinks, its awning orange and its glass windows protected with wire mesh, she turned to face me. There were a lot of people rushing by, most of them workers beginning the trip home. Later, when it had been dark for a couple of hours, the only people left here would be hookers, drug dealers, and old grizzled men who carried the boxes in which they lived on their backs like turtles. Perhaps my future, if I couldn't figure a way out of this.

"How long are you going to let this go on, Dr. Obler?" Callahan said. Her head was tilted up to me, green eyes flashing, red hair swirling. "I want him."

My stomach clenched. "I want you to have him."

"Two words, that's all."

"I can't," I replied in a hesitant, agonized voice.

Her smile was close to a sneer. "I was thinking more of a first and last name."

"I can't give you that. You know the position I'm in. If I help you, then. . . ."

I had to stop: it was useless to continue. I felt useless, because Callahan believed I was the key to solving these murders and preventing more of them.

The way this tough cop was glaring at me, I felt ashamed. I had agonized for so long. I didn't know if I was doing the right thing. In her world it was cut and dried. Not in mine. Whichever way I went led to ruin. I thought she understood that. Maybe she did, but right now she didn't care.

Callahan took a step back. "Why did you agree to meet me?"

"Because you asked me to." My shrug turned into another shiver. She saw it, but her glare didn't soften. "I keep thinking I'll figure out an answer," I explained.

"I know the answer: put the animal in a cage."

The sun was disappearing behind the buildings along the Hudson River. A blast of wind hit us, making my eyes water and her hair stand almost straight up. Her hands were in the pockets of her long brown coat. I wondered where she kept her gun and her handcuffs and her Miranda card.

"I can't do it," I said softly.

"You have to, damn it!"

"I'm sorry."

Whatever would happen would happen now. I turned away and began walking. I heard the click of her heels; then her hand gripped my arm. Maybe she was putting me under arrest.

Her face was close to mine. A few strands of her hair whipped my jaw. Her breath felt warm and moist on my face.

"There is a serial killer on the loose, Dr. Obler," Callahan said fiercely. "You know who and where he is. If you don't help me bring him down you'll be just as responsible as he is when he kills again. Don't you under-stand that?"

"Yes."

Her grip on my arm tightened. "So what are you going to do?"

Chapter 1

High Tide

The nightmare began innocently, on a cool, bright morning in late September.

I was in my office waiting for my new patient to arrive, gazing out the window. The office was located on the top floor of a five-floor walk-up in Greenwich Village. The large window overlooked a street of mostly brownstone houses and small shops.

This was a section of Manhattan that was primarily residential and considered relatively free of crime. The safety factor was important for my patients, who more recently were of an economic and social class that did not want to feel vulnerable on the way to a therapist.

This would be my first appointment of the day. The rush hour was already over. The few people on the street walked rapidly, late for work and dressed in conservative business suits and swinging dark leather briefcases while glancing repeatedly at watches that glinted when exposed to the strong sunlight. Others were homemakers or students who wore a wide variety of casual clothes and walked more slowly. The homeless and night workers struggled by to whatever they called home.

There was a pervasive sense of relief that summer seemed to have ended in the city. The last heat wave had moved on, making room for the Canadian air that forecasters assured would cool us off.

Below, at the entrance to my building, I saw a flash of a blond pony tail and broad shoulders before the door closed behind him. From what I'd been told, that would be Devon.

I sat behind my desk toying with my pen. It would be several minutes before he entered the office. First, he would have to scan the directory for my office number since it was his first visit. The elevator never seemed to be waiting on the first floor, and it was so rickety that its descent to the lobby and then rise to my floor would certainly slow his progress. Even more so considering this young man probably was nervous and reluctant to go through with this appointment.

He might even pause for a minute or two outside my door, contemplating if there was some way to avoid going ahead, before pressing the bell. And I would wait a full minute before buzzing him in. In my profession, it was embarrassing to appear anxious or eager, even though the fact was I felt a bit of both about meeting Devon.

He would enter a small anteroom containing four uncomfortable wooden chairs, a table laden with out-of-date magazines on inappropriate topics like boating, skiing, and bridge, a lamp with only a forty-watt bulb, and a small square window that displayed a portion of the brick wall of the adjacent building.

For some time I had been planning to find another office, one more contemporary and upscale, but I just hadn't gotten around to it. Part of me didn't want to. I knew this neighborhood. I felt comfortable in it, and I still wasn't completely comfortable with my increasing success.

Perhaps my insecurity was why I'd gone along so readily with Erwin Pomerantz's telephoned request. Dr. Pomerantz was the Dean of Counseling at a major university nearby with a national reputation in the psychology field. When he requested something, especially from a younger colleague who did indeed owe him a favor or two, only the most self-centered and disinterested person would refuse. And, in truth, he had also aroused my curiosity.

I heard the elevator creaking down to the narrow lobby. Knowing I had several moments before Devon would enter the anteroom, I reviewed my conversation with Pomerantz a few days earlier.

"There's a graduate student at the university I'd like you to evaluate," Pomerantz had said.

"What's the matter, is your staff on vacation already?" I jokingly replied.

His voice remained serious. "An initial, short-term consultation is all I ask. I'd appreciate your evaluation."

The *your* was emphasized in his reply. That's always flattering, especially from an esteemed and experienced professional.

"What can I do?" I asked with the intent to be polite even as a small voice in my head complained, *Marty, you fool, you've already committed yourself.*

Pomerantz told me the student's name was Devon Cardou, that he was twenty-seven and that he was pursuing a doctorate in psychology. He added that Devon was a fine looking young man "with an extra dose of charisma" and that he was the one of the most brilliant students in the university's program.

"Maybe *I* should consult with *him*," I offered, with a sinking feeling that humor didn't stand a chance.

Pomerantz sighed, and the implication was that this was the last snappy line he would tolerate. I pictured his bushy grey eyebrows knitted below a thick shock of white hair that made the nest above his pushed-up black-framed eyeglasses.

"Dr. Obler," he said with intimidating formality. "This young man has the potential for a great career. He has clear advantages in his background as well as his intelligence and energy. A generation from now you and I may be adhering to standards he has set."

"But?"

Pomerantz gave a different sigh this time. "But he is disturbed."

Okay, Marty, get him to tell you more. "In what way?"

"There is no clinical evidence," Pomerantz said quickly. "Yet there are reported behavior problems that I believe need to be addressed if he is to successfully continue in this program."

I waited for him to elaborate. Pomerantz was a gruff, direct man. His stature in the field meant he never had to worry about stepping on toes or, in fact, refrain from asking for a favor, which I knew was the reason for this call.

"What are the problems?" I finally asked.

He lowered his voice. "They are of a sexual nature. Because of student confidentiality rules at the university, I cannot be specific."

Now I sighed. "Dr. Pomerantz," I began, feeling suddenly like a graduate student myself, "of course I will do an evaluation simply because you want me to. However, if you are genuinely concerned about this Devon, you must realize that I have to know what the hell I'm supposed to talk to him about. If it's sex, have him take a class or talk to his father. I'm uncomfortable talking to my own son about it."

He laughed, caught off-guard, then sobered abruptly. "Marty, how about this part of the conversation never happened."

"What conversation?"

"Okay. Devon has a way of intimidating his fellow students. It's a combination of the force of his personality and his superior intellect. One result is they would not confront him directly about a problem."

"And the problem is?"

"Reports have come to me from others in the dormitory that he has frequent liaisons in his room. The sexual partners are male as well as female."

The discomfort in Pomerantz's voice was evident.

I said carefully, "Obviously, there are health-related concerns or the complaints may be fueled by envy. In college young men and women do a lot of sexual experimentation. Why are you getting involved?"

"The complaints include reports of strange noises, including screams, cries, and other stuff," he replied. "To be blunt, I'm afraid there is perverted acting out going on that may very well include violence. One especially nosy student claims that a couple of Devon's *conquests* were much younger males who were not seen again after they entered his room."

"Casual sexual partners wouldn't necessarily lurk around or return," I offered. Of course, Pomerantz knew this, but whatever else there was I wanted him to come out and say it.

Instead, after a pause he added, "Marty, I'm convinced you are the only one to work with this young man."

"Work with him?"

He backtracked, fumbling. "I should have said, give an evaluation. I would be grateful for a report from outside the university."

The underlying meaning was clear. Devon, for reasons that weren't obvious to me, couldn't be handled in-house. The university had the option to just boot him out, but there were good reasons not to, such as his brilliance and potential. Another option had to be found, and apparently I was it. Yes, I was curious. And it was more than flattering that such an esteemed colleague was turning to me for the answer.

"I can see him next Wednesday at ten o'clock."

"Thank you, Marty." Pomerantz's sigh expressed even more appreciation than his words. "I don't want to lose this young man. And, of course, I have to think of the university."

"Yes."

"I'll messenger over what information I can about him," Pomerantz had said.

The bell rang, forcing me to break away from my thoughts. I imagined Devon standing in front of the outer door, perhaps tugging at his clothes, smoothing his hair, or even peering into the peephole. I *was* anxious and eager to meet him, but I held back from pressing the button under my desk.

The information Pomerantz had sent over wasn't too revealing. Devon did indeed have an excellent academic background, nearly all A's and his IQ was 154. Early on he seemed to be on a fast track to becoming a leader in the psychology field, or whatever other profession he chose to pursue.

I felt momentarily insecure. I reminded myself that I had handled a variety of cases in the last few years. Sexual dysfunction and related aberrant behavior were my specialities. The papers I had, of late, published in professional journals had been viewed as significant advances in the field and my practice was thriving. Professionally, I was advancing.

Probably it was no coincidence that my personal life was not. A too early marriage, which had produced a son and daughter, the finest children parents could have, had dissolved. The fault was largely mine. My devotion to my career and lack of involvement with the family were the primary reasons my wife had divorced me. I was completely committed to helping others, and the price paid along the way was spending too little time with the people I should have loved without reservation. For a while I was alone.

Then I'd met Rachel, a beautiful and giving woman. She and a boyfriend had participated in a workshop I conducted at the university. They had some problems, sexual and otherwise, to be worked out before they got married. I had been attracted immediately. So had she. The boyfriend had faded away. I was falling in love, and so it seemed was she, but I still was unsure about any future. The memory of my previous failings unnerved me. I figured we should take our time and be sure.

The last thing I needed now as I tried to balance my need to forge a new relationship with my children and the woman in my life was a difficult case. I could choose from among fairly simple and lucrative ones. There was no need to take on a challenge; yet Pomerantz had stirred not only my curiosity but flattered me by saying I was needed. I was still young for a therapist, rising in my profession and believed, as my father used to say, the world was my oyster.

Then I nearly drowned.

Chapter 2

Fateful Meeting

He had been waiting long enough so I pressed the buzzer that let Devon Cardou into the anteroom. There was no hesitation on his part: a moment later a firm, loud knock sounded on the office door.

"Come in!" I called.

In walked Devon—strode was more like it. I'd been wrong to envision a nervous graduate student, hunched over and shifting eyes. The air in the office seemed to disassemble and reform when he entered.

"How are you?" he asked, grinning.

I walked around my desk and shook his extended hand. It was a strong grip, his hand dry and cool, and the strength of his muscled arm was evident. He wore a tan blazer, a denim shirt, jeans and loafers. His clothes were well made, expensive looking, and fit him perfectly.

I realized that even if I were blind I would have sensed by his heavy steps a physical strength. Looking at him more closely I saw a slightly muscled chest, slim waist, thick thighs and long arms and legs.

He was taller than I by three or four inches, and I had to raise my eyes to meet his. They were a vibrant blue-green, almost shining, changing color, and during the time we shook hands they did not blink until, as though realizing they should, the lids sank slowly and then rose quickly, the eyes becoming even brighter.

"Dr. Obler," he said, "I presume."

I winced and he laughed, a boisterous guffaw. "I know," he said, his voice a bit too loud, "you've heard that before. *Stanley and Livingstone*, Spencer Tracy, 1939. Do you like old movies, Dr. Obler? Tracy's easy, but knowing Charles Coburn was in it is a real test."

He continued to grin at me, finally releasing my hand. I didn't know what to say first, to answer the question and get sidetracked or get down to business. He appeared quite charming with a flavor of grandiosity; a young man one would enjoy meeting at a party. However, this wasn't one.

I murmured that I was pleased to meet him and motioned him to the only other place to sit in the office, a straight-backed wooden chair. He glanced around the room, taking in the half-dozen bookcases that lined the wood-paneled walls. Only recently had I been able to afford to fill the shelves with books, and now I didn't have the time to read any of them.

"What, no couch?" he said, still grinning as he settled into the chair. He crossed his long legs and clasped his large hands in his lap.

I sat behind the wide mahogany desk. "Surely you know that has become a rare feature in a therapist's office."

"When I practice, I plan to reintroduce it," Devon

replied. "Perhaps wicker instead of leather, trendy as well as comfy."

I realized that I felt uncomfortable while he appeared to be completely at ease, as if we had traded places. Maybe the university therapists had felt the same way. Or maybe Pomerantz's confidence in me was misplaced.

After a few general questions on his background, family life and living conditions, I decided to take the initiative and be direct. "Devon, I've spoken to Dean Pomerantz and apparently there is some concern about your completing the doctoral program, let alone practicing psychology."

"Oh, I see. Why?"

I took a deep breath and slowly let it out. It was obvious he wanted to play a game. Basketball was my passion, and I compared Devon to a player who dribbled around and faked once too often before taking a shot. I went right to the hoop.

"Apparently, he has received reports from other students about your behavior. Specifically, that you have entertained visitors in your room in the dormitory for sex. These 'liaisons,' as he termed them, are with males as well as females."

I looked directly at him. There was no reaction. I went on, "Despite the evidence of academic achievement, there is concern that you are not directing all of your energy toward your studies and, in the process, are creating problems with other students. I can surmise that Dean Pomerantz feels these activities and problems do not support the training you need to successfully complete the program."

I hadn't intended to be so longwinded, but I wanted to choose my words carefully. Maybe Devon, even with his

high IQ, had to digest them slowly because he didn't at
once respond.

In fact, even after a minute passed, he didn't say anything. That minute stretched to five. It wasn't an awkward
silence necessarily, though I felt a drop of perspiration course
down my spine. There was a slight smile on his smooth hand-
some face as he gazed clear-eyed at me. I was starting to
count the seconds between blinks when he finally spoke.

"Let me ask you this. Do you have confidence in
Pomerantz's abilities?"

He sat forward, uncrossing his legs and placing his
hands (I noticed the fingernails were well manicured) on
his knees.

"I'm aware of his reputation," Devon continued.
"Everyone in the program reveres him. But now, today, is he
still regarded as a pioneer in his field?"

He had made a quick, surprising thrust forward and I
felt him getting past me. "Dr. Pomerantz is viewed as a
remarkable professional," I said quickly.

"A pioneer?"

"Well. . . ." The issue here wasn't defending a colleague but to discuss Devon's situation. "Yes, at one time.
His work is found in many texts. Is he breaking new ground
today? I'm not sure that's true."

Devon smiled and sat back, crossing his legs again. I
couldn't see his feet, but I heard the subtle sound of one
loafer slapping against his heel. He ran a hand through his
hair, flinging it over one shoulder.

"I respect your candor, Dr. Obler. I believe we'll get along
just fine."

"You do."

"Yes. I'm aware that you are to evaluate me, which may require several visits." He placed one long finger against his chin. "I've also done some reading and asking around. Your star is ascending. Some colleagues envy you, perhaps more so than mine envy me. That's not idle boasting. My relationships with fellow grad students and with Pomerantz are the issues here." He stopped smiling. "I'm genuinely pleased that if I'm forced to . . . if it is recommended that I be evaluated, that it's by you."

The flutter of response I felt to the flattery was disturbing, indicating a vulnerability I had to guard against. I sensed in that moment that his intelligence was very supple and varied, and that I also had to guard against feeling intellectually inferior even if it turned out that I was.

"I appreciate your comments, Devon. However, I would like to turn back to. . . ."

Quickly he leaned forward, an earnest, almost pleading expression on his face. The blue eyes appeared larger.

"Dr. Obler," he said "I am in a very difficult position. Forgive my bluntness, but I am someone with an enormous amount of energy who requires—is not distracted by, but *requires*—that there be more in my life than my studies. Am I strongly interested in sex? Yes. Am I bisexual? I don't know. Don't young people engage in experimentation?"

It was as if he'd heard my response to Pomerantz a few days before. "Yes," I said uncomfortably.

"And as a psychologist, I would be surprised if you were opposed to homosexuality," he said.

"Not per se. Do you view yourself as a homosexual?"

"No."

A direct, forceful statement. Then he relaxed, leaning sideways in the chair and throwing one long arm over the back.

"Let's put this situation in perspective, Dr. Obler." He raised one finger. "One, other students on my floor, male and female, are jealous of several aspects about me, including my ability to attract sexual partners. Let's face it. Many of those nerds couldn't get laid by their own shadows." He laughed loudly and exclaimed, "Though God knows in the supposed privacy of their rooms they try!"

"Do you think what they do is shameful?"

"Of course not. You do what you can in the absence of other willing flesh. However, they apparently feel I should be ashamed of my conquests and my conduct, or they wouldn't be crying about it." Then he added, tossing it off, "And obviously Pomerantz has his own problems."

I didn't disagree with him, until he mentioned Pomerantz. Keeping my voice even I said, "I'm very interested in learning what those problems are."

Again he gazed expressionless at me for a long time. By this point our conversation seemed very long, though it had probably taken no more than a few minutes. Then he grinned.

"Dr. Obler, can I match you in complete candor?"

"Please."

"I accept that Pomerantz has had a distinguished career. There are hundreds if not thousands of people walking around today who are leading more fulfilling, satisfying lives because of his therapeutic innovations. He may well be a hero, as you could be one day."

"But?"

"But he's old news. Yesterday's textbook entries. As a person he is old-fashioned, restrained and probably repressed. He is unable to handle the changes in social mores as well as those in his profession. Frankly, I believe he finds my activities, behavior, interests, whatever you want to call it, inappropriate because they do not conform with his version of morality."

His voice slipped into a hesitant, southern twang. "What we have here is a failure to communicate.' Strother Martin, the prison boss in *Cool Hand Luke*, 1967."

Devon grinned and shook his head. "Sorry, I know I'm being silly. Growing up I spent a lot of time in movie houses. Sometimes alone."

It took a moment for that comment to register with me. I wanted to pursue it, but he straightened up in the chair, making the wood creak.

"In all seriousness, Dr. Obler, to use an archaic phrase, the problem is not so much communication as it is a generation gap. The reports Pomerantz received should have been dismissed for what they were, expressions of envy. That they have not been indicates to me that he is at least or I should say, at best, uncomfortable with the sexual activities of today, and especially mine."

My head was almost spinning. Devon had indeed not only gotten past but around me several times. "Why should he single you out for disapproval?" I asked with less authority than I intended.

"Well, I'm complained about more," he said as if instructing a slow pupil. "Other than that, I think you should ask him."

He leaned forward, the almost-pleading expression

on his face again. "Will you?"

"I believe I will."

Devon gazed at me for a few seconds, then slowly nodded. Maybe I misinterpreted his expression, but there was a hint of disappointment in his bright blue eyes.

"I would also like to resolve this problem," he said with clear sincerity. "It's interfering with what I want and need to do. Will we meet again?"

I stood up, my legs itching with pins and needles. "As you know, one discussion is not an evaluation. Shall we meet next week, same day and time?"

As his eyelids slowly lowered and rose, I noticed how long and fine the lashes were. "Your place or mine?" he said.

I laughed, trying to hide my nervous release. "I look forward to seeing you again, right here."

"I do too."

He rose from his chair and we shook hands across the desk. Devon offered one last quick grin, then turned and strode out of the office, leaving the door open behind him. I heard the outer door quickly open and shut.

I realized I had been holding my breath and slowly exhaled. Devon was very special. At that moment, however, I couldn't define what "special" meant other than to acknowledge with a sinking feeling that at the same stage in my life I hadn't been that special.

Gazing out my window at the gleaming sunlit street, I wasn't sure if seeing Devon again would be all that useful. For all his intelligence, perhaps eccentricity, and reported strange behavior, he might very well be one of the gifted young men often found at major universities who liked to push the envelope a bit. Would it really be helpful, to him or to the university, to address what could be side issues at the risk of thwarting the development of a brilliant career?

Even if the answer was yes, did I have the ability to intervene and help him?

Looking out the window, I saw the front door of the building open, and again I saw the flash of bright blond hair and broad shoulders. Then he was gone. Damn my curiosity and whatever else in me would not allow this to be the end of it.

I called Pomerantz. He was in a meeting. I told the departmental secretary that I was inviting him to lunch on Friday. Sorry, his calendar was full. Monday then. She copied down the name of a restaurant close to the university, where I planned to meet up with Pomerantz.

I returned to the window. There was a half-hour until my next appointment. The sun was higher in the sky and its light bathed both sides of the street. I saw a man remove his jacket and a woman wiping a hand across her forehead. It might turn out to be a summerlike day after all. But for some reason I felt chilled.

Chapter 3

Spooked

I arrived at the university fifteen minutes before my scheduled meeting with Pomerantz. He had given me permission to go through Devon's academic file to find a little more personal background than he had supplied to me.

I'd wanted more. Specifically I wanted reports from any previous psychological testing or evaluations, but Pomerantz had growled, "I don't want a lawsuit on my hands. His family has friends in high places."

An attractive secretary, whose skirt was much too short for an office that saw a lot of hormone-crazed grad students, smiled as she handed me two files, and pointed to a bench against the wall. Then she retreated behind the partition that hid the inner workings of first-level administration from view.

The information in one of the files was more thorough but no more revealing than what I'd already learned, namely, that Devon's IQ was light years above average and at every previous academic level he had been at or near the top of his class. Other people would kill for such grades. Certainly when I was in school I would have.

I noticed two curious things in the reports: one was the lack of honors Devon had received and the few organizations in which he had participated. No big deal—with his grades, the extra-curricular activities that helped other students' portfolios and impressed admissions officers weren't needed. Odd though that someone with his charisma and energy hadn't gotten involved more with school activities or been more frequently recognized for his achievements.

The other thing I observed was that twice during his undergraduate career he had taken a semester off. This was probably insignificant too, because students sometimes have to interrupt school to work. I still winced thinking of the menial jobs I'd taken on, often two or three at a time, to support a young family while I was in graduate school.

The second file held only two sheets of paper. One told me the names of Devon's parents and a brother, a home address in Connecticut, Devon's status at the university, and other routine information like his Social Security number. The other sheet contained financial information about tuition and payment. Remarkably, given his academic accomplishments, Devon was not on scholarship nor had he taken out any loans. The family was footing the bill. It was also noted as an aside that Devon's grandmother, Sarah Bouvard, was a trustee of the university.

I returned the files to the secretary who accepted them through a slot in the partition. I walked over to the building which housed Pomerantz's office. He was just emerging from the building as I arrived, struggling into his overcoat and patting a hat down on his white hair. It was a misty, gloomy day. Summer's heat was only a memory.

"Are we going somewhere nice?" he asked.

"Of course."

"Then it's your treat. The university is cracking down on expense accounts."

"I would treat you anyway."

The Italian restaurant was three blocks away. We hurried, the damp breeze bathing our faces. As we handed our coats to the maitre d', drops of water fell from the end of Pomerantz's pipe. (As a student of his I'd idly wondered if he ever removed that pipe from his mouth, even for sex.) At the linen-covered table he ordered a scotch neat. Mineral water for me: I'd never cared for the taste of hard alcohol, which hadn't helped my popularity as a grad student.

"So you perused the files," Pomerantz began.

"Not much in them," I said. "Apparently tuition isn't an obstacle."

"Devon's family is of French extraction, prominent and rather wealthy. The father is in manufacturing. Clothing, I think. Took over from his father. Married into society. Not as much green on the mother's side, but the blood is blue."

The drinks arrived. Pomerantz inhaled half of his. After we ordered, he pushed his glasses to the top of his head.

"So what was your impression of Devon?"

I described our first meeting and concluded by saying, "My impression was a good one. He is extremely intelligent, obviously, and has charm and physical presence. There's some grandiosity and pretension about him, but God knows that would fit a lot of students operating at his level. Devon seems like an exciting young man. If I were a fellow student, I'd want to be around him."

"I felt the same way. However, it seems his fellow students do not." He finished off his drink and signaled the waiter for another. "He is not well liked. I would even say he is actively disliked and avoided."

"Envy? Jealousy?"

"No doubt some of that. But there are frequent complaints about his behavior and rumors about his nocturnal wanderings and activities in his room." Pomerantz shrugged. "By choice he has his own room. He can afford it."

I lowered my voice, because the tables were small and close together. "I'd like to bypass a fishing expedition. During our conversation last week you mentioned 'perverted acting out' and 'liaisons' with members of both genders. After seeing him, I'm not surprised that Devon has no difficulty attracting sex partners."

Pomerantz was about to interrupt when his drink arrived. He sipped it as I continued, "When you said 'strange noises' and the like, what were you dancing around?"

He put the glass down with most of its contents gone. "Marty, there is little specific information I can give you."

"Because of ethical concerns, or you don't have it?"

"Both."

Pomerantz rubbed his face, leaving a glistening trail of condensation on one cheek. The glasses slipped down. The lenses did not hide what I saw in his eyes, and it startled me: he was afraid.

"Marty, he has undergone therapy before to address issues stemming from childhood."

"That wasn't in the files."

"I can't release such information."

This time I shrugged. He was ignoring the discreet ways that we both knew to pass on confidential information. Pomerantz was genuinely nervous.

"Anyway," he went on, "there are, I believe, unresolved childhood issues that affect his adult outlook and behavior. I do not have direct evidence, but I also believe that his sexual encounters include violence. To what extent I don't know."

I mulled this over. It still wasn't what I needed. "I'm not freewheeling enough, as a psychologist or as a person, to accept 'rough sex' as normal," I said. "But people his age do a certain amount of acting out that really can't be construed as perverted. It doesn't mean that there is real damage occurring, physically or psychologically, or that they will be lifelong practices."

Pomerantz drained the rest of his drink, pushed his eyeglasses back up, and smiled. "You've done so well lately that you can lecture me."

I felt myself reddening. "I'm sorry. Of course I'm stating the obvious. I'm just trying to gauge what you're asking me to get into. My initial impression was that this is a bright young man who may think he's invincible, and maybe he's engaging in some sordid practices. I'm sure he's not the only one."

"I agree there." Pomerantz was about to order another drink when our food appeared. He hesitated, then sipped from a water glass. "But I strongly suspect that Devon is very disturbed. If I tell you more, I put the university at risk. If I don't tell you enough, I'm worried something might happen that would also jeopardize the university *and* someone else *and* result in Devon being tossed out."

He sighed. "Marty, I do want to see this young man do well. He may be at a crossroad where one path leads to a brilliant career."

"Okay, I believe you. But I need a little more, so let me go first. In our session last week, Devon contended that your attitude toward his perceived or rumored behavior is based on generational conflict. People in their twenties are doing all kinds of things now that ten years ago no less thirty or forty years ago were considered inappropriate."

I laughed, trying to lighten the mood. The scotch hadn't seemed to do that for Pomerantz. "Hey," I said, "I feel cheated that I didn't do more carousing when I was in grad school."

Pomerantz cleared his throat and slipped the glasses back down over his eyes for a moment before pushing them back on the top of his head again. "I met with Devon to talk about this. It was the strangest session I've ever had. It was almost frightening."

"In what way?" He had me now. An expert fisherman couldn't have used better bait. "You were scared?"

"Well . . . no, not exactly. Perturbed is more like it." He paused, then spoke rapidly. "We talked. I expressed some of the concerns that had been brought to me, Devon immediately apologized for distracting his fellow students and admitted that he was less than discriminating in his sexual interests."

"There you have it. We all have youthful regrets."

"No!" Pomerantz exclaimed. "Hell, if it were that I could've left it with a simple reprimand: be more goddamn discreet. In fact, I was about to do that. I almost felt sorry for him, thinking he was more a victim of jealousy. I put my hand on his shoulder and was about to offer sympathy when he suddenly twisted away, jumped up, and glared at me." Pomerantz paused, then added, "I've never seen a look like that."

"Did he say anything?"

"He said I wanted to fuck him."

"What?"

"He accused me of . . . well, he went on in a very descriptive fashion, Marty. I was truly unnerved."

Pomerantz didn't have to explain. In his long and distinguished career he had handled and consulted on the most difficult cases of psychological distress. His expertise and resilience had established his respected reputation. After thirty years at a major university, he had to have seen everything. Until, apparently, now.

I also recalled that in our discussion last week Devon had mentioned that Pomerantz "has his own problems." But any implication that he had anything other than a sympathetic interest in Devon was ridiculous.

"After he left, I was shaken and didn't know what to do," Pomerantz continued. "I went over our discussion, reviewing what had occurred, looking for misinterpretations and exploring my own behavior. Finally, I listened to instinct. I am convinced that this young man is deeply troubled and also amazingly promising. If something isn't done one will win out over the other. I fear which one may be conqueror."

"Yes." I nodded. I didn't know what else to do except agree with Pomerantz's initial evaluation.

We had only picked at our food, and it was apparent that neither one of us was hungry. Two fashionably dressed women at the table next to us, who had tried not to be obvious about listening to our conversation, asked their waiter for the check. I did the same. Pomerantz and I rose and got our coats. We put them on and he popped his hat on slightly askew, tilted at an angle opposite from that of his protruding pipe.

Outside, the breeze was stronger, but drier. Huge gunmetal clouds raced across the sky and gave fleeting glimpses of the sun. We walked back toward the campus until Pomerantz turned down a side street.

"Marty, can you spare a few more minutes?" he asked.

"I've got a little time."

He led me south, away from the campus, then east and south again. Every few minutes, without speaking, he raised one arm and pointed. I saw dark-windowed bars and small nightclubs that either were not yet open or displayed no signs of being open other than dull, dirt crusted, flickering neon signs in the windows advertising beer.

At the corner of Spring Street Pomerantz paused. Somehow in the stiff breeze his hat had remained on his head, still at an angle. He removed his pipe and appeared about to comment further. His eyes were unfocused.

I tried another joke. "Tell me, Spirit, the meaning of these travels."

"From what I've been told," he began, allowing a brief smile, "what you see here are some of the haunts Devon frequents regularly—places other students avoid."

"Does he come here to buy drugs?"

"No." It was difficult to hear Pomerantz's hoarse voice in the wind. "Perhaps people."

"Meaning?"

"These are pickup bars and clubs, patronized by a rough crowd. Incidents are routinely reported to the police of fights and other activities, and we can only speculate about what doesn't get reported. Men and women of various ages are known to pick each other up here for sex, in any combination."

"Idle gossip? After all, if the students you encounter avoid such places, how do they know what goes on there?"

Pomerantz stuck the pipe in his mouth. "It *is* hearsay at best. And God knows jealous peers will concoct any story to damage the reputation of a brilliant fellow student they've targeted."

I let a few seconds pass.

Then I said, "I think you're right; it is best if someone outside the university does an evaluation of Devon."

Pomerantz looked at me, one bushy eyebrow raised. "You think we've lost our objectivity?"

"Maybe." I added quickly, "But if so, you're professional enough to recognize the possibility and take other action for a student's sake."

"And I've asked you."

"Yes."

"Because I think you're the best for this particular case and I know you have experience dealing with very difficult situations while keeping a balance."

I nodded, knowing he was referring to Moira, one of my early patients. While trying to help her, I'd come up against a formidable obstacle.

"Devon is to see me the day after tomorrow," I said. "I'll schedule enough additional sessions to do a full evaluation. You'll have my report in about a month."

"Thank you, Marty." The hand he extended for me to shake was cold and moist. "Walk back with me?"

"I have an appointment uptown, so I'll catch the subway."

"Good luck."

Pomerantz turned and walked away, huddled inside his bulky coat and pressing his hat down low enough so that it made his ears stick out. It appeared that he didn't want to be noticed in this neighborhood.

I shivered as I walked quickly west. The street was littered with pieces of newspaper and other garbage sent skittering by the wind. In doorways quivering old men were sprawled out asleep. Loud music blared from narrow delicatessen doorways interspaced with shabby clothing stores. A group of twentiesh young men dressed in black leaned against a row of street phones, watching me approach. I crossed the street and picked up my pace.

The sun appeared, sending shooting beams of lemon light that lasted for several seconds at a time. Out of the corner of my eye I saw a flash. It wasn't the light or a reflection but something else. Glancing across the street, I saw a flicker of breeze-blown blond hair. Then it was gone, disappearing around the side of a boarded-up building.

Was it the image I'd seen before outside my office last week? I shook my head. This was silly. Pomerantz had gotten me spooked too.

Chapter 4

Voices in the Night

The phone rang, shattering sleep. I roused myself. In my profession, calls after midnight come from time to time. It is never good news. But if you are a psychologist dealing with troubled people, you know that in the blackness of night fears often rise to the surface.

Reaching for the receiver, I groggily noticed the time: two o'clock Monday night. No, Tuesday morning.

"I might be in some sort of trouble." Devon's voice was strained and tense.

For a moment I wondered how he'd gotten my home number. Then I focused on his message.

"What sort of trouble?"

"I'm not sure if it's. . . ." His voice trailed off. Background sounds indicated hurried activity—people talking in quick bursts, swift footfalls made by soft-soled shoes, doors banging shut, a name called on an intercom.

"Devon, where are you?"

"I'm not telling," he said petulantly.

"A police station?"

"No one can connect me with the guy," he urgently cried.

"What guy? What's wrong with him?"

"He got hurt, and I brought him here. Good Samaritan, that's me. Now what should I do?"

Okay, I thought, a hospital. I sat on the edge of my bed. "Is he alive?"

"He got hurt, I told you!"

"Okay, okay," I said as calmly as I could. "We'll figure something out."

"There was a lot of blood."

"Did you hurt him, Devon?"

"I'll take care of this myself!" he said, his voice rising, growing out of control.

I was losing him. We'd met only once so I didn't know how best to soothe him. "I'll go wherever you are, to be with you," I said as calmly as I could. "Do you want that?"

"No. I don't know. No."

"I'll call someone else. A friend?"

"I have no friends."

Petulant again, like a little boy left on the front stoop while everyone else in the neighborhood headed to the movies or Yankee Stadium.

"Do you want me to call your parents?"

Mistake.

"Keep them out of this!" he screamed. Then his voice lowered. Weakly, he said, "I knew I couldn't trust a shrink."

"Devon, you can. . . ."

With sudden confidence he said, "Anyway, it's only a little blood. Just a blot really. Not a lot. I said a blot of blood, not a lot."

Strange laughter, beginning as a gruff exhalation, breathlessly escalated to a high pitch and pierced the line. For a moment I thought it was someone else on the phone. Then with a chill I realized it was Devon. The laugh evolved into a howl almost like a wolf call. I gripped the receiver. Chills raced up and down my spine.

I heard a click, then a dial tone. Other than being almost sure Devon had called from a hospital emergency room, I had no idea where he was or what had happened. I didn't get much sleep the rest of the night.

When I got to my office the next morning, my first call was to the university hospital. No one matching Devon's description had been there overnight. I tried other emergency rooms, choosing hospitals closest to the campus. A deep-voiced woman at the third emergency room said she thought the person I described sounded familiar, but couldn't tell me more.

I took a taxi there. It was a lukewarm morning that hinted of an Indian summer day to come. I had my jacket slung over my shoulder and tie loosened when I entered the emergency room.

I apologized to the receptionist for looking disheveled.

"You look all right to me," the husky nurse behind the wide desk said, smiling.

"Thanks, but I could use some help."

I described Devon, mentioned the time of the call and that he had apparently brought in someone injured and bleeding. "It's very important that I find out about the incident," I told her. I identified myself as a psychologist and mentioned the name of an administrator at that hospital whom I knew and said he would vouch for me.

"Let me call Dr. Perez," the nurse said, shrugging. "He's been on duty since yesterday."

A few minutes later a man in his early thirties emerged from behind double doors. He wore a blue smock, had curly black hair, and needed a shave. His red eyes implied he'd been on duty for a long time.

"What can I do for you, Dr. Obler?" His voice wasn't much above a whisper and had a Spanish accent. After I repeated what I'd told the nurse, he asked, "This Devon. Is he a patient of yours?"

Without hesitating, I replied, "Yes."

He nodded, then paused, then shook his head. "There isn't anything I can tell you. Like you, we've got confidentiality concerns."

"I understand. I'm not really asking about the patient you treated. The person with him, I'm interested in."

The way Dr. Perez looked at me, I knew if I wanted to bribe him all I'd have to offer was two hours of sleep. Finally, he said, "Good-looking guy with long blond hair, late twenties? Yeah, he was here. Brought in a kid about eighteen years old, also white, some scarring, rough life."

"What were the injuries?"

He shook his head again.

"Let's just say lacerations. Looked more serious than they were. Treated and released."

"And Devon?"

"He didn't stick around."

"Any chance I could see the paperwork?"

Dr. Perez grinned. "Assuming it's been done and you could read my handwriting?" Then the grin faded.

"Personally, I don't care. But I've got people to answer to, including the administrator you mentioned to the nurse." His expression grew thoughtful, and he added, "We've all got to cover our asses." He grinned again. I wondered if his remark was a clue.

"Sure," I said, feeling like I was missing something. "Thanks for your time."

He started to walk away, then turned back. "The other guy—this Devon. Be careful."

"Why?" I said warily.

He was still shaking his head as he pushed open the double doors. The nurse smiled at me. This time I shrugged and held out my hands, silently asking, "Can you give me more?" She shook her head negatively and kept her eyes down, studying a clipboard.

The rest of that day I had to make myself concentrate on my other patients. The day after that, Wednesday, was Devon's appointment. He didn't show up. I waited worriedly past the time and then made several calls to the university: to the psychology department office, Devon's dormitory monitor, and the counseling office.

I even called Devon's mother, using the number I had copied from the file. I got an answering machine with a deep male voice curtly instructing the caller to leave a brief message.

The only call on which I connected was to Pomerantz. After I told him what happened, he said he would call back. When he did, he reported, "No one has seen him. He's skipped classes. No sign of him coming in or out of his room. It's like he's vanished."

"If you could leave my number with. . . ."

"I may have called you in too late," Pomerantz inter-rupted, sighing.

"Or just in time. Something's going on."

"If I find out anything, I'll let you know," he said curtly.

For some reason I doubted that. There was a hint in his voice that he had lost interest and wouldn't be too sorry if Devon never appeared again. That bothered me, and I wondered about Pomerantz. Maybe Devon didn't get a fair shake from him. Don't wash your hands of a young person who might need help, I told myself.

I felt more and more tight and tense as the work week progressed. I needed some physical exercise. I wanted to feel a basketball between my hands and headed over to the university gymnasium. There were only a few other people there, none of whom I recognized, so I just shot baskets for a while.

It wasn't all that much of a workout, but it felt good to be lofting leather—or whatever it is they make basketballs out of these days—for an hour or so. While it's better to play a game, an advantage to fooling around on the court by yourself is your imagination can run free. In that hour I won a career's worth of NBA seventh game finals for the Knicks!

Years ago I'd played outdoors. Sometimes I was bold or foolish enough to try the West Fourth Street courts on Saturday mornings. There's a rigid protocol to those courts that must be followed if a player hopes to return. Some of the best basketball players in the city come there, and the games are tough enough to imagine playing in Madison Square Garden—but without full stands and big salaries.

As the day goes on, the players and the games get better and better. You start to notice a real difference by mid-morning. At 10:30, guys are jamming and, if they don't feel like choosing sides and playing a game right away, they hold contests, like swiping quarters off the tops of the metal backboards.

My skills are okay. I know how to play and love basketball. My wind is good, and I can consistently knock 'em down from fifteen to twenty feet from the basket. But once I get past twenty-five feet, it is crystal clear that my skills are one step above rudimentary.

When I reached thirty I started playing indoors because you're out of harm's way there. Not physical harm: ego hurt. It's easier to maintain daydreams when you can't glance aside and see players doing things as if they were afterthoughts that you can't do with every ounce of effort.

Leaving the gym that Friday evening, my imagination was still creating sports scenarios. I imagined I was leaving the Garden through the players' gate. Of course, no autograph seekers here. I was still in a hoop mood and there was some daylight left on the cool, crisp evening. I knew there was a public school playground a few blocks away, so I wandered over.

As I approached the tall chain-link fence around the court, I saw a game being played at one basket. The metal chains rattled as shots fell in. The players looked like high school kids. At the other basket was another group of high schoolers and one taller guy. They all smoked cigarettes. I couldn't see them clearly because the sun had gone behind the large red brick school building.

As I walked through the gate onto the court the group of high schoolers turned and walked away, all except the tall, lanky guy. He had long blond hair tied behind his head in a pony tail. As I came nearer, he gave me an uneasy grin just as I recognized him. He said, "Hello, Dr. Obler."

"Devon! What are you doing here?" I said, surprised.

He shrugged. "Just hanging out with some guys. What are *you* doing here?"

"I just wanted to watch."

"Yeah, that can be fun, huh."

The others had stopped and were leaning against the fence on the opposite side of the yard. Though I couldn't see their faces in the waning light, I could feel their eyes on us.

The one time I'd seen Devon he had been well dressed. Now he wore torn jeans, a stained white sweatshirt without sleeves, and untied moccasins without socks. He hadn't shaved in a few days. Walking closer to him, I noticed that the skin around his blue eyes was pinched as though he hadn't slept in a while.

"Devon, I've been looking for you."

"So I hear."

He appeared uncomfortable, as though I had interrupted something. "I wanted to. . . ." I began.

"Do you play?" he suddenly said in a loud voice, pointing to the ball under my arm.

"Not too bad. Not too good either. You?"

His slight grin faded. I had a strange feeling that he hadn't wanted to see me. I glanced over at the teenaged boys, feeling the intensity of their stares. They might have been staring at Devon. His shoulders were slightly hunched forward. He looked behind him at the kids, then stopped. Whatever was going on, I was the intruder.

"You're so-so, huh?" he said.

"It's exercise. I sit behind a desk so much that I like to

run the ball when I can." I started to back away. "Listen, I want to see you. How about we try again next week?"

He suddenly grinned and said, "Let's play."

"What?"

The grin grew wider. He straightened his shoulders. It was obvious he was speaking to our audience. "Want to play with me?"

There was an edge to his voice, but I couldn't read what it was. Maybe he felt a need to impress the youngsters by beating the executive-looking, desk-bound stranger. He stood a good chance. He was eight years younger, taller, and physically more powerful. The expression on his face now was total confidence and something more. He didn't just want to play and win, but dominate. I hadn't come here for that.

"Devon, it's almost dark and I have to get back to the office."

"Don't be scared, Dr. Obler. A friendly game, to seven. Five minutes, max."

Something was going on here. I agreed, not because I wanted to play but because I hoped if I went along Devon would be more likely to keep his next appointment. Tests of manhood usually weren't part of the therapy process, but this seemed important to him.

I tossed him the ball and unzipped my sweat jacket. "Take it out."

"Winner's out?"

"Your court, your rules."

"Fine." He gestured grandly toward the top of the key. "Then I'll let you go first."

The other game had ended, so there were over a dozen

people watching us. Devon got into an awkward defensive stance, bending his knees slightly with his hands dangling below them, his head straight up, balancing on the back of his feet. I dribbled toward him, then pulled up and launched the ball. The chains rattled.

Seeming genuinely hurt when I motioned for the ball, he asked, "Loser's out?"

"You made the rules. Play them."

He rifled the ball to me; strong, yet the motion indicated that he really didn't know how to play. I hit another jumper. Devon's face was turning red. "Go to the hoop," he said loudly.

"Win the best way you can. That's the game."

"Let's go."

He came up on me. Before he could set himself, I dribbled right around him and to the basket. That made him more angry. I didn't know what game he was playing, but I would play mine.

After a few minutes I allowed Devon to steal the ball. He grunted with satisfaction and, barely remembering to dribble, rushed to the hoop. His shot banged off the backboard and I chased it. He was breathing too hard to make the effort. I repeated the maneuver a few times and his moves to the basket didn't get any more graceful. I put two more in from the perimeter. He didn't come out at me enough through concern that I would go inside on him.

Devon wasn't catching on and it was obvious the game was pissing him off. Perhaps he would've been pissed off anyway, but it was apparent from the quick glances he threw to the spectators at the fence that it was worse losing in front of people he'd intended to impress. I couldn't figure out why he cared about the opinion and admiration of kids seventeen or eighteen years old. Maybe that was why—losing to an old man?

When I sank another shot, Devon didn't appear as angry. This was disturbing, as if he was humiliated. I decided it was best to end this game quickly. I sank one from about twenty feet, feeling all the eyes on me and thinking for a nanosecond that if I'd really pursued basketball in college, maybe. . . .

As Devon turned to me with the ball, I said, "That's seven. Game. You okay?"

His face was beet red and his breathing was harsh and rapid. Strands of damp hair that had come loose from his pony tail stuck to his face. He clenched his fists, straightening up. "Why game?" he asked.

I walked over to him. He looked lost and confused, like a kid betrayed by clumsiness he couldn't help and thus humiliated. I almost put a hand on his shoulder, but I recalled how he had reacted to a similar gesture from Pomerantz. "It's over, Devon. The sun's gone down. My tired old eyes can't see any more."

"Don't you pity me, Doctor!" he said through clenched teeth.

"I don't. You're too. . . ." I tried a smile. "You're too interesting and strong for that. I do want to see you again. Maybe when we're not sweating so much."

Devon straightened up and his face changed. He lost or managed to suppress his anger and shame. For a few seconds he gazed impassively at me.

"I'll be there Wednesday, Dr. Obler." The confident grin was back. "I want to try your court."

"You're on."

"Winner's out?"

I sensed that at this moment something had changed between us. Or would, if I went along. So I nodded and took the ball from his hands. "You want a rematch, come and see me."

Devon almost laughed, then stopped himself as though aware of the other eyes. "I won't lose again."

Chapter 5

Old Movies

Devon arrived for his appointment on time the following Wednesday, and again his appearance surprised me.

This time he wore the businessman look. He had on a perfectly tailored, dark blue suit that nearly matched the color of his eyes, a red and blue striped tie with what looked like a gold clasp, and brown loafers with tassels. His long blond hair was combed straight back and tied in a pony tail. He carried a small brown leather briefcase. His handshake was firm, and on his face was that slight smile.

"Very impressive," I said, indicating his outfit. "You look ready for Wall Street."

He laughed. "I was trying for Cary Grant in *North by Northwest*. 1959."

"I know, directed by Alfred Hitchcock. One of my favorites. I like suspense."

"Oh, you do? Just in movies?"

"Most of the time, that's the only time I encounter it."

I tried for a slight advantage. "Who played the older man who saves Grant and Eva Marie Saint at the end?"

"Leo G. Carroll. Too easy. *Man from U.N.C.L.E.* is on cable." He closed his eyes. "Who played one of James Mason's henchmen who later made it big in the *Mission Impossible* TV show? That's on cable too." He waited, grinning, then gave the answer. "Martin Landau."

Advantage Devon. We had switched from basketball to verbal tennis, and he'd made a sharp return.

"Please sit down," I said. "May I ask, other than Cary Grant's influence, why you are so well dressed today?"

"I did want to impress you with what a fine, upstanding citizen I really am."

I sat behind my desk. "I get the feeling that it's important to you to impress me. Why is that?"

He shrugged, then waited, gazing at me silently. His suaveness or good attempt at it bothered me. I even felt some irritation and that bothered me more. I tried another tactic.

"Devon, when you said the other evening that you 'heard' I was looking for you, was that a message from your parents?"

"My parents?" He raised one blond eyebrow.

"Yes. I had called and left a message."

"Why?"

"After the hospital incident, I wanted. . . ."

"The 'incident.'" He leaned back and crossed one long leg over the other. The tassels on his loafer quivered as he shook one foot. "You knew it was a hospital."

"Yes. And when I went there. . . ."

He leaned forward. "I haven't been in contact with my parents for quite some time."

"Were you ever going to come back here? To see me again?"

He leaned back. "Dr. Obler, if I wanted to see you, I could any time."

"That's not true. There are appointments."

"I could *see* you, and you wouldn't see me."

The room suddenly felt colder. "That makes me uncomfortable. It's almost as if you're describing a stalking situation."

"Dr. Obler, if I were to 'stalk' someone, he wouldn't see me. Or at least, shall we say, I wouldn't make my presence known."

"Why wouldn't someone see you?"

"They just wouldn't," he replied, grinning.

My annoyance was growing again. He was back in the Cary Grant mode. Damn his masking. I didn't want to spend this session playing parts. I wanted to get on with the evaluation and get at the truth.

"Devon," I began, placing my elbows on the desk and my chin atop clasped hands, trying to gain control over my emotions and regain my objectivity. "Who did you take to the hospital? How badly was he hurt? And what happened to him?"

"Which question do you want answered first?"

"Take your pick. Any answer would interest me."

He shifted in the chair, gripping the sides of the leather briefcase on his lap. "I overreacted."

"At what point?"

Devon stared at me. Once again, I found myself counting the seconds between blinks. A scintilla of past knowledge suddenly sprang to my mind. I had been taught that psychopaths stared for long intervals of time as they scouted, almost sensed their surroundings, evaluating what was presented to them, especially potential danger.

I shook off the thought. I did not present any danger and, of course, I did not consider Devon a psychopath, particularly after encountering the vulnerable clumsy boy of last Friday evening. It was more likely that with his intelligence he was choosing how to respond, perhaps equating possible responses with the suave character he was portraying today.

"I'll be honest with you, Dr. Obler."

Now it was my turn to silently gaze. Finally, I said, "I would appreciate that. Remember, if we are to work together. . . ."

"Oh, I know. You need to know the truth," he said a bit petulantly. "Well, that night there was a situation. I overreacted. It's over, no harm done, and I think we should go on. Certainly you must have more to offer than inconsequential chatter."

"I don't think anything we discuss here is inconsequential."

He shrugged and smoothed back his hair. "It's your court. I guess you can decide."

"Why did you feel the need to beat me at basketball last week?"

"More chitchat," he sighed. "It wasn't a need, I assure you. I simply wanted to. It felt right at the time."

"How carefully do you weigh consequences?"

He smiled. "Usually, pretty carefully."

"Why did you 'want' to beat me? Are there others you seek to impress?"

"Isn't that true of everyone?"

He was parrying confidently, enjoying this game much more than the previous one. With mind games, he felt an advantage.

I shifted in my chair and in direction. "That evening, when I said I'd been trying to find you, you replied, 'So I hear.' So your parents informed you."

He gritted his teeth and spoke as he had on the basketball court. "I told you. I haven't been in contact with my parents."

"What about your brother? He's younger, right?"

"Same thing," he almost hissed.

I backed off but filed away the idea that this was an avenue to pursue later. "So it must have been messages I left at the university."

He relaxed. "Must be. We're in the information age, right? It's hard to keep track of where stuff comes from."

I leaned forward and said, "What are we doing here? Do you want help?"

His eyes focused on me and he reached back one hand to twirl stray strands of hair. My speaking sharply and abruptly had gained an advantage. I filed that away for the future, too.

"We're here," he said, almost sighing, "because that old goat Pomerantz wants me to be evaluated. Beyond that, I'm not quite sure. Do you think I need help?"

I smiled, putting some warmth in my voice. "I'd like to find that out. The other night, on the phone, why did you laugh like that?"

"Like what?" We gazed at each other. Then he said, "I don't remember that."

It grew quiet in the office. I heard the ticking of the

grandfather clock against the wall next to the door. There was another clock, digital, on one side of my desk which I used to keep track of sessions—this one was nearly half over, though it seemed to have begun only five minutes ago. As I watched Devon squirm in the chair, I saw the long bronze pendulum of the grandfather clock swing from one side to the other and back again.

"You don't?"

"No."

"Devon," I said with concern, "I'd like to know more about the incident."

His lips curled.

"You make it sound so sordid, like a crime."

"I don't mean that."

"Anyway, there are some things I'm not prepared to tell you. Yet."

Then he grinned, flashing an expanse of perfect white teeth. I felt the mood shifting, almost as if a cool breeze had found its way through the closed window.

He leaned forward and said, "There is a lot you want to know, isn't there?"

"That's why I'm here."

"No, that's why *I'm* here. Pomerantz and those other jerk-offs at the university brought you in because they don't have a fucking clue. I guess you're the heavy hitter, the one to clean up the mess I am."

"Are you a mess?"

"To them I am. If you listen to them, I'm Leopold and Loeb rolled into one. *Compulsion*. 1960. Orson Welles and Stuart Whitman."

"Devon, I don't want to get sidetracked by talking

of movies."

"But they're part of *me*," he cried, not with anguish but with triumph. "Dr. Obler, if you are to truly help me. . . ." He smiled for a moment. "And if I am to be of some help to you, you've got to accept the whole package."

His sky blue eyes stared into mine. "Can you do that?"

The balance had shifted. Now I felt cornered. Suddenly, I realized that the contest of mind and wills had not wilted Devon but had instead energized him. He had resources, and no doubt secrets, I couldn't yet fathom. At that moment, I wasn't sure I wanted to.

Still, I replied firmly, "I want to."

"Good." He sat back, smiling, straightening his tie. "I want you to also."

"Why?"

He shrugged. "Maybe because I really think you can." He appeared to relish the thought.

I clasped my hands and rested my chin on them, trying not to acknowledge the frustration I felt. Devon was back in control. He knew it and he was enjoying it. I could push a couple of buttons that I'd learned were there, but I questioned whether doing it would ultimately help him or myself in our sparring. I listened to the grandfather clock ticking, reminding myself that because of my training and my own instinct the patient's welfare had to be the highest priority.

"Devon, I don't think we can work together unless you are completely candid with me."

He tilted his head to one side. "I agree."

"So I hope you will be."

He laughed grandly, as though about to bestow a gift.

"Dr. Obler, please don't be like the others. You must ask the questions—the *right* questions—to receive useful answers. Is that requesting too much? I don't think so."

"So my questions must improve?"

"Of course. I don't think I'm a terrible person. If others do, I can't really help that. It's their problem." He raised one eyebrow, a trick that was impossible for most people. "Am I to fall at your knees?" He grinned, then added, "To confess?"

"Is there something you want to confess?"

"We all have something to reveal, things that we wish we had done differently. Even you."

There was time left, but suddenly I felt drained and exhausted. He had hit on an area that was sensitive to me. It was possible that I was no match for his intelligence and resilience. Inside I suppressed the quiver of defeat.

"I will try to be a more formidable inquisitor." I tipped the water jug on the desk and poured myself a drink.

"A rematch?" he asked.

"Next Wednesday."

He stood up. "I'll be here. I do want to continue, if you do."

"Yes."

He tucked the briefcase under his arm, tugged at his suit jacket, and smoothed a few strands of loose blond hair back over his head. Then he waved to me and walked to the door.

"Devon?"

He turned, smiling expectantly. "Stuart Whitman wasn't in *Compulsion*," I said. "You might be thinking of Bradford Dillman."

His smile thinned, and the corners of his mouth turned down. With some irritation he muttered, "You're right." As he left he closed the door quickly behind him.

Some advantage, Obler.

I stood and gazed out the window. He hadn't yet left the building. I still felt his presence. I knew I should make some determination as to whether Devon was a vulnerable young man who could be helped—whom *I* could help—or someone with a serious mental condition to be addressed. However, at that moment, as I pressed my forehead against the hard glass and felt my fingers twitching, I wanted to think about anything else but him.

Chapter 6

Falling Leaves

The cinnamon smell of autumn was in the air on this Sunday morning. An amber hazy sun shone against a muted cadet blue sky. My children—Mark, who was twelve, and Selena, who was ten, whom I'd just stopped by to get at their mother's—were excited about going to Madison Square Garden. They were even willing to postpone until later trying on costumes for Halloween, which was less than a week away. So what if the Knick game we were going to see was only an exhibition? I had planned it so we could do something together. I was now one of those divorced fathers seeking to keep alive a bond diminished by no longer being part of their everyday lives.

It was an afternoon game, so we had to get going. We walked hand in hand, the children and I. They lived in the apartment I had once inhabited with their mother on the outskirts of the Village. Today was a typical Sunday morning in fall. There were many other people on the streets with children, coming back from church, heading to a playground or perhaps going to brunch. Of course, most of the family groups were composed of a father, mother, and children while ours was not.

It was more reassuring than usual to see people with children walking around. There are always reports of violent incidents in the city, some of them murders. However, in the last several months, there had been reports of young people killed in and near the Village. Most of the folks living there were concerned. There was talk the murders were the work of one person, or so the media insinuated. The police weren't saying much.

The victims were young men and women. Of course, I didn't like the fact that anyone was being killed, supposedly in a most vicious way, and so close to my children's home, but I didn't see where my family was at great risk. Still, as we walked, I held my children's hands a bit tighter than usual.

At the corner I hailed a cab and we went north at a leisurely pace. "Who are the Knicks playing?" Mark asked.

"The Bullets."

"Do they stink?" Salena wondered.

"Well, they're an improving team."

Mark whispered to her, "That means they're not that good."

"Can we have hot dogs?" Salena asked.

I nodded. Probably by the end of the first quarter the kids would lose interest in the action below, but food and soda would prevent restlessness, I hoped.

The Bullets had some good young players. But my earliest memories were of the Knicks and Bullets being evenly matched and how they went to war in the playoffs. The Bullets were based in Baltimore then and had Unseld

and Monroe, Marin and "Mad Dog" Carter. The Knicks had
Reed, DeBusschere, Frazier, Bradley, Barnett, and Russell.
Even after Earl the Pearl went to the Knicks and they were
on their way to their second championship in four years, the
Bullets never quit. I remembered with pleasure those warm
spring nights in Brooklyn when I hid under my sheet in bed
clutching a transistor radio, breathlessly listening to every
word Marv Albert said.

Outside the Garden we stopped at a concession stand
for pretzels. Then we found our seats about fifteen rows up
from the court.

The stands were only half full. The season opener was
still ten days away, and most local sports fans were still into
football with the Giants and Jets. Mark was content. His
large pretzel had mustard on it, and it was dripping unnoticed
on his striped shirt. Salena had not only passed on the mustard, but was finicky enough to be picking off every piece of
salt which fell into the lap of her pink dress. God, how I
missed them.

The Knicks, with Ewing dominating inside and
Starks hitting three pointers, were out to a big lead midway
through the second quarter. Maybe it was the lack of competition, or my thoughts would have turned away anyway,
but I started going over my last session with Devon. Lately,
a good portion of my at-ease moments were spent thinking
of him, more so than all my other patients combined.

"Daddy, can we have hot dogs now?" Salena asked.

I signaled for two, then a minute later came an
identical plea for sodas. "Okay," I said as they sipped,
"all set now?"

The kids nodded, stuffed.

I smiled. "Great. Let's watch the game."

But I thought instead about Devon. I began to review our recent sessions. For the last few weeks he had been reliable, showing up for his appointments on time. But they hadn't been very productive. We talked. We kidded around. I sought to draw him out, but he parried and teased. It was like we were a couple of guys who met for a drink after work and conversed without much conviction about our jobs, politics, and families to pass the time before going home.

Such idle conversation wasn't good for dealing with whatever was going on inside Devon. And I was convinced there was a lot of chaos under the surface. The upside was I felt we were establishing an essential foundation of therapy: trust. Establishing trust was extremely important. Trust was the jumping off point. But where? And how do we leap together?

My initial impression had been that Devon was a decent young man who was looking for, and needed, to trust someone. His experience as a consistent head-of-the-class student who was envied (and worse) by peers had resulted in barriers that wouldn't let anyone pass through. I'd also gleaned, from the little he allowed himself to reveal, that Devon's relationship with his family—parents, a younger brother and extended family—was not a warm one, or supportive. He did well; in their eyes he was *supposed* to do well. Whatever he did, they wanted him to do more. He sought solace in the cinema. Modeling the behavior of characters on the screen, his personality formed from the outside in. He had grown up fast, prodded by very high expectations and influences I couldn't yet fathom. Emotionally he hadn't caught up.

So on the outside he was brilliant, charismatic, hand-some, and enjoyed displaying wit to the point of flaunting it. Inside, his demeanor indicated (and I suspected) that he was confused, lacked confidence, and was emotionally vulnerable, especially when he was uncomfortable in his surroundings.

And that was the crux of the problem that I thought had developed in our recent sessions. On the surface Devon had begun to feel comfortable. He came in playing a role and left the office with the role intact.

But when would he reveal the truth under the mask? Be patient, I told myself, trust takes time to develop.

Mark leaned close and murmured, "Hey, Dad, it's halftime."

I forced my attention back to the Garden.

"Game's over, huh?" Salena commented.

"No, gang, this means more hot dogs." I stood up. "Right?"

"I'm full," Mark said.

"I have to go to the bathroom," Salena said.

This was the kind of tricky situation that required a mother. Something I had deprived them of. Guilt over-whelmed me. I couldn't leave Mark alone while I accompanied Salena, and, even so, which bathroom would my daughter go in? She was too old for the men's room and too young to go into the women's room by herself. Well, divorced fathers with kids deal with this every visiting day, I told myself. My solution was to say to them, "Hey, it's time for dessert." I signaled to a ven-dor selling ice cream. "Okay, here we go. Just hang on."

"But, Dad, I have to go."

"Look, there's a show."

Female dancers in glittering jewel—colored costumes were executing turns and kicks on the court as colored lights swirled. The combination of lights, loud music and ice cream sandwiches proved irresistible for the children. With Mark and Salena occupied, inadvertently my thoughts turned again to Devon.

What bothered me was not knowing how much he concealed, both consciously and unconsciously. I sensed there was a great deal. However, our discussions had been so surface skimming that I couldn't with any certainty gauge the depth. Pomerantz *was* old-fashioned and probably in overdrive, but he wasn't the self-absorbed fool Devon portrayed him. Maybe there was more to the so-called "liaisons," and of course, there had been that call from the hospital, which Devon continued to laugh off.

If it weren't for my instincts, I would just write up an evaluation saying that Devon could cope sufficiently enough. Let him proceed academically and in his personal life as long as there was no clear harm to himself and others. It would be so easy to do that. There was plenty more on my plate. I knew of professionals whose entire careers were based on passing patients from one stage of the process to another and collecting staggering fees for it.

However, I couldn't. I'd rather quit the field than enable, ignore or let things slide toward bookkeeping. I'd never get that complacent or compromise my integrity, I promised myself. There had to be a way to break through to whatever was below the surface in order to help a troubled patient.

Salena tugged at my jacket. "Dad, I really have to go to the bathroom."

"My stomach is making noises," Mark said.

I glanced at the scoreboard. It was five minutes into the fourth period, and the Knicks were up by twenty-two. We left the Garden with its intoxicating odors of food, smoke, uniforms, and sweat. The cab ride back took less time, perhaps because the driver had other plans and bothered to stop at only two of seven red lights. Mark and Salena appeared to enjoy this ride more than the game.

"Would you like to stop for a bite?" I asked, not wanting the visit to end.

"Dad," Mark said, obviously not wanting to hurt my feelings, "Mom said we have to be home by four." In the lobby I lingeringly kissed each of them, thinking about the interval till I'd see them again. I winced. "Be good till next week."

Mark and Salena stared at me. Talk about instincts. I would wager they knew my feelings. "When?" Salena asked.

"Next Sunday. I'll call you every night."

Mark put out his hand and we shook. That gesture, implying that he was already the man in a broken family, was more painful to me than the hurt look in their eyes. I pressed the elevator button. As the doors closed, neither of the children looked at me.

I walked east from the building and caught the subway to the station at 77th and Lexington. Rachel, the woman I was becoming more and more interested in, lived in an older twelve-story building between First and Second Avenues. It wasn't big enough to have a doorman, and the elevator was slow and creaky.

I didn't have to take it this afternoon. From half a

block away I saw her sitting on the front steps. Rachel was a beautiful woman, a combination of grace and intelligence, seeming more mature than twenty-six—certainly more so than I had been.

She wore a long khaki skirt, a long-sleeve denim shirt and brown shoes. Her short dark hair, still wet from the shower, glistened in the afternoon sunlight. In her hand she held a large straw bag which probably contained an early dinner, though I had said I would be glad to take her out.

Rachel was quite independent in her thinking and behavior. As a publicist working for a publishing company, she didn't make much of a salary, yet she was reluctant to accept gifts. Perhaps it had something to do with being the girlfriend of a divorced man and not knowing for sure if our relationship had a future, ignoring that most likely we had already gotten to a point of no return.

Rachel smiled when she saw me approach, making my heart skip a beat, a terrific feeling, one I hadn't felt for a very long time. It skipped again when I got closer and could clearly see Rachel's large, expressive brown eyes. She stood up, swinging the basket, and seemed ready for the kiss I gave her.

"You're a little late," she said, her voice low and soft.

"You were waiting."

"Oh, on such a lovely day I just wanted to watch life on the street."

"Anything interesting?"

"Always."

We turned and walked west. She wasn't being coy about why she was sitting on the steps. Rachel genuinely liked to observe life in the city. She had moved here four years ago after college to try living in New York. Coming from a small town in the middle of Pennsylvania, she had a continuing fascination with her city surroundings. Not all of it was pleasant, but she was intrigued and wanted to explore.

Sometimes I worried about her being too naive and open to the urban experience—though she reminded me she'd managed fine before there was me to worry about her. Still, I suspected she hadn't fully accepted that there really were dangerous people doing evil things in this city. As a psychologist, I didn't exactly believe in evil people, but as a city citizen I knew one shouldn't court trouble.

When we had met months ago in one of my group therapy sessions, she had brought her boyfriend with the intention that by talking out their problems, sexual and emotional among others, they would resolve them. In an unexpected way, they had been resolved. They had broken up and we had become involved. Now she and I were trying to figure out how to do what was right for ourselves and others. We hadn't made much headway other than realizing being apart wasn't the answer. So much for my being a wise psychologist.

"Marty, how about we hit a museum first?" Rachel asked. "I read in this morning's *Times* about a new exhibit at the Whitney."

I shrugged, and she led us on. I was about to vote for the Metropolitan. Rachel enjoyed and seemed to understand new trends in modern art. I liked the classics, preferring the rarely changing exhibits of work by eighteenth and nineteenth century artists, especially van Gogh, Cezanne and, on the American front, the Hudson River School.

Her appreciation of very new work made me more aware of the difference in our ages.

As we walked, Rachel asked, "Did you read in the paper about that new murder near here?"

"I didn't read the paper this morning. I took my kids to a Knicks game." I paused. "But I know there have been several in the Village area?"

"Another kid, an eighteen-year-old, was killed."

"Another?"

"That's five, the story said."

I shrugged it off. "Let's not talk about it and spoil our day."

"I mention it only because it happened near where your kids live."

"Let's discuss it later."

In the museum, other than the ever-present Calder sculptures, I was not impressed. The works appeared half-formed, not thought through, dashed off as if to meet a curator's deadline. Even the more complicated and occasionally bizarre paintings, which from my perspective should have resulted in psychological intervention, appeared slapped together, a muse out of control.

However, Rachel swayed deliberately from one foot to another, one finger gently stroking her lower lip, sometimes shaking her head slightly and other times smiling as if deciphering a message. I wondered if she also spent time pondering our relationship. I purposely, because of my own confusion, did not bring it up. It was there between us, we both knew it. I suspected she had many questions. But we just went along. She may have been looking to me for answers, but I wasn't ready to give them.

"Want to go?" I finally asked, picking up the straw bag.

"This doesn't do it for you, huh?"

"Well, it's such a great fall day out there. . . ."

"Okay, okay. The park it is."

We walked to Central Park. Once there we trod upon orange and brown leaves which made a crunching sound under our feet, until we came to the lake. We stayed on the side where the jewel-leafed trees didn't block the sunlight. We found a smooth patch of grass beneath a large tree within calling distance to other couples, some of them with children, who were also picnicking.

"This is heavy," I said, lowering the bag.
"Expecting company?"

She had an infectious laugh. "Expecting an appetite."

Rachel sat with crossed legs and reached into the bag. Emerging from it were plastic containers which turned out to hold fried chicken and salad, a long loaf of Italian bread and a bottle of white wine.

"I like a woman who plans ahead," I said, reaching in and finding a corkscrew.

"Only like?" she said, eyes crinkling.

I took a deep breath. "In general terms, yes. With you. . . ."

She smiled and turned her head away. I knew that she needed to hear I loved her, yet the expression of such deep feeling still made me uncomfortable. If you weighed the doubts, the scale would tilt her way. However, once burned twice shy. I couldn't blame her for wanting commitment. I too wanted it. I just wasn't able to voice it yet.

There were blue paper napkins, paper cups and plates in the bag. We settled back against the tree with our food and wine, our shoulders pressed together. Sunlight found its way through the partially leafless branches to our extended legs.

"This is especially nice," Rachel said.

"Yes, it sure is."

And then it happened. It shouldn't have. The company was special, the food was delicious, the wine smooth and cold, the breeze mild and full of the fallen-leaf scent, the water in the lake glittered, picnicking and passing people chatted languidly in several languages, even the flies were politely waiting their turn. It was a first-rate, pleasurable afternoon seeing a woman with whom I was falling in love.

But I started to think again about Devon.

I drank more wine, hoping to drown the thoughts. After a period of silence, Rachel put her plate aside and asked, "Are you okay?"

"Sure."

"What is it?"

"Nothing. More vino?"

"You can have the rest, if you want. But I want to know about that faraway look."

"Just . . . things."

She leaned against me. I knew she wanted more from me at that moment. But I couldn't. So, I began to talk about Devon.

Not everything, of course. There was confidentiality to consider, and I felt myself acting like Pomerantz, a nice turn of the tables—what a double-edged sword confidentiality was. I had been circumspect about discussing my work with Rachel. Now I tried to balance this sudden need to talk about Devon with not opening a door too wide. I described Devon physically, knowing she would never meet him, and in general terms the reasons why he had essentially been turned over to me and what therapy I might seek to provide.

"What do you suspect about him?" Rachel asked.

"'Suspect' might be an inappropriate word."

"Okay." She was pensive, a finger on her lower lip as at the museum. "What do you want to learn from him?"

Though I might have asked for it, I hadn't expected such a perceptive question. Inwardly I tried out several answers, but none sufficed. I just started talking again.

"That's the whole matter," I said. "I still don't know what the right questions are. Then, if I were to find them, would I get useful responses—useful from a therapeutic standpoint. Devon is extremely intelligent, he can probably run rings around me. He can give me an answer that's a detour and I'll follow it. He can give me an answer that's on target and I might not realize it. Part of me believes he's a messed-up young man who may be experiencing victimizing behavior and truly needs help from someone who will listen carefully without judging. Another part of me wonders if he's playing a game, and I'm nothing more than the most recent player to come along."

Rachel squinted at me. The sun was setting behind the russet and gold-leafed trees and a soft reddish glow was on her face. "Why is this man so different from your other patients?"

Sincerely, I replied, "That's a good question. I don't know. I could write this case off or get further involved. . . ."

"But you will."

"You know that?" I asked seriously.

She smiled at me. She looked so lovely I had to

fiercely resist the urge to lean over her and kiss her.

"Yes, because. . . ."

"I need to know," I finished for her. "The way we are now, we could go for months, even years, on a surface level, just playing his game."

"Don't you play games with other patients?"

"Sometimes," I admitted. "Darn your smartness. Some just play games. That's all they need to cope and function, and that's all I can provide."

"But Devon is different."

"I really do think so."

"So what will you do?"

"I don't know. I do know that it's helped a lot to talk to you about it. And that you're interested." Guilt stabbed at me because of the implication that my wife had not been interested in my work—or was it more accurate to say that I had told her less and fewer times had sought her opinion?

Rachel squeezed my hand. "I won't pry into your business, but I like when you talk to me about what's on your mind."

"Only like?"

She laughed. "In general terms, yes. With you. . . ."

It was my turn to smile. "Now what?" I asked.

She looked at me sideways, the slight irresistible smile flickering. "Well, how much time do you have?"

The truthful answer would spread beyond the question. I shrugged, got to my feet, and then helped her up.

Chapter 7

Count Backwards

It was the grunge look this time. Devon entered the office wearing baggy corduroy pants, unlaced boots, a Pearl Jam T-shirt, and a torn denim jacket. His hair, probably deliberately, was unkempt. There was a large dark green knapsack slung over one shoulder. He let it drop to the floor next to the chair as he sat down. There was that familiar feeling of the room being suddenly smaller with him in it.

Nothing that he wore bothered me except a pair of aviator sunglasses, which he kept on. A sign of evasiveness, masking boredom, and perhaps, diminishing expectations.

"Do you like Pearl Jam?" I asked.

He shrugged. "I listen to a lot of different music, depending on the mood I'm in."

"Is that how you choose how to dress too?"

He flashed a wide grin. "Sometimes. But I also told you I like disguises."

"Devon, do you trust me?"

The grin faded, replaced by a sincere expression.

"Yes, Dr. Obler." He leaned forward. "Why do you ask that?"

"I want to try something, because I'm concerned that we're not making progress, after all we've been meeting every week for nearly two months."

It was as if he was trying to comfort me when he said, "I've enjoyed coming here."

"That's my point, Devon. This has become little more than a nice place to visit, to. . . ."

"Kill some time?"

"Yes. I don't feel that we're working toward something. We're drifting. That's not what therapy is about. At least, the kind I'm interested in practicing."

He gazed at me, and even though I couldn't see them I knew his eyes weren't blinking. Finally, Devon said, "I won't disagree with you. In fact, I've been reevaluating my overall participation in psychology."

"Meaning?"

"I seem to have lost my enthusiasm for it." He leaned back and crossed one leg over the other. "One consequence of our 'visits' is I've stepped back to reconsider psychology as a career. I'm not sure that I want to continue to follow it."

"Have you spoken to anyone at the university about this?"

"No." He laughed softly. "Wouldn't that be like telling a chef you don't like the way he cooks?"

"Maybe the menu can be altered to suit your tastes."

"My tastes." He lowered his head for a moment, peering at me above the green lenses. "I prefer to explore my tastes here with you."

While what Devon was telling me was a surprise and

worth pursuing, I sensed that again our discussion would descend to idle repartee. I had to shake things up.

"Devon, have you ever undergone hypnosis?"

"No." He straightened up in the chair. "I've been curious, but haven't gone beyond that."

"I would think in the psychology program you might have had a chance to experiment."

"I don't care for the prospect of losing control."

"I'm not suggesting that. However, let me ask you again: do you trust me?"

After a pause, he replied, "Yes, I do."

"Good. What I *am* suggesting involves hypnosis, but not going so far as to enter a fully hypnotic state. You will be aware of everything we do and what is said. I will not be able to direct your behavior."

He grinned. "No standing on your desk and shrieking like a disemboweled pig?"

"Not even close. It will be a state between hypnotic and being awake."

"Then why do it?"

The answer was I wanted to break under the surface of his defenses and root around in whatever I found. But the answer I gave him was, "I don't think you should continue in therapy, or at least continue with me, if certain issues aren't addressed."

Warily, Devon said, "What issues are you most interested in?"

"That's just it." I kept any hint of frustration out of my voice. "After all these weeks, I'm not sure what they are. Yet I am. . . ."

"Convinced they are there." He smiled at my surprise.

"I think I know you, but you don't know me. That isn't very sporting, is it?"

"This isn't a sport."

"All right, okay." With some exaggeration, Devon sighed. "What are you suggesting?"

"I would like to try a technique that is experimental in therapy," I replied. "It involves placing a patient in a hypnogogic state."

"I've heard of it at school but. . . ." He squirmed in the chair.

"The procedure is more simple than the term implies. It's as if you were entering a hypnotic state but you stop just before you go under. That way you are able to be aware of everything going on between us and can participate fully in the treatment process."

I knew I had to reassure him that nothing would come from his unconscious without his participation. His concern about control was clear; without it he wouldn't chance the procedure, trust or no trust. I hoped he was unaware that what I was trying to control now was his underlying paranoia.

Recently, I had been experimenting with the hypnotic technique in my private practice and even in group therapy. The results were outstanding. Patients who had been completely blocked in therapy were showing signs of opening repressed material that up to that point had been entirely unavailable to treatment.

This paralleled claims being made by the research psychologists on the West Coast, most notably the Gestalt movement. Fritz Perls, among others, had claimed that traditional talk therapies were too focused on the past or at least on how the past manifests itself in the present. Proponents encouraged the use of exercises designed to help the patient bring out repressed and conflicting material and, at the same time, relax about it coming out.

I had taken their approach and integrated it with the hypnotic innovations of Dr. Lewis Wolberg and Dr. Martin Orne at Harvard. Both of them independently had developed the idea that hypnosis was essentially a strong suggestion technique in which a patient allows material to emerge that he hides in consciousness to emerge. My idea was to encourage this conscious emergence by emphasizing the patient's participation at all times in the process so there would be control over what is asked and what is revealed.

Another innovation I was trying was to measure the brain wave patterns of the patient while he was in a hypnogogic state. Generally, in a normal conscious state an individual produces patterns called beta waves that measure eight to thirteen cycles per second. Under hypnosis, the activity decreases to approximately one to three cycles per second, equivalent to deep sleep called delta. In a hypnogogic state, the pattern measures four to seven cycles per second, an alpha state—this is when a person is most creative in his thinking.

This also meant I could monitor more carefully the efficacy of the patient's reports and distinguish them more easily from a fantasy state. With Devon, this would enable me to determine if his reports were imaginary or truthful.

"Why don't we try it right now?" I said. "That way

you can see directly the benefits of the technique and compare it to our usual sessions."

He appeared nervous but tried to hide it, perhaps out of a display of manliness. Then he shrugged and said, "I'll go along. I'm curious. Also, if it's something you want, I'd like to please you."

"This isn't just about me."

"Of course, Dr. Obler. I realize that." Then he grinned slightly. "I should warn you, though."

"Yes?"

"Be prepared for what you might find." He twisted several strands of long hair. "I don't know what either. This could be fascinating, or nothing."

That was a disadvantage I hadn't mentioned—the extent of what might be revealed by going deeper into Devon's mind. If, as I suspected, there were some powerful forces that had long been repressed, whether rage or anguish, tapping into them could be like striking oil. I felt, however, that either an attempt should be made or Devon and I ought to go our separate ways.

"I'll take that chance. Are you ready?"

He nodded. I slowly led Devon through the steps, which are based on behavior modification and borrow a bit from yoga, transcendental meditation, and other deep relaxation techniques. I had him breathe slowly in and out and focus on relaxing every muscle in his body. In his mind this created a sensation of descending toward sleep, but he did not go all the way to sleep.

"Close your eyes and feel that there are steel balls attached to the lids," I said.

He concentrated on my voice, and I spoke more softly

and slower. "Shut out everything else except my voice and think of something pleasant and relaxing. You are sitting against a tree in a verdant, sweet-smelling forest."

Soon he was totally relaxed, slumped in the chair, head tilted back.

"How do you feel?" I asked.

"Nice," he said, his voice calm and even. "This is nice."

I was surprised that Devon had entered the hypnogogic state so easily. Almost half of patients require practice over several attempts. Perhaps it had worked well for Devon because of the trust we had established, or he was especially susceptible for as yet undetermined reasons. There was a hint of something else: it seemed to titillate him in some way to hand control over to me.

His mouth was slack, there was a thin line of the whites of his eyes showing through the green lenses, and his arms hung at his sides. He had the appearance of a vulnerable young boy in need of comforting.

"I'm going to ask you some questions. Please answer them any way you can."

"Yes, Dr. Obler."

I asked him a series of questions with answers I already knew, that I'd learned from his records. The answers I elicited were factual and required no statement of opinion. Devon willingly responded, his voice low and flat.

Then I asked simple queries, whose answers I'd seen in Pomerantz's notes, about his family.

"My father, Jacques, is in his mid sixties," Devon responded. "He's fifteen years older than my mother, Anne. My brother, Andre is six years younger. My only living grandparent is my mother's mother, who is a university trustee. I've very little contact with her."

Indeed, according to Devon, he rarely saw or spoke to any family member. (I intended to come back to that in another session.) He described in some detail his parents' home in Connecticut, which sounded like an estate.

When I asked him about his keen interest in movies, I sensed there was some filtering in Devon's responses. "I enjoy sitting in the cool darkness," he said flatly. "I like being alone."

When I asked if he always went to the movies alone, he replied, "I went alone." He seemed to emphasize the second word. I tried to follow that up but he changed direction, talking about the old movies he particularly liked.

When he mentioned *Rebel Without a Cause*, I asked, "Did you like James Dean? Did you identify with him?"

Devon laughed softly and said, "I preferred Sal Mineo. He was a much better actor. He died, you know, violently."

Trying to remember, I said, "In the movie?"

Devon only laughed again.

I moved on, keeping to simple questions. The session was almost over. It would probably be best to stop here, I thought. I had established a connection and would return to it next time. But I wanted to try one more thing to determine if there really was some value to this strategy or if it was just another sidetrack.

"Devon, before we end, I'd like to ask about the incident several weeks ago."

"Incident?"

"Yes. What happened that night you called me from

the hospital?"

Suddenly, his body went rigid in the chair. He struggled to sit up. The sunglasses slipped off his head and clattered on the floor. A thin film of sweat appeared and glistened on his forehead. His blue eyes stared wildly.

"Th-that was just a guy I met," he stammered, his voice ragged.

"Where?"

"At a bar."

I tried to keep my voice soft and low. "What happened?"

"We left. Together. Then he got hurt."

"How did he get hurt?"

"I don't know."

"Devon, I want to help you. You trust me. Please tell me what happened."

His lips quivered. Drops of sweat coursed down the sides of his face. He leaned to one side in the chair, reaching. His fingers crawled into the knapsack and he pulled out an empty glass soda bottle. It shook in his lap. I heard his boots tapping on the floor.

"What are you feeling?" I finally asked, astonished by the transformation.

A violent shaking seized his body. He pushed his glasses aside with one foot, I heard the sound of metal bending, but kept my attention on Devon's face. The pupils of his eyes rose toward the ceiling until only the whites were visible. I had witnessed similar convulsions in hospitalized patients experiencing extreme anxiety attacks.

This was going too far. I was about to lean over the desk to bring him out of the state when his right hand tightened around the neck of the soda bottle. Clutching it, he rubbed the neck up and down continuously, as though masturbating. The movements intensified. His legs and feet were extended. It was silent in the room except for the eerie squeaking of the bottle and his rapid, ragged breathing.

"Talk to me, Devon."

He laughed. It was similar to the sound I'd heard that night on the phone, though it didn't reach a peak. Except for his hand, his entire body was quivering and rigid. Sweat darkened his T-shirt.

"Do as I say, you little bastard!" he suddenly shouted.

"Who?" I kept my voice calm.

His voice became stronger, the words faster. "Give me your ass. Tie you up! Blindfold—where's the fucking rag? Blood?"

"Devon, tell me what. . . ."

"Blood? Blood! I'm. . . ."

"Who is the little bastard?" I demanded.

Devon went silent again. His neck twisted and his head swung from side to side. The whites of his eyes flashed.

I asked, "Where is the blood coming from?"

"From his ass, you prick!"

He shouted again, "The glass up his ass! Hurts, doesn't it!" Through clenched teeth he added, "It hurts, it hurts." Then he began mumbling until his voice trailed off. He stopped rubbing the bottle and his head slumped down. Sweat dripped onto the bottle with tiny tapping sounds.

I walked around to sit on the edge of my desk and let out my breath. Slowly I brought him out of the hypnogogic state, counting backwards in a soft voice. When he raised his head, his eyes were clear and dresden blue, indicating an amazing resiliency.

"What happened?" he asked hoarsely.

I was asking myself the same question. Never before had I seen such an abrupt switch in personality. Something deep inside Devon had suddenly shot up to the surface, so fast that he couldn't contain or even filter it.

"Devon," I began as I shakily returned to my seat behind the desk. "Were you aware of what just happened?"

Without looking at the soda bottle, he stuffed it in the knapsack. He straightened his clothing and pushed his long hair back with his fingers, all the while gazing at me, unblinking.

Finally, he stood up. "See you next Wednesday, Dr. Obler." Then he left.

I sat back, exhausted. What had I tapped into with Devon?

What had been related to me, I was convinced, was real. Other than that, I was sure of nothing.

Little did I know that a life and death struggle had begun.

Chapter 8

An Eerie Feeling

It was probably fortunate that I couldn't reflect on what had happened during the session with Devon until late in the day. There were other patients to see, a group therapy session at an uptown counseling center, consultation conference calls, and everything else that made up a typical day. This allowed time for me to regroup a bit and gain a little distance.

Finally, I begged off meeting with a colleague for a quick drink and instead returned to my office. It had been a cold, blustery day, perhaps an indication of an early winter. Daylight-saving time had ended, so it was already dark by six o'clock. There was an eerie feeling about this night as if Halloween, which was a couple of days away, had decided to come early.

Inside my office I lit only my desk lamp, propped my feet up, and leaned my head back to gaze at the ceiling. Okay, what the hell *did* happen, and who *is* Devon?

Though during the "episode"—at present, I didn't

know how else to refer to it—I had compared Devon's physical responses to that of an acute anxiety attack, I doubted that's what it was. He seemed to be literally reliving an intense experience, which for now I had to assume was a sexual encounter violent enough to result in having to take his partner to the hospital. Remembering what Pomerantz had passed on to me, I also had to assume this was far from being Devon's only experience with rough sex. However, possibly, this one was the most violent.

In the trance Devon had undergone a total personality shift. I had not before witnessed such an abrupt shift nor one that was so overwhelming to me personally. I wondered which personality was the real Devon—the witty, charming and vulnerable young man or the angry person I'd seen this morning, almost consumed with rage and horror.

I bit my lip pondering the scene. Perhaps the bottle had been a phallic prop. Or was it more than that? He had repeated the word "blood," and had shouted "glass up his ass." Had a bottle or some other glass object been part of a sexual encounter? I felt some revulsion imagining the scene as well as nervousness about exploring with Devon what he had been experiencing. Apparently he had moved close to the edge, and there really was the risk of going too far.

Yet, there was that startling recovery, the sudden and total shift back. He had left my office amused by my reaction to the session or maybe he had surprised himself and was delighted.

Then there was that strange look he had given me when I asked him if he knew what had just happened. He should have known at some level, because he hadn't been under complete hypnosis and I was convinced that he was aware of what he had revealed. Reflecting, I realized his gaze possibly contained several meanings: he may have revealed things he hadn't intended to (and perhaps never had before to anyone else, certainly in a therapy setting); he had simulated masturbation and there was some embarrassment associated with being observed; and he had for a few minutes lost control of his actions and essentially had placed himself at the mercy of another.

However, if anyone else had undergone such a transformation and been so unguarded and vulnerable, they would have been almost shattered by the experience. Not Devon. I sensed there had been no guilt or lingering shame and that nothing had really changed inside him.

Except one element: both of us had been involved in the experience, and because of that we were more deeply connected than before. I hoped that if anything this had strengthened the bond of trust, because it was clear to me, and I suspected to Devon, that there was now no turning back.

It was going to be difficult for me to wait until our next session. Even though somewhat repelled by what I had witnessed and then by extension imagined, I was fascinated.

I picked Devon's sunglasses up from the desk. Apparently, he had forgotten they were on the floor when he walked out. The next patient, a matronly woman separating from her fourth husband, had found them and handed the glasses to me, saying with more truth than she knew, "Hey, Dr. Obler, you didn't tell me some wild stuff can go on here."

Now I stared down at them. Aviator sunglasses. I'd like to wear such a pair, but doubted I'd wear them with the same panache as Devon. The dark green lenses stared back at

me as though taunting me, daring me to discover
hidden secrets.

I went home that night unable to relax. I tossed
and turned in bed immersed in strange dreams bathed in
green lights.

I wondered further about his inner reserves when in
the next two sessions Devon insisted again on being put
back in hypnogogic states. Again there was no resistance.
The procedure took only a short time.

However, there were no more personality shifts.
Perhaps that was his reason for trying it again—he was
testing himself or to him it was an exercise. The same way
one works on a muscle by flexing it repeatedly until it
grows stronger, he wanted to test and build up a barrier.

"I'm at your mercy, Dr. Obler," he said, grinning. "Be
gentle with me."

"Do you really want me to be gentle?"

He laughed and said, "Oh, I trust you. Do what you
will."

"Devon, I'm not trying to *do* anything to you other
than help you."

"Then let's have at it. 'Come on, men!'" he almost
shrieked, then grinned again and spread his arms, holding
them aloft with one eyebrow raised, waiting. Then with a
hint of disappointment he lowered them.

"Think sand, Turkey—the country, not the bird—and
World War I. David Lean?" He waited, then shook his head.
"Peter O'Toole in *Lawrence of Arabia*. Dr. Obler, you really
should get out of the office more."

"Another movie made before you were born."

"Maybe a lot of things were better then."

"Why?"

"Why don't we try that procedure again?"

I'm not sure if it was because this was the best path to follow or I was hesitant to go too far, but in the sessions, once he was in the hypnogogic state, I stuck to questions that elicited factual information. Some of his responses were startling, yet I kept in mind that he could—and certainly had the inner resources to—filter the information offered. Apparently, Devon chose not to hide behind a barrier.

Or what he told me he wanted me to know. A part of me couldn't help feeling I was part of a new game that was intriguing him and he wanted to keep playing until it became tedious.

Devon began speaking of his childhood. Growing up, his father held almost total power in the family. As the son of a self-made man, Devon's father was used to having control, exercising power, and having his demands met. The demands on his children focused mostly on Devon, the oldest. He would have to be brilliant and, as it happened, fortunately or not, he was; he would have to prepare for a career full of accomplishment, though, oddly, not in the father's profession; and Devon had to carry himself as if he were a hell of a lot better than anyone else. The father was a gruff, emotionally cold, and domineering man whose high expectations could never be met.

Nevertheless, up to a point, Devon had come close. He excelled academically and spent most of his time studying, at the expense of play and otherwise socializing with his peers. One escape from the disciplined routine had been staying up half the night, after his parents had gone to sleep, and watching movies on cable television and videos. When he was older, he frequented movie theaters.

His mother, despite the advantages of inherited social status, was readily submissive. She catered to her husband's and children's needs. She was a nervous, physically frail woman who Devon determined fairly early on was now close to being useless. She had essentially served her purpose to her husband by bringing "class" into the marriage and then bearing two sons. Everything after that was little more than existence. She was a presence to be tolerated in the family and not, I surmised, respected or loved.

The younger brother, Andre, named after the father's grandfather, was just there. At least, that's what Devon indicated. He did not seem to serve any purpose other than to be insurance that the family name would survive should something happen to Devon. Ironically, the mother doted on Andre, lavishing him with much more attention and emotional connection than she did with Devon. It was disturbing to watch Devon struggle when discussing Andre, to filter out expressions of jealousy and anger. There was something else, too, but Devon wouldn't reveal it and I hesitated to pursue the subject.

Okay, not a "normal" family, whatever that was these days, but certainly not the most dysfunctional I'd encountered. I sensed during the sessions in which I collected this information that Devon was enjoying the offerings, as though for many years he, or a part of him, had been awaiting the opportunity. In the telling he observed and reflected upon the details and his own reactions.

In a way, I felt like a lawyer questioning a cooperative

witness. Devon would, for the most part, answer what I asked. I just had to ask the right questions, as he had advised me weeks ago at the beginning of our sessions. If I didn't ask, he wouldn't volunteer information. The answers he provided were as much or more interesting to him as they were to me.

Sometimes, other than feeling like a lawyer, I felt like a tool. Devon was playing a game that included me but was mostly with himself. He was interested in and pondered inwardly what he said and held it up for examination. I did not know what the purpose was. But as long as he was cooperative, I went along.

The only time his composure broke—though "broke" is too strong a word, because it was nowhere near like the earlier episode—was when I asked about his parents' relationship with each other. Devon had portrayed it as rather distant, almost like a Victorian marriage of convenience. Did they love each other?

"Love?" Devon said. He repeated the word several times, only his mouth moving as he slumped back in the chair. "Do you mean did they have sex more than, obviously, twice?"

"No, not necessarily."

"They did, you know."

"What?"

"Oh yes. They did. And, oh, they thought no one knew. Not me, for damn sure." Then one eyebrow went up in that trick of his, and his lids fluttered. "Maybe they did. They are true degenerates. Yes, they wanted me to. . . ."

After a minute of silence, I asked, "What did they want?"

"That I knew they were doing it."

His large hands clasped at one knee and tugged. "I was

only three. Maybe four. Still precocious, huh? I slept in their room, a little narrow bed against the wall. Their bed was like a great expanse, with a canopy and curtains, but they were never closed all the way."

"Why did you sleep in their room?"

Devon laughed. "You'll have to ask them. I think they wanted me to see."

"See what?"

"Them doing it."

"So you saw them having sex. That isn't unusual."

His laughter interrupted me, though it was kept at an even level. "Unusual? I leave that to you. He pulled his pajama bottoms down, lifted her nightgown up, she was on her stomach, sort of mewling like a cat, an animal. He started thrusting. Big Dad. Willing Mom. He did it and kept doing it. Pig Dad. Both animals. She kept crying out. He was grunting, a rutting animal. She made all sorts of sounds. He had to be hurting her, right? But he kept at it. They both made sounds, higher, louder. . . ."

His head lolled to one side and he was silent.

"Devon, did your mother ever complain about being hurt? About your father hurting her?"

"No." He added bitterly, "She never complained about anything."

"Isn't it possible that with those sounds she was expressing pleasure?"

"He was hurting her. Do you think it's pleasant to be fucked up the ass?"

"Are you certain that's what they were doing?"

"Don't be so obtuse!" Devon suddenly shouted, his body stiffening and his eyes wide open.

I waited, breathing slowly and quietly, expecting another personality shift. Then he relaxed a bit, tilting his head as if considering his own reaction, examining it from various angles. He gradually slid back in the chair.

"Dr. Obler, let me clarify. There are times when you seem to be easily confused. That is disappointing."

There was a hint of warning in his voice, but I let that pass. "Please explain."

"At the time when I observed these *encounters*, I wasn't aware that my parents were screwing. To me, one was hurting the other. When I got older, of course, I understood that sex was involved. However, pleasure was not. Or I should say, my mother's pain was pleasure for my father."

"How did that make you feel toward him?"

Devon smiled slightly. "I had a healthy hatred for both my parents."

"You consider hatred healthy?"

"It can be quite useful. Let's move on."

In these two sessions, I learned more about his school experiences. Devon was sent to private schools where the students came from families of wealth and social privilege, so he didn't have an edge there. Also, most of his peers were intelligent. Devon's intelligence, however, seemed to be greater and more agile than his schoolmates'.

To cope with his own feelings, the jealousy of other students, and even the behavior of some of the teachers toward him who apparently found him difficult and disrespectful, Devon played power games. He was simply quicker than others. Offering friendship and then withholding it, he shifted among his peers, finding weak spots to exploit and playing one student or teacher against another.

As he related these experiences, he didn't express any guilt or remorse about his behavior. And I sensed that he had none now.

When this last session ended, Devon stood and stretched, the muscles of his arms and chest straining the fabric of his shirt. "Ahhh," he sighed. "Was it good for you too?"

My voice sounded hoarse.

"I've found it most illuminating."

"Now that you know me better, what do you think?"

I sat on the edge of my desk, looking up at him. "I may know you better than two months ago, but I can't say I know you. We still have a lot of road to travel."

He raised an eyebrow again. "Such a dilemma."

"What is?"

"You don't know enough, so you really must find out more." He leaned toward me, gazing down unblinking. "And learning more may make you unhappy."

"My happiness isn't a. . . ."

"Poor choice of words. Disturbed?"

"Devon, at times like this, I have the feeling that there is something very important you want to tell me. Why don't you just say it?"

"Oh, that wouldn't be any fun." He stepped back. "But I'm trying to help you, really I am. More so than I have with anyone else. I don't want you to be disappointed either."

"Then we'll keep having at it."

He grinned and threw his jacket over one broad shoulder. With his hand on the doorknob, he turned sideways. "I'm glad it's daytime. And I feel safe here. Do you?"

"Yes. Why wouldn't I?"

Devon spoke quietly. "There was another murder, not far from here. I bet most people are apprehensive. The victim—what a way to go."

"Do you feel sorry for him?"

Devon shrugged. "What is he to me?" Then Devon opened the door and left.

Late that afternoon I was on my way to meet Rachel for dinner. Having spent most of the day sitting behind the desk, I decided to walk to the 14th Street subway station. People walking by held up arms and briefcases against the wind. The cold gusts made my eyes water. I was barely noticing where I was going anyway, deep in thought about Devon.

I was sure that he was indeed concealing something powerful, and it wasn't necessarily any specific act or bit of knowledge. I suspected more than ever that it was a deep core of anger or even rage. Whether it was directed at himself, his family, others or cumulatively all of the above, I couldn't tell. I compared him to a volcano. So far I had heard only rumblings.

Taunting me, daring me to find out. If I found out, would the discovery be disturbing, as he had said? How messed up was he? There was a disorder, I was certain, but how deep and serious was it? Even the casual way he mentioned the murder victims was indicative of a lack of compassion, of feeling. Again, a disturbing thought came to me. Psychopaths have no conscience, no empathy. They can manufacture feelings but, in reality, have no real feelings for others.

I stopped walking and glanced up at the darkening sky and swiftly moving clouds. Could Devon be a psychopath? Just asking the question of myself made me very uncomfortable. I had to remain open to every patient, and stay objective. The patient is the top priority. A psychopath? I shook my head as people brushed past me. It was wrong to think of Devon that way.

As I resumed walking, the station two blocks ahead, the feeling of being watched, perhaps followed, came over me. I quickly looked around. There was someone across the street, a tall man with blond or white hair, who appeared to be staring my way.

I couldn't see him clearly. He was just a face fleetingly appearing between passing cars and buses. The stinging wind had blurred my vision. When I rubbed my eyes and looked again, he was gone.

Imagination. I was being silly. Yet, when I reached a bank of phones, I called Rachel and suggested she meet me at the restaurant instead of at her building.

I bought a newspaper and leafed through it during the ride uptown. Despite what Devon had said, there was no mention of a new murder. That struck me as odd. However, I tried to think only about seeing Rachel again. I willed myself to push thoughts of Devon aside. But they kept intruding.

Chapter 9

Life and Death Challenges

One day passed. Friday morning I awoke early and stepped outside my door to get the newspaper. There was a front page article about the newest body found. Dead about forty-eight hours.

LINK HINTED IN NEW SLAYING
Neighbors of Murdered Man
Tell of Stranger

Residents of the Lower West Side neighborhood where an eighteen-year-old youth was killed Tuesday night have told police they had seen a man in the area who strongly resembles a suspect in the sexual mutilation and slaying of three young men several months ago in the same or nearby areas. The composite sketch was one of several different ones drawn by a Police Department artist at the time of the murder of the three young men.

The suspect in the murder of Karl Jones, whose slashed body was discovered on top of an apartment house, was described as wearing a hooded blue jacket and sunglasses, 6 feet tall, muscular build and medium complexion.

Residents indicated to the police that they had seen a man in similar garb talking to some boys near a basketball court on West 14th Street.

Although no witnesses to the slaying of Karl Jones have come forward the police questioned 100 suspects to obtain lead.

The police said all the victims have been mutilated and sexually molested and that there were similarities to the other slayings. They would not divulge the similarities.

Thoughts of Devon whirled through my mind. A psychologist does not jump to conclusions. Of course, in many occupations, people, especially if they have learned to rely on instinct, have to reach quick conclusions—police officers, firemen, emergency room personnel, shopkeepers, basketball players.

However, not in psychology. Practitioners (the good ones, anyway) work with patients in a deliberate fashion, gradually collecting information and then mixing it with perceptions, observations, and professional experience to form a theory about the root of the patient's problem. That theory is tested in subsequent sessions, and the practitioner must be open to altering or even throwing it out the window and starting over to develop a more suitable one.

I had tried not to jump to conclusions in Devon's case. We had now met twelve times. Sometimes, however, there are signals and signs which are hard to ignore. When Devon arrived for the next session, the first thing I asked him was, "How did you know there was another murder?"

"What murder?" he said, appearing genuinely surprised.

"Last week, when we were finishing up you mentioned it."

"Oh, that." He shrugged, then leaned back in the chair and crossed his legs.

I prodded him. "It wasn't in the newspaper until two days later."

"Must've been on the radio or maybe someone I knew mentioned it. Big deal."

"Okay."

I felt my face reddening and hoped he wouldn't notice. What was I doing? Was I thinking he knew something about the murders—as disturbing as they were, *I* hadn't paid much attention to them—because of a casual comment? This was embarrassing. Some professional I was. I was happy to move on; then I saw that Devon was grinning.

"Who do we have here, Dr. Obler or Dr. Watson?" he said, wagging a finger at me.

"Just idle curiosity. Your remark stuck in my head and I felt like asking."

Now he laughed, his shoulders shaking. "Sometimes you're so transparent!" he chortled. Then he stopped laughing. "And I'm supposed to trust you."

"That was an inappropriate question, Devon. I'm sorry."

He raised the one eyebrow and leaned forward with a slight smile as though about to reveal a secret.

"It would create an intriguing situation for you if you had a patient who was a murderer and actually told you, wouldn't it? I mean, it's confidential. You couldn't tell anyone. Could you?"

"Hypothetically?"

"Of course." He leaned back, chuckling.

"No, but the laws are always being redefined. For instance, if I'm informed of child molestation going on or it is clear that someone is about to be harmed, I as a therapist am obligated to go to the authorities. But that's not ironclad, because"—I ticked off one finger—"there has to be a clear and present danger, and that is subject to interpretation by a therapist who presumably is completely objective."

I ticked off a second finger. "Also, most professionals, and I'm one of them, are trained to make the patient's health the top priority. If the therapist is not absolutely certain, he, by training and philosophy, is obligated not to discuss what is said or divulged in sessions. The consequences are serious, both to the patient and to the professional who has broken confidentiality."

"My, what a dilemma." Devon mused for a few moments, idly scratching one cheek. "Makes me think of *I Confess*, the Alfred Hitchcock movie, 1953. Montgomery Cliff plays a priest. Some acting job, considering his freewheeling personal life. A killer confesses that. . . ."

"I've seen it," I broke in, somewhat irritated by the way he was toying with me. "I'm not a priest."

"Oh, don't I know that!" Devon crowed.

"You do? May I ask how?"

"Dr. Obler, with all due respect, are we here to talk about you or me?"

He had me twisting in the wind, and flustered. "I'm sorry. Let's get down to business."

"Before we do, I want to reveal something."

"Yes?"

"Today I signed the forms and officially left the university." He held up his hand as though pushing away an expected protest. "I know. I should've discussed this with you first, instead of just springing it on you."

After a pause I said, "My participation in your decision or reaction to it isn't important."

"But you're upset."

"Well, yes. I know how intelligent and talented you are, Devon. It is impossible to know how far you can go in this field, but I suspect you would have done very well."

He gazed at me, then said, "And?"

To make sure our trust remained strong, especially after what I'd said earlier, I had to be honest, to confirm what he had apparently sensed. "And I feel that I have failed you in some way. We began with the intent of having you remain in the doctoral program."

"Why we began is irrelevant now," he said sternly. "We're moving in a different direction."

"And that is?"

He smiled. "Let's find out, shall we?"

I glanced at my watch, happy to see our time was up, and my next patient was waiting.

When I had a break between sessions later that day, I called Pomerantz, who confirmed that Devon had dropped out. I did not mention that in our morning session Devon seemed disturbed about my expression of having failed him and the session had not been productive, but I did admit to Pomerantz that I wished I'd had an opportunity to discuss the matter with Devon before he acted.

"Marty, I'm sure it has nothing to do with you."

"Why is that?"

"This young man has trouble sticking to things. He loses interest." There was a knock against the receiver, probably the dean's glasses slipping down his face. "It was just our turn. Maybe it's for the best."

Perhaps he was right. I recalled from Devon's records that his schooling had been interrupted at least twice before, and I knew he could become bored easily. "Did he give a reason to anyone there?"

"No. Cold and distant is what he was. Did the paperwork and left. No goodbyes, more like good riddance. You?"

"I tried to ask but he didn't care to discuss it and I didn't press the issue."

"Do you think he'll stay in therapy with you?"

"I don't know," I said wearily.

"Are you making progress, Marty?"

I did some quick thinking. If Devon was no longer a student at the university, then technically he was strictly my patient and mine alone now (we'd have to work out the details about the change of status, and payment), and anything I told Pomerantz risked breaching patient-therapist confidentiality. I would give him an evaluation report based on the initial sessions and nothing more. On the other hand, I suddenly felt cast adrift and could use some input from a respected, more experienced colleague.

"How about we discuss it over dinner?" I said. "I'll even treat again—but add it to my bill, of course."

"Just send the bill." Pomerantz said curtly.

"You have other plans?"

"Marty," he began gruffly, and I pictured the glasses pushed up on his head again, "I'm not sorry Devon dropped out. He did, he's out. The university is happy to close the book on him." He paused and then said, "And personally I have a bad feeling about him."

"A 'feeling'? How about the patient?"

"He's your patient now. Good luck." Abruptly Pomerantz hung up.

Despite my worry about his continuing therapy, especially after I told him I would now have to bill him personally, a fact he took in stride, Devon was more gregarious and willing. He readily underwent the hypnogogic procedure the following week.

I had been prepared to insist. The more I'd thought about Devon, which was during every unoccupied moment, the more questions I had, and the stronger was my desire to come up with answers. I needed Devon to help me, an uncomfortable situation for a psychologist. Pomerantz could wash his hands of the situation. I had to persist.

Perhaps what bothered me most was that we had taken a few steps forward but now might sink into inertia again. Whatever Devon's disorder was—and I was now thoroughly convinced there was one—if we drifted along I would never have insight into it and might even be enabling it.

Devon was both a professional and personal challenge. I was growing frustrated at feeling at a disadvantage, of being inadequate to draw him out or ascertain the truth. Whatever I was to find out, I was ready for it, and *could* handle it.

Or so I thought.

This time I went in another direction. I first asked simple questions and Devon offered trivial details. It was apparent that he was barely interested. He'd dropped out of the psychology program, maybe he'd next drop out of our sessions. My gut feeling was this was the worst thing that he could do.

"Tell me a fantasy," I said.

He raised his head, keeping it from lolling, and asked, "You want what?"

"A fantasy. Everyone fantasizes."

"You too?"

"Sure."

He laughed softly.

"You live your fantasies, don't you?"

I ignored whatever he was implying, though a small voice in the back of my mind cautioned, *Be careful.* Trying to be the patient-oriented professional, I ignored that voice too.

"Devon, tell me about any fantasy you want."

He was silent for a minute. His head slowly lowered, and only the whites of his eyes showed. His arms hung at his sides, though once he began talking his fingers twitched.

"I'll tell you a story, Dr. Obler. It's about sex. Do you

want to hear it?"

"Please."

Other than the twitching fingers, he didn't move. "Dark movie houses. Alone. The cool anonymous darkness. I told you about the movies, old ones. Then I went to other ones. I was sixteen. On and around 42nd Street. All that fornicating, rampant, closeups, details, disgusting. Men. Deserved what they got, in the mouth, up the ass. Me, watching, just there, you know. All eyes.

"Holy shit, look at that! Movie over, these guys were on stage. Naked. Real guys naked. Except this one guy, more like a kid, small and skinny. Bends over. Wow, were they going to hump him right there? Oh, wait, a freaking bottle, long neck. They're putting it up his ass! Must hurt. No! He likes it! More, stick it in more! Oh, man, feels good. Can't believe I'm seeing this. All eyes."

Devon laughs softly. "Guy sits next to me. Feel him there, try not to look. Smell of leather, his jacket. Smell of greasy hair, wet jeans and shoes, must've been raining, just came in, saw me, sat down. Puts his paw on my pants. Tried to unzip me, can't do it, pants too taut. Watching."

His hands stopped twitching. "Hotel around the corner. We did it. Like a movie. Hurt me. Did it again. He kept the jacket on. Smell of leather. Smell of sex. Smells. I made my way home. No one notices I'm different." Devon's pupils appeared. "That's good."

"Do you like being different?"

"Am I?"

I sidestepped. "That really happened?"

"Yes. Do you appreciate that I'm honest with you?"

"I do."

Despite my shock, I wanted to take advantage of this opening, to try to glimpse what he concealed. "Thank you for that recollection. Let me ask about a dream. Or are they the same? That was so much like one."

"You'll have to figure that out."

"Maybe next time we'll do the dream."

"Okay, okay," he said somewhat irritably. It was interesting to note that he would object to any expression on my part of disinterest. "Up the ass."

"You told me that," I challenged.

"No, shrinkface, *me* doing it."

"That's your dream?"

He laughed, then mumbled for a few moments, the words gradually becoming clear. "I'm doing it. Feels good at first. But it stops. 'Butt,' get it? It stops. Can't feel it. Okay, stay still. Got something here. You like it? Sharp. Careful, might cut you. No, don't move! Stop it! That's better. So close, careful, delicious. We're on the edge."

Devon was sweating. His hands appeared to be reaching, but nothing was next to the chair. The fingers keep quivering. "It's okay if it hurts," he said, almost whispering. "My turn? Oh no, Oh no!"

He sat upright in the chair, rigid except for his hands making twisting motions. Foam formed at the corners of his mouth. His head began to quiver, then shook violently. His fingers were curled, grabbing at air. Then they fell limp into his lap but the rest of his body continued to quake. Foam spilled over his lower lip. I was suddenly afraid that he was having a seizure.

I got up and went around the desk to bring him out of the hypnogogic state. Then I paused, observing.

Devon shook himself. It wasn't involuntary. This time I was certain that he was causing the violent shaking. His head bobbed and jumped on his shoulders, and his eyelids fluttered furiously. His feet were planted on the floor but the rest of his body shuddered as though he was about to hurl himself up and through the ceiling.

Then the motion subsided. He raised his head and stared at me. "That's enough," Devon said.

"I want to ask you about. . . ."

"I'm not 'under' any more, Dr. Obler." His blue eyes were bright and focused on me. "You requested a dream. Take it or leave it."

I returned to the desk. "I'll take it. Thank you."

He stood up and thrust his arms through the sleeves of his thick, dark blue sweatshirt. "Sometimes I leave here spent and sweaty. Kind of like sex, isn't it?"

"Are you all right?"

He laughed and turned to the door. "Up your ass, poke, with a bottle of Coke!" Then he left.

I went to lunch at a pub on Bleecker Street and sat at a table against the window. I ordered a burger and a beer, but when they came I wasn't hungry or thirsty.

Never, either in individual or group therapy, had I encountered someone who could bring himself out of a hypnogogic state. There were a few reports in the professional literature of it happening. The subjects were all psychopaths.

Devon had literally shaken himself out of it by force of will, or indeed had experienced a seizure that was so powerful that the electric impulses in his brain had broken the hypnogogic state. The cause of the seizure? Perhaps he had gotten close to revealing what was in a sealed-off compartment and strong resources in his mind had hurled him away.

I did not want to think of Devon as a psychopath. I didn't want to jump to conclusions or suspicions. Another reason, I admitted to myself, had to do with avoidance. I did not want to accept the possibility. But he was the most unusual patient and person I'd ever come across. I was almost afraid to think about him beyond that.

The pub was crowded. Maybe it was just coincidence, but most of the patrons were young men. My mind revolved backward to Devon's fantasy. If I was to believe him, considering his interest in keeping me off-guard, he demonstrated intense sexual arousal while watching men perform sex with each other. Also he said he'd had sex with a male stranger.

Did he concern himself with the possibility of contracting a venereal disease or the HIV virus? I doubted it. Further, I would wager that Devon felt more powerful and invulnerable than any disease.

A waiter stopped by and looked at my full plate. "Is anything wrong?"

I stared at him. "With the food?" he added.

"Thanks, no." After he walked away, I stood up and tossed money on the table.

As I left the pub, the scene in Devon's fantasy of the bottle entered my mind, and Devon's comments from his "dream" replayed. I didn't want to think about them. Actually I did, but I had other patients and responsibilities. Yet everything else I did was becoming like a sideshow to the main event, my encounters with Devon.

In the next session, I decided not to go over what Devon had related in the last one. Devon could become bored, or perhaps anticipating such questions he had formed defenses against them.

Instead, once he was in the hypnogogic state, I kept my voice light. "Devon, I am grateful to you."

"Really?" The eyebrow slid slowly up. "Why?"

"You have engaged my interest more than any other patient. It's rare for a psychologist to look forward to sessions with any one person as much as I look forward to our meetings."

He appeared genuinely pleased. "I do want to make you happy, Dr. Obler."

"I am particularly intrigued at the prospect of exploring more dreams with you."

"Hey, it's like I'm Gregory Peck and you're Ingrid Bergman in *Spellbound*." He smiled. "Not that you're a woman. Do you think Hitchcock was bisexual or homosexual?"

"I don't know. Please, could you relate another dream?"

Devon lifted his shoulders and let them fall. The pupils of his eyes had disappeared. His legs and arms were crossed. He was silent for a few minutes. I listened to the tall clock tick.

"The situation is vague," he finally said, speaking slowly and carefully. "I'm in fog, or a smoky apartment. Facing me is a young boy who looks a little like Andre. He's naked with a large dark mole on his back. At first I think he's two years old, then he's a teenager. He grew up right while I was looking at him."

"If he's facing you," I interrupted, "how do you know he has a mole on his back?"

"I just know it's there." Devon is silent for another minute. "The kid—he's maybe seventeen or eighteen—picks up a large bottle and begins to rub the neck up and down. I'm infuriated with him, but I don't know why.

"Suddenly, I grab the bottle out of his hands and break it against the base of the big wooden bed. He is startled. The top of the bottle is large, jagged edges. Hey, it's like in westerns when cowboys are having a barroom brawl."

When his smile fades, Devon continues. "The fog or whatever gets thicker and I'm really tense trying to see. Where's the kid? I wander around the room, then I see him standing to one side sucking on a large banana. As I get closer, I see blood dripping off the other end of the banana. Oh man, I want to fuck this kid. When I turn him around the jagged edges of the glass begin to dig into the mole. Blood is running down his back and down through the crack of his ass. I think he has cancer."

After a few minutes of silence, I asked, "What comes to mind when you think about this dream?"

"Nothing, you bastard!" Devon shouted.

"Okay. What else? Does it continue?"

His head lolled to one side. "No more."

While he remained in the hypnogogic state for the remainder of the session, he refused to discuss any more dreams. When I brought him out of it, he stood without a word, walked to the door, paused and turned.

"Dr. Obler, did you really mean what you said about me?"

"Yes, I did."

There was a bemused expression on his face that made me uncomfortable. Then he left.

I stayed at my desk to make notes, but after only a few minutes I got up and went to the window overlooking the street. Devon had just walked out of the building. He didn't bother looking to the left or right before crossing the street.

Chapter 10

Distorted Vows

"I'm part of a motorcycle gang," Devon said, his voice in the hypnogogic state, slow and flat. "I'm the leader. Like Marlon Brando in *The Wild One*."

"Please go on with the dream," I said.

"Okay. So I'm in this gang, and we're not out in some dusty town somewhere, but right here in Manhattan. We round up some appetizing young girls to be our sex slaves."

I cringed. "Go on."

"I've got to be careful, make sure the gang stays afraid of the leader or they're going to turn on me just like we're going to turn on the girls we've captured. So I come up with an idea. I tell the gang we've got to get rid of them, pointing to the girls, but it's. . . ."

His voice trailed off. His arms were limp, fingers extended toward the floor. It was raining hard outside, a cold rain with torrents battering the window. I had to strain to hear him.

"Yes, Devon?"

"So my idea is to sew up all their cunts. I've got

surgical thread I stole from a hospital. Then, after that, they all begin screaming. It's most annoying. Kind of exciting too, but mostly they're hurting my ears. They should be killed to shut them up. The gang members are looking at me. They want me to do it. I'm the leader."

He was silent again.

Finally, I said, "What do you do?"

"I go up to the girls and ask what they want as a last request. They all ask for money. One by one, going down the line, I stare into their eyes. They're pathetic—fragile, vulnerable, helpless, completely powerless. It's time to kill them one at a time. A gang member hands me the weapon. It's a huge glass bottle."

After a few moments of silence, he added, "Then I woke up."

I was glad when the session ended and my next appointment appeared. I wanted to postpone interpreting what Devon's dream meant.

Even after the last patient had gone, I stayed at the office. I wasn't hungry. I filled up the hours by compiling notes about Devon.

For every hundred words I typed into the computer I spent ten or fifteen minutes staring at the ceiling, the tall clock, or out the dark window. The rain had slowed to a harsh drizzle; a few degrees colder and it would turn to sleet. I had made notes all along on the sessions with Devon, but tonight my mind was boiling over with thoughts. I imagined that if I stuck my head out the window, the exposure to the drizzle would create a steam cloud similar to the way water gushes out of a street grate.

Exploring Devon's dreams had, I believed, been quite rewarding. Precisely what they revealed, if they offered unprecedented insight into his psyche and the connections to

be made were what I hoped to figure out by hours of unin-
terrupted thinking and writing.

Did Devon have deep-rooted conflicts about his
sexuality? Was Devon bisexual, homosexual? I recalled
that several times in our sessions throughout the last
three months when he had mentioned women he had
done so in a very negative, bitter way. Not hatred—it
was more like disdain, even contempt. Okay, I could
connect that with an attitude toward his mother. Of
course he talked of men the same way. I was sure that
Devon never had a real personal relationship that
involved any positive feelings like friendship, respect,
or helpfulness with a woman or a man.

What was even more intriguing was the question
of whether Devon had any genuine feelings at all. No,
that wasn't it. It was more like he could manufacture
the impression of feelings, and might convince himself
for some moments that they were genuine, but those
feelings were not deep or profound. Maybe the capacity
to feel had not developed in him. There might be only
the basic urges of hunger, survival, sex, control of his
surroundings, and perhaps self-protective fear linked to
survival. Devon seemed a fascinating mixture of high
intellect and animal instincts.

A predator possibly. A psychopath?

I believed there *was* strong feeling harbored deep
within him, and that it was rage. At what he raged and how
it had developed I still had to determine, along with whether
or not he recognized it. I suspected he did not, or at least that
his intellect prevented him from acknowledging it. He
thought and acted in a completely self-justifying manner. If
he did indeed feel trust for me, it was probably because for
now it suited him.

Based on material elicted during the sessions and the dreams offered so far, most likely his rage had begun developing in childhood. However, it was more complicated than that. Most young children, for a variety of reasons, feel anger at their parents. Commonly, it's mixed with fear of abandonment. The child is angry because he or she *might* be abandoned. Many children divert that fear and anger into anger against themselves or anger against a weaker figure: a child certainly can't be angry with its powerful parents. In Devon's case he had done both, turning the anger inward and also at his younger brother.

I shook my head. That doesn't create a psychopath. If it did, more than half of us could be classified as such. What happens is, at some point, say around six years old, children essentially outgrow these feelings and move on. We might not completely lose resentment and anger toward our parents, and God knows older siblings take delight in roughly teasing and "torturing" younger ones, but, as we grow, those feelings assume their proper place among many other feelings. A balance is struck. When we mature we have a better understanding of family dynamics as well as "normal" life, and become adjusted.

I theorized for the moment that Devon never turned the corner most boys turn. He remained stuck. His mind and body grew, both becoming quite imposing, but his undeveloped feelings evolved into rage and went no further. Was it possible that since he could not hurt himself he had turned instead to hurting others? Yes. But there was no evidence of that other than his dreams. Moreover, having dreams that included violence did not mean Devon was violent. Even the most "adjusted" people have dreams in which we harm someone else, even those we love.

Not only had his dreams revealed furious feelings

toward his parents, but at his brother Andre. This was supported by other information that had come out of the hypnogogic experiments. He had observed his parents having intercourse, powerful father dominating compliant mother. He had interpreted the sounds they made as giving and expressing pain and the position as anal entry (which may not have been the case). He developed a hatred for the father for "hurting" the mother, but, of course, could not challenge him or do anything to prevent the act from happening over and over again. Still, I remembered Devon also expressing rage at his mother for enjoying the act, calling them both "degenerates."

The glass or bottle theme kept repeating. In one session, Devon had mentioned in an offhand reminiscence that I hadn't considered too important at the time, that soon after his brother was born and was home from the hospital, in a fit of jealousy Devon had picked up a baby bottle and tried to smash his new rival with it. He was stopped by his father just in time.

What was unusual in Devon was that in his fantasies and dreams, especially the motorcycle gang dream, he had used glass or sharp objects. And similar objects were also used in his fantasies about sex.

As an early object of hatred, Devon may have sexually abused Andre to some extent, perhaps with a bottle or a penetrating sharp object, without causing serious damage. This could have ended at the time when Andre was old enough to either resist or report the abuse, or the urge was confined to Devon's fantasies and dreams.

Devon had also said in a session that one time after his parents had sex he thought he saw blood on his father's penis and blood around his mother's anus, further associating sex with violence. This spurred more anger toward his father and contempt for his mother for submitting to such apparently harmful treatment. What Devon might not have known was that his mother might have been menstruating or that there had been a cut caused by an otherwise pleasurable act.

Devon may have felt that if he expressed his anger, his father might attack him in a similar way and his mother desert him. His choice was to direct his anger toward his brother and possibly elsewhere, harboring it for other opportunities. What should have happened over time, along with some insight and maturity, was the development of conscience and feelings of guilt and remorse for his violent thoughts and cruel behavior. At this point I saw little evidence that Devon had developed a conscience.

My thinking, at this point, was that in Devon a conscience hadn't developed because his narcissistic self-wounding resulted in intense anger toward himself which was then redirected toward wanting to hurt others. In the standard psychology texts, that would brand him as a psychopath. The latest evidence in psychodynamic research is that a psychopath becomes fixated during the period in childhood before the superego or conscience normally develops.

I stared at the dark window dotted with hundreds of droplets. Was I really ready to form the conclusion that Devon was a psychopath? Was I ready to turn that corner?

There was no indication other than in dreams that Devon had hurt or sought to hurt anyone. Perhaps he was teetering on the brink. My job was to help him, to bring him back from the edge. For all his intelligence, how difficult and painful his life must be.

And he said he trusted me.

My hands were pressed against the sides of my head. The digital clock mechanically informed me that it was after one o'clock in the morning. Even for me, it was time to go home.

"Marty, I need to talk to you," Stella, my ex-wife, said on the phone much too early the next morning.

"Mark and Salena have just left for school," she said. This was a "good time" for her.

I poured another cup of coffee and said, "Yes?"

"While the kids got ready for school, I watched the news. And it made me afraid."

This was uncertain ground. I sat at the small counter/partition that separated my kitchen from living room. Once again I was living in a tight space, as in the Brooklyn days, but this time alone. "Why?" All I could manage were one word replies.

"It was reported there's been another murder."

"So?"

"The body was found only three blocks from here."

"And?"

"This time it's a young woman, a so called 'model' who's been mutilated."

"Mutilated," I echoed.

"Yes, God knows how." Stella was trying to keep frustration—and, I suddenly realized, genuine fear—out of her voice. "Try to focus, Marty. This is about our children."

Silence filled the line. I didn't trust myself to speak. My head was swimming. I didn't know what to think. Had Devon read of the girl's murder in the newspaper and spawned a dream to entice me or had he done it?

"I'm sorry, Stella. Really." I was going to mention having worked very late the night before and feeling somewhat overwhelmed by my concern for one of my patients, but since such concerns had led to the end of our marriage, it was best not to get into it. "From what I've heard about the crimes, which I admit is very little. . . ."

"Marty, the girl was nineteen. Okay, Salena is only ten, but it's frightening. What's to say, all right? Something very bad is happening out there, and it's getting closer."

"Why are you telling me this?" I asked her. "I mean, I don't like it that young people are being murdered. . . ."

"There's a serial killer out there. *Here.*"

"Yes, okay, say you're right."

"They said so on the news."

"Yes, but serial killers have a pattern. Does Salena or any of us fit it?"

Stella paused. "I don't know. But this girl was killed with a soda bottle, just like the others. Maybe the killer is changing his pattern. Marty, can you find out anything? You're a psychologist. Do you know someone who has information? I don't want us hurt!"

Now her terror was obvious, and however busy or distracted I was I wouldn't ignore her or our children. "I'll try to find out something, okay?" I said. "It's a good thing you take the kids to school."

"I know. But there's an awful feeling here in the neighborhood. I'd really like to know something more about what we're dealing with."

"I'll try. I promise."

I really didn't have any good sources to consult in law enforcement. Given the confidential nature of my profession, the less contact I had with police officials the better. First, I thought of that day's newspaper. Of course the story on the

murder of which Stella had told was there. To learn more
about the murders, early that afternoon I hiked over to the
university library and looked through back issues of a couple
of newspapers.

It was only after the fourth murder that there was an
article of any consequence. The victims had all been seventeen to twenty. They had probably been stabbed. The details
were vague, and there was the implication that the victims
were mutilated during what one reporter termed "rough sex
that went too far." Subsequent articles said basically the
same thing.

They had occurred uncomfortably close to home. The
most recent article about the girl's death said people in the
Village were scared and were being more cautious with
their children.

RIVER DEATH RAISES
NEIGHBORHOOD FEAR

**The discovery of the body of nineteen-year-
old Jennifer Chantilly floating in the Hudson
River off Greenwich Village has further
heightened this neighborhood's anxiety. Five
additional murders, though of young men,
have been reported in recent months. Police
announced there were similarities to the other
murders, but they once again refused to comment further.**

**The dead young woman, whose occupation
was listed as a model, was found Wednesday.
Ms. Chantilly lived at 15 Hudson Street. She**

**had been stabbed numerous times and
mutilated in a killing police are referring to as
a "rough sex" encounter.**

Still, that wouldn't be enough for Stella, and I
felt a pang of remaining love for her that she should
be so protective of our children. So, later at my office
during a gap between appointments, I called Todd
Shapiro. He and I had been good friends at Brooklyn
College. He was a trustworthy comrade in fun, frolic,
and sometimes scholarship. We had expected to
remain solid friends. However, he had chosen the
path into journalism, and I had followed the path of
psychology. The two worlds can be very far apart.
Now he was an assistant managing editor at *Newsbeat*.

After preliminaries about our families and careers, I
said, "I don't know anyone in your business."

"Then you don't know anyone worthwhile."

I laughed. "Okay, I'm at your mercy. Listen, Stella's
worried about something."

"For her, I'll help."

Todd chuckled, but I knew he would. Those
Brooklyn and dating days were a bond. Now a further bond
had developed. We were both divorced, and he probably
didn't like his situation any more than I liked mine.

"These serial killings in and around the Village. She's
worried about them. Worried about Mark and Salena."

"They're very nasty," he agreed. "We've been following them here. Sounds cold, but there has to be a certain
amount of gore to interest a national magazine." He covered
the phone to yell something to someone else, then he got

back on the line. "But we're close to doing a piece. Not me, a real reporter." He laughed again. "Anyway, Marty, it *is* getting to be big news."

"Why is it nasty?"

"Jeez, it's enough to be killed, but these young men and now this young woman have been mutilated, cut up like crazy. Local press is probably cooperating with the New York fuzz, not publishing the down and dirty. But it's bad. Real sick. Makes Son of Sam and the Zodiac Killer look like Mother Theresa."

"The details are worse than what's in the paper?"

"You can't imagine, even in your sordid, twisted profession. Hey, maybe it's one of yours."

A moment of silence. Then I recovered myself. "Nah. These days I just do therapy with rich broads who want to screw their husband's chauffeurs."

"I can drive. Give 'em my number." His voice lowered. "Just between you and me, the victims have been sliced to ribbons, capital 'N' nasty. This ain't no surgeon but a real angry bastard. If I were you, I'd be on the safe side and find reasons to move Mark and Salena for a while."

"Thanks, Todd."

His voice lowered again. "Marty, you okay? Something we should know?"

"It's me. I did it."

"Don't I wish. Hello, Pulitzer Prize!"

He was laughing when I hung up. My hand was shaking. I was starting to be afraid for my children, but there was also something else. "One of yours?" Todd had asked. No, I didn't want to begin that line of thought. Devon had bad dreams that was all.

Devon's dream conversation weighed on my mind up

to the next session with him. I wondered again if Devon really wanted to be helped. Our relationship continued to be a game, a contest, a power struggle. For him, it was a challenge and fun. He had found an adversary who interested him. His likely underlying wish was to do battle with a father surrogate and finally defeat the powerful, hated foe. I didn't want any of this. We were going in a direction I never anticipated. Should I continue, try something else, or send Devon on his way?

But those murders. What if. . . ?

My conflicting thoughts continuing their battle in my brain when Devon arrived for his appointment. He took off his bulky black coat and vigorously rubbed his hands. He was grinning.

"What's got you looking like the Cheshire Cat?" I asked.

"I had a most intriguing dream, Dr. Obler. You're in this one."

Suddenly I felt a chill, as though he hadn't closed the outside door behind him. "You want to tell me about it?"

"Sure." He sat down and crossed his legs and clasped his hands behind his head. "I'm being driven by a headmaster toward the outer gates of a private school. I'm afraid of being kicked out. The big headmaster says I've acted too horribly to remain at the school. You're standing by the gates, looking on but doing nothing to defend me.

"Then the headmaster turns me around and we start walking back to the school building. I feel relieved, no, *ecstatic*, like I've fooled everyone and gotten away with murder. At that point you start calling to the headmaster, vehemently protesting that I shouldn't be allowed back in school. 'You're making a mistake!' you yell. 'He's the one!' I turn to look at you in disbelief, wondering how I could ever have trusted you."

Devon gazed at me, his face impassive. My hands were cold and clammy. I would interpret the specifics of this dream later, but we both knew its general thrust. I tried to return his gaze and waited for him to blink. He didn't.

"You would not turn me in, would you, Dr. Obler?" he finally said, his voice soft.

"What have you done?"

"That's not what I asked."

"Devon, I am a psychologist and bound, as you know, by doctor-patient confidentiality."

"Yes." He smiled, white teeth flashing. "We're linked, stuck with each other. Sort of like a marriage, isn't it? Not quite like your marriage. Here we have trust, right?"

"What do you. . . ?" I stopped. My own eyes blinking furiously. How had he found out details about my private life? I stared at him. What else did he know? About Stella, about my children?

He laughed. "Till death do us part," he said.

Chapter 11

Growing Fear

The acrid scent of murder was in the air. All the newspapers screamed headlines as the numbers of deaths mounted.

NO CLUES ARE FOUND IN THE MURDER OF TWO MORE
by Frank Bonavieda

The police said yesterday they had no immediate clues as they pressed their investigation in the murder of two young people found yesterday. One nineteen-year-old male and a twenty-year-old woman were the victims. They have not yet been identified. Their slashed bodies were discovered atop the roof of an apartment building in Greenwich Village.

The medical examiner placed the time of death of the woman and man between 1 and

4 a.m.

The police said the slayings appeared to be related to the recent string of murders in the area by a suspect dubbed the "Soda Pop Slasher." There were similar signs of sexual molestation and mutilation.

The bodies were discovered at 6 a.m. Friday by a woman walking her dog on the roof, according to Sergeant John Richards.

Parents on the Lower West Side of Manhattan were increasingly afraid to let their children out by themselves. To parents, any youngster walking to or from school, playing in the street, bicycling or going to a candy store was a potential victim. The Police Department was circulating flyers, warning residents. The media seized on the murders, linking them and dubbing the perpetrator the Soda Pop Slasher, because the victims were mutilated with broken soda bottles.

The streets teemed with suspects. More careful than before, people in Lower Manhattan locked their doors and windows. Sketches of the murderer were created, but they weren't too useful, reported the media, because the police really don't know who he is or what he looks like.

Two more victims, one a man and the other a woman, had been killed. Even the few details of their deaths released were gruesome. My children were fine in the morning going to school. It was coming home in late afternoons of shorter and shorter days that scared my son Mark and daughter Salena. Night approached fast this time of year, a more somber sign of winter than declining temperatures. For kids afraid of a new "bogeyman," the rapidly dying light meant the monster was about to strike.

If I wasn't sufficiently concerned after my conversation with Todd Shapiro, I surely was when I heard the fear in Mark's voice over the phone and then saw it in Salena's eyes at our next meeting. Stella and I decided she would take the kids to school every morning, and I would escort them home. Whoever of us had Salena and Mark on weekends would keep an eye on them every second.

This took some juggling of my hectic schedule, forcing me to inconvenience a few patients and clinic colleagues, but it was well worth it when I saw how pleased and relieved Mark and Salena were as they emerged from school and saw me standing by the gate.

"Who wants to go for a hot chocolate?" I asked cheerfully.

They looked at me with serious expressions and replied, "We just want to go home. Okay, Dad?"

How could I argue? Whatever made them feel safe.

As I walked around in the neighborhood more, stopping to chat with folks if I was early or on the way back with the kids, I found they were not the only ones fearful. Almost everyone was worried, and a few were downright panicked. A killer was on the loose, a werewolf who hunted at night. The body count was mounting and unspeakable things were being done to the victims. Men, women, and children felt vulnerable.

Even Fred Hawkins, a big middle-aged guy who ran a candy store, declared, "If I run into this bastard, there'll be one last mess for the cops to clean up." I could see his eyelids twitching and heard the hollowness in his voice.

From what had been reported it appeared that the killer preyed mostly on males, but also females between the ages of seventeen and twenty who had placed themselves or been lured into the risky situation of being out at night, perhaps at bars and other nightspots. With this scenario, it was reasonable to think that most of the people in the Village didn't have to be afraid.

That could lead one to conclude that older women, older men, and children were unlikely victims. But that kind of logic didn't count for much. I knew MO's could change and I suspected the police were withholding some information. In fact, there were whispered reports that some children had been "approached," though these might be only rumors concocted out of paranoia, or incidents unrelated to the murders. However, they also might indicate the killer was enlarging his search for prey.

No one could be certain about anything except the fear that hung like a dank element in the air. People *were* being murdered and mutilated (or the other way around), it had to be the work of an insane monster, and no one really knew who was safe. It was best not to find out the hard way.

"Watch your back, buddy!" an acquaintance who managed the coin-operated laundry on Bleecker Street called to me one afternoon.

"Friggin' cops, why can't they catch this animal?" lamented the old man I'd meet every day as he walked home from feeding the birds at Tompkins Square Park.

"I told my husband if we don't sell and move I'm taking the kids and getting outta here," I overheard the woman behind the stationary store counter say when I stopped to buy a newspaper.

The murders were on everyone's mind and lips. Pervasive fear made the frigid air feel even icier.

Even in the worst days in my birthplace, the Brownsville section of Brooklyn, where violence was no stranger, I hadn't experienced anything like the tension and paranoia now present in the Village. I learned that parents were not permitting their children to be alone outside their buildings and brownstones. Teenagers' movements were restricted to going back and forth to school or the local Y. No hanging out. It was disturbing to hear people talk about buying guns to protect themselves.

More than once I heard someone say, "If the cops can't do it, we'll do it ourselves." I doubted it was just frustrated talk. If the killings continued, it wouldn't be long before vigilante groups formed, patrolling the neighborhood and reacting, maybe without thought, to any suspicious activity.

"Hey, Dr. Obler," said Gail, a clerk at the local library, pulling her coat close around her, "how can someone do these things? What kind of sicko is this?"

I tried to shrug and look equally exasperated. She and others probably wouldn't understand or really care that much about the clinical explanation for serial criminals. I doubted they wanted to hear that there wasn't any such thing as a monster, that the killer was someone who for psychological reasons had become a psychopath and couldn't help himself. That would be most unsatisfying. The villain was evil and had to be executed, end of story.

"The Soda Pop Slasher's," crimes were highlighted in stories and broadcast reports about the investigation and lack of results. Providing so few details made matters worse, because with a moniker like that most of what he did to victims was left up to the imagination. Ironically, I had the feeling that however far one's imagination went, it still might not come up to what was really happening.

On television and in print there were more tentative sketches of the slasher. The sketches were so nondescript I felt they could have fit thousands of people, and because they often changed there was a sense the police had nothing to go on but fantasy. Posters that appeared in store windows one day were replaced with revised ones two days later.

Still, I learned that more and more men were being hauled in for questioning—black, white, Hispanic, and Asian, businessmen and shopkeepers and homeless, people with alibis and those who couldn't remember what they had done five minutes before.

Community leaders and politicians were demanding an arrest. I sympathized with the police for the pressure they were under, and wondered how long they could hold out before grabbing someone simply to lower the heat, if only for a few days, until the Soda Pop Slasher struck again.

I took some comfort in that none of these early sketches resembled Devon. I felt like I had gotten past my initial, hesitant suspicions. How could I have entertained the thought that he was a violent psychopath harming others? A good psychologist doesn't make a tentative diagnosis based on speculative material, I told myself. A diagnosis must be definitive and symptoms have to be validated prior to reaching a conclusion. I was obligated to work with my patients and assist them in overcoming their mental disabilities—*that* was my top priority. A big roadblock to doing that was thinking that one of my patients was capable of such evil acts.

There was another distressing aspect to such a line of thought: by correlating the behavior of a patient with current homicides, I was not being objective. My decisions were less rational. My own emotions had intruded upon the relationship with a patient. The situation was not far removed from believing and then accepting that a patient has an emotional interest in the therapist. We are not supposed to be swayed by our own emotions and suspicions.

"I'm glad you're here, Dr. Obler," said Salena's

teacher one grey, blustery afternoon when she walked Salena to the front gate where I was waiting.

"Me too," I said.

"Look around," she said, motioning.

Obeying, I understood. As the children emerged from the building, some holding teachers' and administrators' hands, dozens of parents and a few grandparents, probably some aunts and uncles too, were congregated on the sidewalk. A turnout like this was most unusual. In an ironic way, the Soda Pop Slasher had caused some family members to reacquaint themselves with how precious and vulnerable children were.

"Salena's not so scared now," the teacher said, speaking low. "Probably not Mark either. You're making a difference."

"I'm trying. Thank you for saying that."

A few days later when I walked my children home again, a hot chocolate, even a candy bar, couldn't tempt them to stop on the way. I had mixed feelings: pride that I was consistently putting aside my workload worries to be with them during this tense time, and regret that my relationship with their mother had ended and I was not always with them.

As a professional I had dealt with many people whose marriages had ended and explored with them their pain and confusion. As a person, I hadn't resolved my own feelings about the past, except to know for sure that I loved my children and would to the best of my ability support them in any way I could, even if it was just a hand to hold on the way home from school.

That night, after finishing a couple of evaluations and recording notes about some patients, I sat in a comfortable wing chair in my apartment with a large mug of tea and a small pile of newspapers. Though time was passing since the

Soda Pop Slasher had claimed another victim, articles about the case could still be found, usually on about page ten.

Sketches of the suspect were no longer being published; either the cops realized they were useless or they had some details of what the man really looked like and were repressing them for later use. The short articles somewhat wearily recounted how many murders there had been to date, who the victims were, and vaguely mentioned the condition of the young men's and women's bodies when found—deep cuts and mutilations.

Reporters were speculating that the killings might not be all the work of one person, or maybe the first few were but afterward came "copycat crazies." It was indeed scary to contemplate that in this city or maybe in society it took only a few sparks to set off a flame of violence.

Perhaps that had always been true. If so, then I felt even sadder and more frustrated. It was discouraging to me to think that one of my patients or perhaps anyone under treatment could be implicated in murder and that a therapist could in some way be contributing to fear and pain in society. I began to wonder if psychotherapy, like parts of the legal field, was in actuality protecting the criminal rather than the victim.

There was one bit of amusement. *Newsbeat* had done a story that began, "A murderer labeled the Soda Pop Slasher by law enforcement authorities is not only claiming victims but cutting a swath through any sense of security residents of Greenwich Village in New York City have about their otherwise trendy, upscale neighborhood." It was my old friend Todd Shapiro's kind of phrasing, and knowing that, I read on with great interest.

As lurid as the lead was, I knew it was accurate. Fear had gripped my neighborhood and the neighborhood of my ex-wife and children. I could not protect Salena and Mark completely. My sadness was compounded by the realization that the harshness of the world had been shown to them much too early—their parents' divorce and now surroundings filled with anxiety. Whatever else, however, I was sure they knew they were loved and we would do everything to protect them.

Well, maybe the answer wasn't throwing ourselves in the path of danger but making sure danger didn't get too close. It was almost eleven o'clock, probably too late to find Stella up, but I suddenly had an idea to share with her.

The phone rang when I was almost to it. "Marty, are you okay? It's Rachel."

I couldn't suppress the sigh that escaped.

"Yes, I am. Why?"

"Well, you picked up the phone so quickly."

I couldn't help laughing and then pointing out that she had apparently called me out of concern that I was waiting by the phone. "Anyway," I said, "I really appreciate the call."

"Thanks, but we haven't talked in days, let alone seen each other." Her voice was throaty, hoarse. "I was worried about you."

"I'm fine, really. You know, this harem I have takes up a lot of time and energy."

"Marty, don't joke."

"All right. Well, not exactly 'fine.'"

With some guilt, realizing that I had closed a door to her, I explained to Rachel about trying to spend more time with my children and described some of the fear and anxiety of people in their area. She did not interrupt.

When I finished, she said, "You're doing the right thing, Marty. Helping children feel secure is very important."

"I think so too, but it means. . . ."

It meant we were not seeing each other, and perhaps

drifting apart. Was I becoming so preoccupied with the murders and Devon that there was no room left for a personal relationship? Or was I deliberately creating distance because I still had unresolved feelings connected with the end of my marriage?

It was all more complicated than I wanted to think about just now. "It means I just haven't been too available lately, and I'm sorry about that," I said lamely.

"I can come over there and you can apologize in person."

"No, don't," I said more fervently than I had meant to.

"Why not?"

Avoiding the real reason, that at this moment I just didn't want to see anyone, even her, I mentioned again the heightened fear and tension in the area. "It's possible no one is safe."

"Marty, you're into this overprotective thing again."

"Indulge me, please? For now?"

After a pause, Rachel replied, "Yes, doctor."

After I hung up, I wandered around the small apartment for a while, a bit ashamed of myself but also feeling justified. Why take a chance?

My concentration was shot, so I decided to turn in. It took a while to fall asleep, and when I finally did drift off I had a powerful dream. Devon was in it.

I was leaning against a streetlight adjacent to one of the city's public swimming pools. I felt peaceful and aloof, enjoying a warm, clear night.

Devon came into view. He was with a group of high school boys who were climbing over the chain-link fence to get to the pool, which was closed for the night. Apparently in a leadership role, he directed the others on the best method of climbing, making sure they avoided the curved metal loops that ended with a sharp point at the top of the fence. At first I admired his leadership and how he was looking out for the others. Then I sensed that something underhanded was going on. They were not supposed to be climbing over the fence, and he was persuading them to do it. I turned away for a few seconds.

When I turned back, I saw Devon standing naked over one of the boys who was gazing up at him. Angrily, Devon raised his fist. In it was a piece of metal from the fence. I began shouting, begging him to stop. "Don't hurt the boy," I called out.

That was when I woke up shouting. It sounded especially loud in the lonely silence of the bedroom.

That weekend Mark and Salena were supposed to stay with me, but I called Stella to say this wasn't a good time. "I have to catch up on a lot of work. Next weekend for sure."

Each of the kids got on the phone. Neither seemed disappointed, more like relieved.

"You'll still walk us home, right, Dad?" Mark asked anxiously.

"You bet, fella. I'll be there. Love you."

I spent a lot of time that weekend catching up on work, and once that was done, reviewing my notes about Devon. My dream lingered in my mind. One of my interpretations was that Devon was luring others to do something wrong and once he had enticed them he turned on them.

I was concerned about my presence in the dream and that I was angry and shouting, playing an authoritarian role or at least one where I was all too eager to call attention to his activities. Was I assuming the role of a controlling parent? In the dream as well as our sessions?

If so, it opened the door to Devon exploiting me to stop his sadistic impulses from being expressed with other people. Would this prove to be true?

Perhaps none of it was, and I was just superimposing my own fantasies on a troubled patient.

So I hit the notes, pondered, and made more notes. It was time to get back on track. Whatever else was going on around me—serial killer on the loose, frightened children, Rachel wondering why I'd become distant—I had to focus on helping Devon.

I had to discover what was really going on in Devon's inner life and try to help him, I told myself.

Chapter 12

Jagged Memories

The next session, my twentieth with Devon did not go well. He seemed disinterested, distracted, and resistant to my questions. It was almost as though he knew or had sensed my renewed resolve to understand and help him, and for some reason didn't want to make it easy. He scowled, stammered, and generally looked bored.

Nevertheless, I was not deterred. Toward the end of the session I made a suggestion. "I'd like you to bring to the office next time several items from your apartment," I told him.

"Playing psychic, Doc?" he said, perking up.

I couldn't help smiling. "I just think it might be helpful."

As usual, when he left, it was an effort to turn my attention to my other patients. In the week leading to our next encounter, the only happy interlude was spending more time with my children. We spent every afternoon and the following weekend together. How odd that a series of gruesome murders would draw me closer to Mark and Salena.

The tension in their neighborhood was still high but

perhaps not as sharp. The Soda Pop Slasher had not struck in several weeks. One police official was quoted in a newspaper as speculating that the killer's blood lust had been satisfied. I knew this couldn't be true, but it offered some comfort to citizens who began to think more about the approaching holidays and a little less about homicide.

My opinion, if anyone in the media had cared to ask, was that all the attention and a more aware, self-protective populace had forced the killer to lay low temporarily. It was also possible that he had left the area, or New York City, to prey on victims elsewhere. It could be the same as if Jack the Ripper had boarded a train out of London to vent his evil in Manchester or Glasgow. Of course, he didn't. Had the Soda Pop Slasher? Well, I couldn't help wishing him, if not caught, far away from those I loved.

The next Wednesday, carrying the large knapsack I'd seen before, Devon strode in. "I've brought a few things for you, Dr. Obler."

"Did you grab them at random or have specific reasons for the selections?"

After removing his large black overcoat and shaking water droplets from his long blond hair—it was snowing lightly and forecasters predicted two inches—he sat down and grinned. "This exercise would be less interesting, wouldn't it, if I told you everything right off the bat."

I returned his grin. "Good point. Okay, let's do some show and tell."

My suggestion that Devon bring several items from his home to my office was aimed at learning more about his inner life. I hadn't been any more specific because I wanted him to choose, the idea being that what he chose and the way he discussed each item would be revealing, at least enough that some heretofore closed doors would open a crack.

Devon had left my office last week like a good student who as a reward was being offered an opportunity to do a special project no one else in the class was capable of completing. I noted it was still remarkable how eager Devon was to please me if sufficiently motivated.

"Before we begin," he said, "a bit of news you might find interesting. I found a job, with Roberts, Hausman and Buchanan, a midtown law firm, doing proofreading. I've been at it almost three weeks now." He tilted his head, appearing somewhat sheepish. "I didn't tell you before because I wanted to see if I liked it."

"Since you just mentioned it, apparently you do."

"Yes." He leaned back and stretched, flexing the powerful muscles in his arms. "Law is fascinating. Guess I never fully considered that before, because I was so wrapped up in psychology. So far, at least with proofreading all this wordy complicated material, I'm damn good at it. Hey, maybe I'll become a lawyer."

"Having something that engages your intellect is good for you," I offered.

"Other than our meetings, you mean?" he asked, his expression coy.

I allowed a smile. Certainly I didn't want to indicate to Devon that our sessions and the overall case he represented engaged my interest much more than I ever expected, probably to the detriment of my other work responsibilities. "Let's take a look at what you've brought in," I said, changing the subject.

Devon reached into the knapsack and pulled out a photograph. "This is about nine years old, from an album given to me by my parents at high school graduation." He pushed it across the desk. "It's the only one I have of all four of us."

The slightly faded photo offered my first look at Devon's family, and the reality was not far from what I had imagined. Devon was essentially a shorter version of how he appeared now, though the features were less formed and distinctive. Andre was dark-haired and pouted at the camera. The father, wearing a dark brown suit, was large and broad shouldered, also with dark hair and eyes, a mouth set in a grim line, and large fists clenched. The mother wore a grey print dress that fell well past her knees; she also wore a slight smile, and her hair was almost as light as Devon's. One hand clutched Andre's and the other was tentatively placed on her husband's thick arm.

I took a closer look at Devon in the photo. For a moment I was startled. His eyes stared intently at the camera, almost appearing to be crossed, as though he were trying to project or repress powerful emotions. The look reminded me of those of incipient schizophrenics I had treated.

"In that one we were in a park, and my mother asked some stranger to take our picture," Devon explained.

"You appear concerned."

"My father was angry that she had approached this strange guy, and he didn't like posing. Well, this time we got him."

"How often do you see your family?" I asked pensively.

"As little as possible." Devon shrugged. "We don't have a warm relationship. Couple of times a year I'll return to the family manse. After a few days, my father offers me money. I take it and leave. My mother and brother are the same helpless, boring idiots they always were."

I waited, then asked, "What else can you tell me about them?"

"Let's move on," he said decisively. From the knapsack he produced a shiny bicycle chain, then laughed. "Cleaned this up for you. One time, after I'd disappeared a whole day on my bike, when I got home my father broke the chain right off and beat me with it."

He let the chain fall to the floor. I asked, "How often did he hit you?"

"Well, not too often. But when he did, he made sure it hurt." Devon laughed again, almost a giggle. "Until I got about as big as he was."

"Did you ever hit him?"

He shook his head sadly. "Even in a dream I can't. But I sure wanted to. He deserved it a hell of a lot more than I ever did."

"Was he ever sorry for beating you?"

"Probably. He always gave me money afterward. That was the answer for everything. Pay, and you can do whatever the fuck you want."

Devon pulled a blue cotton bath towel out of the knapsack. "Yeah, it's just a towel, but I like to smell towels. Cover my nose and inhale deeply. Especially a towel that's been used a few times. There's a damp, funky scent." His eyes shifted from the towel to me. "Sometimes I beat off with a towel. Kind of rough, but not too much. Does the job."

I leaned toward him. "Do you also use a soda bottle when you masturbate?"

"I don't want to talk about bottles. Been there, done that. Okay?"

"We've never fully explored why you. . . ."

"Enough!" His voice rose, cutting my words off.

His blue eyes glared and turned the color of steel, and his body stiffened. I didn't want to risk ending his demonstration.

"Okay, Devon. Please continue."

"I mean, if I'm *boring* you or if. . . ."

I allowed some irritation in my voice. "I'm sorry, all right? Now what else do you have?"

He produced two metal devices that looked like nutcrackers except the handles were padded. "For my hands," Devon said. "I work out a lot, hoisting barbells like a Russian weightlifter. However, I had to fit something in here. You squeeze these things. They make your hands feel like goddamn vises, fingers like redwoods. I could pinch the head right off a cat."

"Do you?"

"What?"

"Do things like that to animals?"

"Not since I was a kid."

Devon, red-faced, looked as if he would become angry again. Then his blues eyes softened. He leaned back and smiled. "Let me tell you this story. It's true, but I want to emphasize that it happened a long time ago." He waited for me to nod. "One time, the gardener was sick, but my father was giving this party for some big shot business types and he had to have the lawn mowed before it began. 'Get out and do it or I'll lock you in your room for a week,' he says." Devon shrugged. "I was only twelve."

"What happened?"

"So I cranked the motherfucker up, some old gas-powered thing, and I was going up and down, up and down, blades of grass flying all over, in my face, in the pool, everywhere. Then I turned it off. I was dying of thirst and sweating like a stuck pig. And in the sudden quiet I heard this little high-pitched sound. I looked behind a bush and there was a kitten. It was orange and white and maybe six weeks old. It was obviously abandoned, filthy, one eye was closed, there was caked blood on its back, no one would want this cat. It saw me and cried like crazy. It cried more when I lifted it up. It wouldn't stop. Weak, annoying, useless thing. Best to put it out of its misery, save it from a wasted existence."

He was breathing hard, almost gulping air. A full minute passed before he continued.

"So with one hand, while the thing's screaming in the other, I dug a hole in the lawn, stuck the fucking furball in it, packed down the dirt until it was stuck good in there."

"You buried it alive?" I said, repulsed.

"Better than that. You think I'm some kind of cruel bastard, let it die slow? No. It was buried up to its neck with its little screaming head sticking up, eyes bulging like marbles. It just wouldn't shut up. Somebody was going to hear it. I powered up the mower. Started at one end of the lawn and mowed a straight line, tall grass in front, short grass behind. I was getting closer. Almost there. Fucking head is twisting and squirming, mouth wide open, squealing but I can't hear it, short white teeth and pink tongue extended, whiskers looked yellow in the sunlight. Then I was there, mower goes right over it, maybe heard a tiny crunch, felt a little tug. Time to move on. Never looked back."

Devon laughed, loud and hard. "Later on, one of my father's guests found a little furry ear floating in the pool. Thought we had rats."

He was a psychopath.

I clasped my hands tight together so that Devon might not notice how hard they shook. "What else do you have?"

He was silent for a couple of minutes, gazing idly at the ceiling. Then his shoulders quivered and he straightened up in the chair. I watched as his eyes refocused. Then he reached into the knapsack again.

He drew out a black leather jacket. It gleamed in the light from my lamp. Devon stood up to put the jacket on, zipped up the front, and turned slowly, then took it off. Sitting back down, he laid the jacket across his legs.

"I wear this when I'm trying to pick up someone."

"Whom do you pick up?"

"Hookers, mostly. Hell, you know that, Dr. Obler. Or ones who don't give a shit about anything, about who they go with, what's going to happen."

I leaned back in my chair. I wished that I smoked a pipe like Pomerantz so I'd have something to do with my hands. "Male or female?"

"That matters to you, doesn't it?"

"Does it matter to you?" I asked softly.

"When I go out, nothing matters." He swept the jacket off his legs, and it slumped atop the towel. "That's all there is. Ain't no more."

"Sounds like a line from a movie."

"Yes, but you can figure out which one. No fun if I tell you everything."

Devon smiled at me, assignment completed. Or was it? His eyes shifted a couple of times to the knapsack. He was playing another game. I thought it best to play along.

"Oh, come on. One more."

"Say please."

"Please. Show me more."

"With sugar on it?"

I nodded and made a begging gesture with my hands.

"Folks, we have a winner!" He leaned down and rummaged in the knapsack and produced a sheaf of papers, about a half dozen white pieces of copy paper. "Take a gander, Dr. Obler. You'll be glad you did."

"I will, huh. Why?"

"I *won't* tell you everything," he said irritably.

I took the papers from him. They contained sketches

done in pencil. From what I could determine they were of young men and women in their late teens or early twenties, but a couple were of pubescent children, but beyond that the sketches weren't detailed enough. They were free-flowing drawings of faces with only hints of shoulders and torsos. A couple of the faces were shaded in, implying that the subject was black. All had dark eyes gazing out at the observer. The mouths were simple, thin, even dark lines.

The sketches were captivating, either because Devon had true artistic talent or their direct simplicity had an unguarded quality. There was no past or future to these images, just the present, and the almost beseeching staring.

"These are most intriguing, Devon. Yours, I assume."

"Correct." His eyes glittered in an odd way.

"Who are these people?"

"Doesn't matter. I've met them. And others. Some I wanted to sketch. Not portraits. I did these from memory. Later. They stayed in my mind. For a while."

"Maybe you should forget law and pursue art."

"Really like them, huh?"

The way Devon leaned forward, knees pressed together and fingers twisting, white teeth flashing, he appeared as pleased as if I'd just suggested he should be crowned king of England.

"Aside from any technical skill, what impresses me is there's a quality that comes through." I paused, then went on. "A feeling."

"Love?"

"I don't know if I'd call it that," I said thoughtfully.

"Dr. Obler," Devon pushed himself back, crossed his long legs and rubbed his face. "I know I can tell you anything, so I'll share this with you. I'm lonely. I mean," his face looked almost as if he were a lost child, "I feel so alone in many ways."

"Apparently, you do spend time with people."

"Sure," he said flippantly. "Like a guy selling tokens in the subway meets people all fucking day. I mean, to really *be* with someone, for a long time."

"To be in love?"

"Yes, yes. That's it. Someone always there with me. 'Isn't it pretty to think so.' *The Sun Also Rises*. Ava Gardner, Tyrone Power. 1957. Errol Flynn's last really good performance. Okay," he shook his head back and forth, "it wasn't as good as the book."

He was going too fast for me. I scanned his face and the preoccupied, eager expression slowly faded. If I could believe what he said, this was remarkable. He might not have developed a conscience—that painful kitten story was strong evidence—but if Devon genuinely felt a need to be emotionally involved on a long-term basis with another person, that was an indication that he might not be a fully involved psychopath.

Such people do not let anyone in. From what I had gathered, the need he was expressing was for a steady relationship, homosexual or heterosexual, and not just promiscuous acting out. Fine, such an interest and related activities were better than repression, which often led to displaced sadomasochistic behavior and pent-up rage.

I ran my fingers over my chin, pondering. Perhaps I had encountered Devon at a pivotal time in his life, when he was poised to but had not slipped over the edge, when he was no more than a borderline personality, not yet a full-blown psychopath. If indeed I could help him before it was too late, I would not only help him but I would have found the method to be instrumental in helping others who would

otherwise be destined to live lives of mental anguish, soli-
tude, and violence.

It was suddenly crystal clear to me that how I
helped Devon was connected to the idealism that prompted
me to go into psychology—to ease and perhaps resolve
pain, and to help people lead fulfilling lives.

"Dr. Obler?"

"Yes?"

"I take it as a compliment that you haven't been
watching the clock."

Now it was my turn to laugh. "You're right, Devon.
And I do have other appointments. Can we continue next
week?"

As he stuffed the items he'd brought back in the
knapsack, he said, "I look forward to it. I sense a breakthrough."

The funny thing was, with this most unusual patient, I
didn't think he was referring to himself.

That night I still felt a glow about what had occurred
in the session with Devon. As disturbing as the session had
been, I sincerely believed that we had turned a more productive corner.

After finishing up on the day's notes and feeling
pretty satisfied with my own role, I bought a huge hot
chocolate on the way to my apartment and, after lapping
up every drop, decided I also deserved a good night's sleep.

I was on my way to having one when on the edge of
consciousness the dream began:

It was a dark, moonless night. (Why didn't I ever
have daytime dreams anymore, a distant part of my consciousness wondered.) A boy was running down an empty
street. At first I was like a camera, simply observing, then I
sensed my body become present, as though I too was on the

street, probably standing in a dark doorway. This was not a
street I recognized in Manhattan or Brooklyn. Something
implied it was another city, maybe not too far away, because
the air was cold.

The boy glanced back. Obviously he was being
chased. He faced forward again and ran faster. There were
other rapid footsteps. The pursuer was large and agile. At a
corner, under a streetlight, the boy paused to look back again.
My body shuddered as I saw that the boy was suddenly taller
and a few years older, and that it was my son.

Mark turned to his right and ran, his body language
more furious and desperate. But he couldn't stay ahead. The
large figure behind him was gaining. Mark entered shadows
and I couldn't see him. Rapid footsteps echoed off buildings.
The figure entered the glow of the streetlight. It was Devon.
His leather jacket gleamed, his face was twisted with rage,
his hands clenched and unclenched. Again, body shuddering,
he paused, then raced off after my son who suddenly was
accompanied by his sister.

"Stop!" I shouted. "Leave him alone! Leave *them*
alone!"

I couldn't move, stuck in the doorway like one of the
bricks, disoriented in a strange city, hearing in the dark distance speeches and vague oratory as though people were
speaking from a podium. The sound of receding footsteps
was mixed with a noise that resembled flags flapping. Then
all was quiet. But I knew that somewhere out in the dark
night Devon would catch my son and daughter.

Suddenly I awoke. My sheets were soaked with sweat. I
got up to get a drink of water and, hands shaking, I dropped the
glass. Shards of glass glittered in the small sink.

As I stood there in the middle of the night in an
apartment I shared only with fear, I had a wrenching gut

feeling that I had overlooked something about Devon, something important. Despite my training and experience and objectivity and my sympathy and idealism, something had eluded me.

Something was very, very wrong. And I had to face *it* or face the consequences.

Chapter 13

Tremor Cracks

Bright colors today—red crew-neck sweater, tan pants, white high-top sneakers, and a tan parka. Devon was full of cheerful energy when he strode into the office.

It was quite the opposite for me. More murders this past week. Male, probably hustlers from the way the papers described them. The media was ablaze announcing them. And the press reports were on my mind. I was going to take some risks with this patient to find out the truth, though I hadn't been able to resolve if I wanted to do this because it was helpful therapeutically or the feeling I couldn't lose that Devon was dangerous and seriously implicated in the Soda Pop Slasher's crimes.

"Ever go skiing, Dr. Obler?"

"No." I gazed at him. "Basketball is my sport."

The cheerfulness ebbed. "Yeah. I remember." He crossed his arms and legs. "So what's on today's menu?"

I wasn't going to skirmish with him. "Have you been following the media reports on the murders that have taken place in this area?"

"Here and there." Devon shrugged. "You spend time reading about murders in this city and you don't have time for anything else. As you know, I have a restless mind. So many things interest me."

"Do you fear for your safety when you go out at night?"

"Me?" He extended his arms back and forth. "It's unlikely some nut will try to pick on me."

"What if it's more like a pickup? He might disguise his true intentions until you are vulnerable."

Devon pointed at me. "I pick *them* up, and no one makes me do what I don't want to do."

"Who do you pick up, Devon?"

He laughed. "You should come with me some time, Dr. Obler. Might be a real eye-opening experience."

"Did you know any of the victims?"

"What victims?"

I kept my voice even. "Of the Soda Pop Slasher."

He leaned back and pushed fingers through his long hair. "What a name, huh? Who knows. I don't take notes. Here today, gone tomorrow, out of sight, out of mind."

"For someone so intelligent, you use cliches a lot, especially when trying to avoid an issue."

His cheeks reddened. "So what am I trying to avoid, Dr. Brainiac? What *is* it we're talking about here?"

I had to stay ahead, jabbing and stepping aside and jabbing, to keep the upper hand. However, at the same time, if I frustrated him too much, the rage might emerge. I remembered how he had reacted during the basketball game months ago. Then, I had let him off easy.

"How angry are you, Devon?"

"This minute? In general? What?"

"How big is it? How badly does it burn?"

"You have no idea."

"Perhaps I do."

He leaned forward and gazed at me. The swinging of the clock's pendulum was the only sound in the room. A minute passed, then another while I returned his gaze. It was okay that I blinked and he didn't as long as I didn't look away.

I had no idea what was going through his mind or what he was trying to learn from probing mine. I thought of neutral things—a band of sunlight on the tops of trees in a forest, waves lapping at the beach, the pendulum shifting, a car driving leisurely on an open road. I was determined to keep this slide show in my head indefinitely so that my gaze wouldn't shift.

Finally, Devon said in almost a whisper, "What do you want to know?"

"Tell me about your anger. Or rage. How you keep it in. Or why you keep it in."

"What makes you think I do?"

"Either it is always being expressed, in which case you would be going around raving constantly, or. . . ."

"Or it would be deeply repressed, but there would have to be an outlet." His voice stayed just above a whisper. "Remember, Doctor, I was on my way to being one of you."

I couldn't let him steer the conversation. "Devon, I know you have had intense anger for your parents, your brother too. Who else?"

"You're on a roll. Any suggestions?"

"Teachers when you were in school?"

He nodded.

"Other adults you encountered, especially if they did not acknowledge or fully appreciate your mental and physical advantages."

He nodded, a bit more slowly. A sudden gust of cold wind rattled the window. I felt sweat breaking out on my neck.

"Other students? What about friends? Certainly someone like you with such charisma. . . ."

"Let me tell you about 'friends,' Dr. Obler," he said forcefully and bitterly. "You can offer friendship. Be nice and open and trusting to girls and guys. Soon as your back is turned. . . ." He made a guttural sound and a stabbing motion with one large hand. "Right in the back. Actually, those are the least hateful ones. The ones who take and don't fucking care, the sorry sons of bitches who think they can pull your strings, who make like you're lower than a slug even though *they* are no more than a piece of filth under a fingernail. They . . . fucking . . . piss . . . me . . . off."

"You don't deserve to be ignored."

He flashed a sudden grin. "You can't ignore me, can you?"

"I've found it impossible. And I wouldn't want to try."

He leaned back, retreating from the brink of rage. "So you want to know about this big rock of anger inside me? It's molten, like the core of the earth. It *is* there. And it's not pretty. And when it penetrates the surface. . . ."

"Volcano."

"Good. Bonus points."

"What makes it erupt?"

Devon shrugged. "Maybe I'm a force of nature."

"How does it erupt?"

"I plead the Fifth."

"Devon, I'm your therapist."

We gazed at each other again. I was on uncertain ground. It was like I was standing on a shifting plate of earth, and if it met another there would be an earthquake. Do

I bring up the murders again? If so, was I prepared if he admitted a connection? And I couldn't help realizing that if I didn't maintain a power position in our relationship and he admitted to a connection—if it was possible that *he* was the Soda Pop Slasher—I was not safe.

I breathed slowly. "Devon, do you hurt people?"

"People hurt people all the time." Suddenly his eyes went wide, he spread his arms and began to sing: "People, people who hurt people, are the most fucked up people in the. . . ."

"Devon!"

"Don't like the way I carry a tune?"

"It's not one of your more apparent talents."

He laughed. "Always liked the old musicals. And dancing, Fred and Ginger. Did you also get the impression that Edward Everett Horton and Eric Blore fucked each other off the set?"

I ignored the drops of sweat spreading across my back. "Why is it hard for you to discuss your sexuality?"

"I'm not aware that we have drawn any conclusions. Anyway, I thought you were trying to get me to admit that I do nasty, despicable things to people."

I leaned forward. "Devon, after all the time we've spent together, I need to know if you're doing something that hurts other people. Young men. Young women. Teenagers."

"Do you really think I'm capable of hurting other people, Dr. Obler?"

"That's what I'm trying to determine."

"Reality check: so what? What could you do about it?"

He also leaned forward, so that our faces were separated only by the short span of the desk. His eyes were glassy and large. A muscle in one cheek twitched. I could smell coffee on his breath and see that he too was sweating, tiny droplets across his forehead.

I leaned back. "Try to help you."

"Like what, hold them down while I do it?"

"Do what, Devon?"

After a few moments he slid back in the chair. "You really have a bug up your ass this morning." Irritably, Devon went on, "I don't like feeling sorry for you."

"Do you?"

"Poor Dr. Obler, he's not sure if he's on to something. His patient might be fucking and mutilating boys or girls or maybe both. No one is safe. Even his family."

I laughed, manufacturing the sound because it was the only way I could stop myself from leaping over the desk and strangling the bastard. I breathed slowly and carefully wiped my eyes, which were wet either from perspiration or tears of frustration. Or fear.

When I looked back at him, he was scowling, probably upset that he hadn't scored a point. He had, but we could both play games.

"Devon, given how intelligent you are and with your knowledge of psychology, you must realize what you said crossed a line. I have to wonder if we should continue."

"Well, the session is almost over anyway."

"I mean everything ends. No more sessions."

"Hold on, let's not be hasty."

"Just acknowledge what you said. It was a threat, Devon."

"Well, maybe I. . . ."

"Threats are unacceptable in therapy."

He lowered his head, long blond hair falling past his shoulders, and his body shuddered. When he looked up there was no expression on his face, but he said, "I'm sorry."

"Thank you. Don't do it again. Are we clear?"

He smiled slightly. "As glass." He stood up and quickly slipped into the tan parka. "Hey, I gotta go. Supposed to be at work. Lawyers. Talk about killers, too. They get paid big time for it. Next week, right?"

I gazed at him.

"Right, Dr. Obler?"

Finally, I said, "I'm here for you, Devon."

We were into our fifth month. We did not meet for our next session. The day before it he left a message on my office machine: "Really sorry about this, Dr. Obler, but the law firm insists I go down to Washington to help out with some big project down there, needs a super proofer like yours truly. I need a few days to prepare. Give me some time, I'll be running this place. Could take more than another week in D.C., but not too long. This is cool stuff. And it's probably good for me to get out of town while *you* cool down. You scared me, Doc. I'll try to be good, send you a postcard of the Capitol Building. The center of power—hey, maybe that's where I belong. Anyway, back on track when I get back."

He called back a minute later. "Dr. Obler, just realized I made two rhymes in that message. Maybe I'll be a lawyer and a writer, like Grisham. Now that's heavy jang."

For the next two days I felt some relief, and guilt for feeling that way. Though I still wasn't sure what had transpired in our last session, even after reviewing my notes over and over, I sensed Devon and I had stepped up to another level. The intensity of it was somewhat distressing, and being able to step back for a bit caused the relief. The guilt was from not being sure I was ready to go on. Whatever was inside of Devon, whatever he was doing, he was my patient and I had to keep traveling this twisted path with him if I was to be of any help.

And, because of my duty to uphold confidentiality, I had to keep it to myself. That was damn hard.

Three days later there was another murder not that far away, but it was a drug dealer gunned down on Broome Street and, if anything, that reassured neighborhood folks.

I continued walking Mark and Selena home every day. They accepted my offers of hot chocolate now, and the choosing of some early holiday presents. Stella and I were on better terms than at any time since the divorce. A few of her comments let me know that she felt I had come through when needed. It wasn't really all that much that I was doing—and, in truth, spending more time with my kids was my reward—but I felt good about the comments anyway.

Unfortunately though, my relationship with Rachel was dormant. I was pretty sure that deep down I loved her, but also deep down, in the few reflective moments I allowed myself, I couldn't understand why she might feel the same for me. I'd already failed in a marriage. It had been mostly my fault, and work still occupied most of my thoughts.

Rachel and I talked on the phone frequently, and she always offered to meet me, but I was always ready with an excuse. The bottom line seemed to be my fear of making a commitment. I was afraid of her discovering that I might not be as noble, nice and giving as I'd somehow given her the notion I was. Was I worthy of Rachel's love and commitment?

It happened that I was in my office writing up notes and thinking when my phone rang late one night the following week. I expected the caller to be Rachel, but it was Devon. Immediately, I flashed back to his call from the hospital not long after I'd met him, especially when I heard what he had to say.

"Dr. Obler, are you there?"

"Yes, yes, Devon, of course."

"I might be in some trouble."

I gripped the receiver tighter. "What is it?"

"Well, it's . . . it's. . . ." He began laughing, that chillingly familiar sound that kept rising.

"Get hold of yourself and speak to me, Devon."

"H-hold of myself. Interesting concept." He had stopped laughing but his breathing was harsh. "Things got a little rough here, Doc. And here I promised to be good."

"Where are you?"

"The big D.C."

"Yes, but where in Washington?"

"A hotel room, if you must know."

"What happened?"

"Details, details. Listen, if I tell you, will you help me?"

"I'll try to do what I can."

"No, doofus, what I mean is, if I tell you can I get into trouble?"

"With whom?"

"With . . . whoever."

"Police?"

"Hypothetically."

"Devon, you are my patient calling during a personal crisis. I am obligated to help you, and that takes precedence over everything else."

"The old confidentiality conundrum, huh?"

"Exactly."

"Exactly. Olivia de Havilland, *The Strawberry*...."

"Yes, Devon. But this isn't a movie. Tell me what happened. Are you hurt? Did someone else get hurt?"

There was silence on the line. His breathing had

slowed. "Dr. Obler, you have another phone, don't you?"

"Yes."

"Without my knowing it, you could make a call and have this one traced, and send the police."

It had occurred to me, so I waited before I replied, "I wouldn't do that."

"Good thing," he said curtly. Then his tone changed. "Hey, when I see the President, I'll tell him you said hello."

"What is it, Devon? Please tell me."

He started to laugh again. "Maybe I was just testing you, Doc."

The laugh ascended, and just when it became a howl, he hung up.

I spent several hours trying to catch up on my notes—my mind was only half on them. Finally I got up and walked over to the window. I gazed at the night, thinking. Staring out at the leaden December sky that threatened the first heavy snowfall of the season, I wanted to be thinking about the good feelings of the holidays and surprising my children with gifts and how I could sort out my emotions enough to get back on track with Rachel.

However, I was too preoccupied with Devon. Thinking about his phone call from Washington, wondering if he would show up for his appointment Wednesday. Had he been "testing me?" Why? Then, wondering if he had been involved with something dangerous or harmful and was I in some way participating in it, and perhaps in other of his acts involving violence? Instead of treating him, was I enabling him? In a strange way, was I in concert with the activities of a psychopath?

Suddenly, I heard the outer door open. Could it be a prowler? I tensed, then a few seconds later Devon entered my office. Shocked, I immediately noticed that he was dressed all in black—large fur hat, overcoat, pants, boots—like a walking shadow.

He swept the hat off his head and bowed. "Dr. Obler, I am back from the political wars." Then he straightened up. "Okay, well, some power proofreading. And how are you?"

"Worried and shocked, I thought you were still in Washington."

"Ahhh, I'm back." With a sigh he settled in the simple wooden chair without removing his coat. "Well, whatever is troubling you, I'll try to help you in a short time because I can't stay." He pretended to put a monocle to his eye and spoke with a German accent. "So, Herr Dr. Obler, what seems to be your trouble?"

"Trouble. During the phone call, that's what you said you were in."

"It was nothing. Water under the Potomac Bridge."

"But you weren't so calm in Washington."

He grinned.

Sitting down behind my desk, I said, "I believe you genuinely were in trouble, Devon."

"Seeing is believing, huh? And you didn't see."

"You are not leveling with me."

"Okay, okay." He pulled his coat collar close. "You can be such a pain in the ass sometimes. Figuratively speaking, of course. Tell you what."

"What?"

"I was still pissed off. Over our last conversation. The shit you were trying to lay on me. I mean, if we really trusted each other, you wouldn't be talking like that."

In a way, he was right. But he wasn't the psychologist in this room. "So what *did* go on there, and why *did* you call me?"

"You are a persistent son of a gun."

He tried to cross his long legs but the overcoat got in the way, so instead he stretched his legs out and folded his hands behind his head. He gazed at the pockmarked ceiling.

"Let's dispense with this and that so I can tell you a dream I had when I was down there. No hypnogogic state, it's a freebie. All right?"

I sensed that I either agreed or there would be nothing else tonight, so I nodded and leaned forward.

"It's night. I'm on a dark street, and it has to be Washington because I know *all* the dark streets here, okay?"

I nodded again, suddenly feeling uncomfortable.

"There is a strong feeling that something is about to happen. I don't know what, but something. This creepy dark street, the surroundings are totally alien. *Something* is going to happen, something bad. I better warn people, though there aren't any around.

"I step out into the street to yell, but I can't. I don't have a voice. Nothing comes out of my throat. I keep trying, no dice. Then this girl, maybe seventeen, maybe more or less, comes strolling along, passes by me with hardly a glance. She looks like a runaway, and yet familiar. I can't quite place where I know her from. Anyway, maybe she knows what's going on, so I walk after her, waving to get her attention because I still can't talk."

For a few moments I had relaxed. Now I was tensed up again, almost afraid of what Devon was about to say.

"The girl hears my footsteps and sort of turns," he continued. "I reach out my hands, trying to indicate that I can't talk. Maybe I look like Frankenstein or something because this girl bolts, heading down to the corner. I run after her because I've got to find out what's going on in this crazy place, and she runs faster. That pisses me off big time. Rotten tease. So I turn on the afterburners, I want to chase her down and teach her a lesson. Ignore me, huh? I'm really angry. She reaches the corner, takes a quick look around, and bolts down another street. I'm still trying to catch the little bitch, so I run like a wild man, like one of those guys in *The Naked Prey*. Remember? With Cornel Wilde?"

I was silent.

"Anyway, I get to the same corner, and I turn right, and ahead it's superdark. I mean black as ink. I hear the running footsteps. This girl is getting away. I run into the darkness, it surrounds me, then it's all over. The dream." He cracks his knuckles and looks at me, smiling slightly. "One other weird thing. I felt like I was being watched. I felt like it was you."

I had to clear my throat it was so dry. "Am I in your dream?"

"No, but I feel you. That you can stop me."

"I can't stop you."

"Damn it, Dr. Obler, you're *in* me now."

It was almost a wail of pain, or at least frustration. He gazed intently at me, either begging for an answer or waiting to be challenged.

Trying to keep my voice even, I asked, "Do you know who the girl was?"

"Probably just some girl I've seen." Then Devon stood up. "Well, you figure it out. I'm gone."

He pulled something from his coat pocket and placed it on the floor and left, slamming the door behind him. I walked around from behind my desk.

A glass soda bottle stood on the floor,
still quivering.

Chapter 14

Police Call

Devon's "dream"—part of me agonized through the sleepless night that followed. Had he made it up, perhaps to send some message that I couldn't yet decipher? Did he want to frighten me? In fact he had. Portions of the dream were remarkably similar to the one I'd had. I feared for my children more than ever. Before, it had been a general concern because an anonymous serial killer was on the loose and had struck in their neighborhood. Now, I feared for Mark and Salena because they were *my* children, and that killer could be Devon.

Was that the message? A warning? If so, what was it he wanted me to do?

The next morning I bought a bagel and a cup of coffee and walked over to Washington Square Park. Still pondering my fears, I ate sitting on a bench across from the large fountain. The water had been turned off for the winter, and without its splash, at this early hour the park was quiet. Though it was clear, bright, dry and not quite as bitter

cold as January can be, I was the only person occupying a
bench. Looking around however, I spotted two ragged men
sleeping under separate benches, wisps of white air drifting
out of their open, toothless mouths.

My mind drifted back to the internal dialogue I was
waging. Okay, I argued, let's say it *was* a dream. And for a
moment, let's say Devon is the Soda Pop Slasher, or at least
has knowledge of the killer, someone who ran with his night-
time pack. The dream had some encouraging elements.
Perhaps Devon has an unconscious desire to warn people, but
because of deep underlying conflict he cannot. That's why he
had no voice. Or he realizes that if he does cry out to reveal
who he is, he'll get in trouble. His dilemma is that he wants
to reveal himself, but at the same time he feels he may be too
far gone.

Another answer could be disassociation, that Devon
doesn't recall what he does and the most violent actions are
blocked out as though they never happened—yet he senses
something is very wrong with him. There have been
numerous cases reported of people with severe personality
disorders, such as multiple personalities, who don't
remember what the "other person" did.

Somehow I sensed that wasn't true of Devon. And
sitting on the hard bench, beginning to shiver, I felt very
uncomfortable contemplating that Devon was a murderer. I
might be allowing personal fears to impair my judgment.
And, my role as his therapist was not to judge Devon but
to help him.

But I had to know. I had to have more "evidence" that
he could or could not be linked to the murders of so many
young people. Devon may have been warning me not to pur-

sue this line of questioning with him. He would stop coming to the sessions—or worse.

I stood up, feeling stiff. The distant sun was just appearing over the tops of buildings to the east. I walked briskly toward my office. My muscles relaxed but I didn't.

While I was walking however, I did get an idea which I put into effect before my workday started.

That afternoon I took the subway to the Upper West Side, got on a crosstown bus to the East Side, then hailed a cab. I'd felt watched before. I couldn't take a chance now, especially where I was going.

The taxi dropped me off in front of One Police Plaza. Pulling my hat low over my head, I rushed into the large gray building. Inside I didn't feel any better. I'd never been comfortable in police stations, the few times I'd entered them.

A few years ago I had taken on a case that involved Moira, a female police officer with multiple personalities. It had turned out tragically, despite my best efforts. The matter had been swept under the rug by high-ranking officials in the city. It had almost ruined my emerging career, and I had been at personal risk. Once the woman was dead, I didn't try to stop the coverup, my involvement had ended. But one official who'd been impressed by my work had said, "If you need a favor, call me."

Earlier today, on the phone, I called in that marker.

Several police at various desks pointed me to the officer I sought, in Homicide. I was to see Detective Kitty Callahan, who was in charge of the Soda Pop Slasher case. I had been informed by the city official that she had risen fast in the department, a "Bronx-Irish broad from a family of cops, got her gold shield at twenty-eight. She's one of the New York City Police Department's best homicide detectives." He had mentioned a few cases Callahan had solved. They were only vaguely familiar, but I pretended to be impressed.

I was escorted down a long corridor by a beefy uniformed cop. The police stations I'd been to before were rundown, seedy, sweat-smelling places with shouting, protesting and crying people who were steered back and forth by paunchy, hatless cops. The cops wore bemused expressions or weary ones. They'd seen it all and couldn't wait for retirement.

It was different here, resembling any business office. The corridor was carpeted. People spoke softly. The dominant sounds were keyboards being tapped, phones ringing softly, and muted conversations. When the cop knocked on the pebble glass door and opened it, I wanted to rub my shoes before entering.

Callahan sat behind a desk covered by piles of folders, and in the spaces between them were pieces of aluminum foil and wax paper containing several days' worth of half-eaten sandwiches. She stood as the door closed behind me and extended her hand. I'd barely touched it when she sat down again.

In that brief moment I saw a slim, tall woman with layers of curly red hair surrounding a pretty, freckled face. Her white skin was smooth, lipstick a bright red, nose small and slightly upturned. Her green eyes, gazing at me, were hard and her small mouth was set in a firm line; I sensed she was trying hard not to scowl. She wore a blue blouse clasped at her smooth neck and black pants. The shield on her right breast shone in the overhead fluorescent light.

"Dr. Obler, please sit. I can give you ten minutes." The

scowl emerged. "Actually, I can give you longer because I've been told to. Let's try to keep it to ten minutes or less."

"I appreciate that you're giving me this time, Detective," I said, sitting in an old wooden chair across from her that threatened to collapse. "I asked for a favor. You're it. I'm sorry it's you because I realize you've got plenty to do."

The tilt of her head implied, *I'm sorry it's me too.* Then she took a quick glance at the watch on her thin wrist and attempted a smile. "So, why do you want information about the Slasher case?"

I told her the story I'd prepared: that I was a psychologist (at least that was true) who specialized in sexual dysfunction (also true). "I'm working on a book about the connection between that dysfunction, rage and violence." (My fingers were crossed.) "From what I've gleaned from media reports, the Soda Pop Slasher fits that profile. I just need details that go beyond what's been reported."

"The problem is that I don't want what I might say winding up in print," Callahan snapped.

"I'm not a reporter for a newspaper or magazine," I said, hearing a hoot from Todd Shapiro in my mind. "And I sure don't know a darn thing about television news. Any information given to me would be put into a textbook and disguised." I tried a smile. "Hell, most people who read it will probably find it too tedious to go beyond the first few pages."

"That makes me feel like my time will be well spent."

I felt the sting the remark intended. "Yes, I was owed a favor, and I'm collecting, and what I'm doing won't benefit anyone but me and maybe a few colleagues—certainly not the police department and the rest of society. So why don't we get it over with?"

Callahan nodded. "I appreciate your candor, Dr. Obler." It was not only her words but the tone of her voice that made me wince. She shifted several piles of folders, pulling one in front of her. "What do you want to know?"

"First, the media reports about the Slasher murders have seemed somewhat," I paused, searching for the right word, "incomplete. Are they reining themselves in, or are you withholding information?"

"A combination of both." She hesitated before continuing. "It would have a negative impact on the investigation to release some of the horrific details. It would also scare the shit out of people, make them spit up their dinners during the six o'clock news to report the details the media does have."

"I'd like to know those details."

She squinted at me, the jade eyes softer. "Have you ever been at a murder scene, Dr. Obler?"

"Yes."

"Was it bad?"

"I expect every one is bad. I don't watch television shows and I don't romanticize murder. No one deserves to be killed, and nobody looks dignified. Yes, it's awful."

"In this case 'awful' is too mild a word. There's a real weirdo at work here."

Todd had used that expression too. I leaned back in the rickety chair. The wood creaked. Callahan reached under another pile of papers and pulled out a cigarette. She didn't light it, but tapped one end gently on the desk. She had short, red-painted fingernails.

"Tell me."

"Do you want to take notes?"

"I'm used to listening to people and making notes later."

She grimaced. "You must have to deal with a lot of sickos in your line of work too."

"My job is to help them be less sick."

"Mine is to take 'em off the streets."

Her abrupt laugh was like a cough. "Make room for more evil bastards."

"How does the Soda Pop Slasher operate?"

"Operate? He'd never make it through medical school."

She opened a folder and stared at it, yet as she spoke it was obvious she wasn't reading anything. The green eyes stared angrily and then she flipped over a picture to me. The small office was suddenly icy.

"As you can see from that one example, there are clear indications, supported by test results, of sexual activity, oral intercourse and anal penetration. We believe that the attacks begin during sex, not after. The killer is physically powerful, and probably watches for his victim's vulnerability and seizes the moment. We also believe that the attacks are planned yet also represent sudden surges of rage. The victims are severely mutilated—before death. They are aware of what is being done to them before they die, usually of loss of blood." She looked at me and spoke softly. "They are conscious, then they pass out. And die. Even if we showed up while they were still breathing, they would die anyway."

"You've been there?"

She nodded. More softly, she said, "Absolute horror."

"What mutilation takes place?"

"It varies a bit. One constant is the anal area and genitals have been sliced to bloody bits by a sharp object. Not a knife. We've found pieces of glass and a couple of times there's been metal inside the bodies. Forensics isn't sure yet if the material was intact at entry and then broke up or if piece by piece they were inserted and manipulated. In either case, the intent was to cause maximum damage." I handed her back the picture. She closed the folder. "As painfully as possible."

I folded my now cold and wet hands on my lap. I respected this detective. Despite her soft, smooth attractiveness she was hard as nails and had seen a lot, but she couldn't close off her feelings for the victims. Now, though, I had to close off mine.

"What isn't a constant?"

She glanced at me with one corner of her mouth turned down as if to say, *Haven't had enough yet, huh*? The pace of her cigarette tapping increased.

"Four of the victims were bound with chains. Again, before death."

"Anything else?"

"With three of the male victims, their cocks were hacked off," Callahan said. "With the women, bottle parts were in the vagina."

"Then stitched with surgical thread?"

Her hard look indicated I had said too much. "How do you know that?" she asked. I shrugged. I had for a moment forgotten I was speaking to a homicide detective, supposedly one of the best. The cigarette tapping had stopped. I tried to answer her next question before she asked it.

"Okay, I didn't guess," I said. "I've done a lot of research on sex-related violence involving mutilation. This fits a pattern."

"Not any I've come across."

Shifting gears, I said, "Is there any indication of alcohol or drug use?"

"Yes. But if you're asking if the victims are drugged, no. They are simply overpowered, in part by physical strength and in part by fury."

"Have you done DNA testing?"

"Sure. But that would only help us if we had a suspect's sample to compare the results with." Callahan leaned back, pushing slim fingers through her mass of curls. "It's not like fingerprints. The FBI doesn't have a catalog of semen samples. Yet."

"But they can identify blood type, and. . . ."

"Yes. If it's something like O negative. That helps, because that type is relatively uncommon. But the only blood we've found on these crime scenes is that of the victims. And plenty of it."

She leaned forward, flicking the unlit cigarette away and planting her hands on the desk. "Ten minutes are up. And, I think, that story about writing a textbook is bullshit. What is your interest, really, Dr. Obler?"

The green eyes glittered at me. I surely wanted to tell her, but my oath of patient confidentiality prevented me. I could give her information that might crack this case. And more importantly, if Devon was the Soda Pop Slasher, I could prevent more horrible deaths.

But I couldn't jump to conclusions. I couldn't

judge. Handing over a patient, even if he might be a
serial killer, went against everything I believed in
and practiced.

"I had a patient once who I thought might be a murderer," I said, my mind riffing. "I'm reminded of that now.
It's a reason why I am working on this book. Turned out
he wasn't. But I had to know. So I gathered more information. I was satisfied. I helped him. Anyway, I could not
have discussed with the police what went on in therapy."

"What if he was the killer?" Callahan asked. Her voice
quivered slightly.

"I'm bound by the ethics of my profession to. . . ."

She leaned back and waved her hand as though
dismissing me. "I can't help you anymore, Dr. Obler."

I tried a grin. "Please call me Marty."

"Dr. Obler," she said firmly, her face serious. "I don't
care who you know and who owes you what. You're full of
shit, and I can't help you anymore."

She was right, and I wasn't a good enough poker
player to hide it. My best bet was to beat a retreat. I stood up
and began to button my coat.

"I'm sorry to have taken up your time. I hope you find
the animal. Really."

"Thanks a lot. Let me ask you a question: where is
your responsibility?"

"What do you mean?"

"You know something. This was all crap. I can subpoena your records, go through every patient you have."

This certainly wasn't a clean getaway. I put my hands
on her desk. "You can try. It won't work."

"No," she sighed, "it won't."

She stood. Our faces weren't far apart, reminding me of when Devon and I had confronted each other in my office. Now I was in hers, and she wanted something I couldn't give.

"But I'm asking you, Dr. Obler, if you can help us catch this freak before he does it again."

"I can't."

Callahan spun away, curls flailing and badge gleaming. She leaned against the dust-covered blinds covering the one window in her office.

"I've got work to do," she said. "Now it's not enough that we've got our own sick killer, we're getting calls from D.C. cops saying they've got a body like the ones we've found. Maybe Houston or fucking Frisco will call in next. Everyone likes a party. And I'm Miss Information. Get out."

My guts turned to liquid. Suddenly everything roared in my ears—the rattling of the blinds as she shifted against them, phones ringing in other offices, footsteps going past in the hall, the rapid clattering of keyboards, a conversation outside in the corridor. The air in the small office became warm, stifling. I had trouble breathing.

"What did you say?"

"I said get out."

"About Washington. A murder there. Was it a young woman or a man?"

"Girl or boy, you mean. Do you have children, Doctor?"

I nodded.

"Girl or boy?"

"Both."

She looked away for a few moments as if staring at some far off sight only she could see. Then she refocused.

I knew her scope was enlarging. "We'll 'share' sometime, Doctor When you're in the mood," Callahan said bitterly.

"Do you know who is doing this?" I asked her.

"No. Do you?"

I backed away from her angry glare. "Thank you for your time, Detective. Good luck."

I fumbled for the doorknob, feeling her electric eyes still on me. As I closed the door I turned and looked at her for a brief second. The accusing glare was nothing compared to the way I felt about myself.

As I walked down the corridor I kept rubbing my hands, as if trying to remove something. A sticky substance like blood.

Chapter 15

Stir Crazy

Stella had gone out of town with the children for a few days, so I didn't see Mark and Salena that weekend. On the one hand, I was glad that they were away. My own suspicions along with what I had learned from Callahan had turned my anxiety into fear for both of them. Especially if Devon was the Soda Pop Slasher.

On the other hand, I wished they were with me so I could reassure myself of their safety, not only from danger but from my turbulent thoughts. Much of what Callahan had told me about the killings matched information I remembered from sessions with Devon. And the murder in Washington, D.C., if the time frame matched, wasn't that too remarkable for coincidence? I should have asked Callahan more about it and tried to pin down the timing, but I'd been too stunned. And she'd have become reticent if I said more. It would have raised her suspicions further, nor would she be ready to talk to me again.

Try as I might to be objective, I was increasingly

convinced that Devon had intimate knowledge of the
horrifying murders, may have participated in those crimes
in some way, could indeed be the killer. I was stuck in a
double bind. As a therapist, I was judging a patient I was
supposed to help—judging him to be a homicidal psychopath. And at the same time, as a human being I wanted
to prevent more cruel deaths. My thoughts ricocheted back
and forth. I wasn't just a person. I was a psychologist bound
by confidentiality and related ethics of my profession. And
I wasn't just a psychologist, I was a father and a man falling
in love with a very special woman.

On Sunday I felt stir crazy alone in my apartment. I
had to get out and do something, and that something was to
go see Rachel. Of course, I couldn't discuss the case with
her, but I needed to talk to her, even if it was only about the
weather or the Knicks who, as luck would have it, were in
a slump, having lost three in a row, the last game to the
cursed Bulls.

I trudged all the way uptown, needing the exercise
and fresh air. It had snowed a couple of inches the night
before, and the city's soot hadn't mixed in with the white
frothy blanket yet. The sky was still cloudy, but there were
hints of sunlight trying to break through. I must have passed
hundreds of people during the trek, and as usual we all
avoided eye contact. Is it any wonder all manner of
deranged people could pass among us unnoticed.

I suppose it wasn't smart to walk, with my past
experiences of feeling watched. The feeling wasn't present
on this early afternoon. Either no one was observing, or I'd
grown accustomed to it. As I got closer, I thought I should
have called ahead to let Rachel know I was coming, but I

just wanted to see her . . . and what if I had called and she had said no?

It had been weeks since we'd seen each other. Not that Rachel hadn't tried to keep in touch. Whenever she had called, I had tried to respond warmly, but something was missing—my mind. It was elsewhere, obsessed with work and especially the escalating dilemma of Devon. These were some of the same symptoms that ruined my marriage. You'd think a supposedly smart guy like me wouldn't make the same mistake twice, but here I was repeating the formula.

I hadn't heard from Rachel since New Year's Day. Then she'd been awkward, stiff, distant. As we traded small talk, I'd tried to be cheerful, claiming that I was getting some important things worked out. I'd said she was lovely, a terrific person, to have patience, etc. I knew even then I was only kidding myself. If I was sincere about wanting to continue the relationship, truly we had to talk face to face.

"Rachel!" I called as I approached her building and spotted her just emerging from it. "It's me! After all this time you might not want. . . ." I stopped in midsentence.

There was someone with her. A man. And as they turned to look at me their mouths opened in surprise. It was her old boyfriend. The fellow she had been engaged to when we'd met.

"Oh, Marty. Hello," she said with sadness or embarrassment in her voice. "What are you doing here?"

I gazed into her large brown eyes for a few moments, then replied, "Nothing. Sorry."

As I walked quickly back the way I'd come, kicking up small tufts of snow, Rachel called to me, but I pushed on, head down. Now there was something else I didn't want to think about. And I couldn't blame her.

On Wednesday morning I sat in my office staring out the window at a murky gray sky. It had snowed heavily the night before and now flakes were beginning again. Last winter, I had promised myself to go some place warm the next January. Bermuda if by myself (or with Rachel), Disneyworld if Mark and Salena could afford a few days' absence from school. Now it was the depth of winter, I was going nowhere, and I seemed to feel the cold more keenly than ever before.

Rachel had called several times since Sunday, leaving messages, asking and then insisting that we talk. "Psychologist, heal thyself," I murmured over and over. I wasn't handling well that she had apparently resumed the relationship with her ex-fiance, and that it was my fault. I had let a caring, wonderful woman slip through my fingers.

Ironically, thinking about Devon, who was supposed to be at my office in a short while for his next appointment, proved a good distraction. I was considering asking him to agree to an elaborate series of experimental physiological tests for detecting underlying brain deficits correlated with sociopathic behavior. Before my judgment was any further impaired, I wanted to look for objective clinical evidence that Devon did possess the capacity for extreme violence.

Physiological testing of sociopaths was a recent innovation in the diagnosis and evaluation of complex psychological conditions in psychotherapy. It was developed at the Johns Hopkins Medical Center in Baltimore; researchers had determined that many people tried faking multiple personalities. The condition had been popularized in the afternoon television talk shows and movies. An effective diagnostic tool was needed to weed out the pretenders from the real multiples.

Researchers discovered that in true multiples each personality had a distinct brainwave pattern. Subsequently, a similar line of investigation had found that most psychopaths have an underactive central nervous system defect which leads them to compensate for this deficiency by constantly seeking excitement. This very often involves violence, with domination and murder being the ultimate thrill. The challenge was to get Devon to agree to participate in such testing without letting on that I thought he was a psychopath, and quite possibly a serial killer. With his sharp intelligence, I wasn't sure that I could carry off the facade required.

Suddenly, my buzzer went off, announcing that a visitor had entered the office. Devon was often punctual but never early, and there were fifteen minutes before his appointment. An abrupt knock sounded on the door, and, to my surprise, Rachel strode into the office.

"What are you doing here?" I asked.

"That seems to be the question of the week," she said. She was very angry. "I can't believe the way you're acting," she said harshly. "You barely speak to me; there's hardly any communication; you cut me off; then show up out of the blue on my doorstep; then you're gone and apparently can't bear to talk at all."

"Well, that doorstep would've been crowded if I...."

"Stop acting like a petulant child."

It was almost funny that as she said this she stamped a snow-flecked shapely foot. However, the look in her dark eyes wasn't at all humorous. It blazed. Hands balled up into fists quivered against her sides.

"Marty, I've decided that I'm not going to explain any-thing to you, because you don't deserve it. Nevertheless, *I* deserve an explanation of *your* behavior."

"You do," I agreed.

Actually, I *did* want to take the time to speak to her about my feelings as well as my actions. But Devon's arrival was imminent. I didn't want him and Rachel to run into each other. I had to get her out of here now.

"Well?" she demanded, her foot now tapping, making me feel even more like a naughty child.

"How about lunch? You remember that Italian spot on Bleecker? Noon. My treat."

"You're putting me off again."

Damn, I was, but for a reason she couldn't imagine. "I can't break this next appointment. That wouldn't be fair." I held up my hand. "I know. I haven't been fair to you either. And what happened on Sunday, I take responsibility."

Rachel tilted her head to one side and put one slim finger to her chin. "What do you think *happened*?"

"I can't get into that now." I heard the pendulum swinging, and the number on the digital clock changed. "Please, Rachel. I'm begging."

She smiled. "Okay. And if you *really* want to find out what happened. . . ." With a quick wave she left.

Only a few minutes later Devon arrived. Maybe there had been enough of an interval after Rachel's departure. I couldn't be sure. His expression didn't betray having met anyone leaving. He appeared rather jovial, surprising considering how our last sessions had gone. I sat back, relieved. That was a close one, I thought.

He shook off his coat, allowing it to fall over the back of the chair. "I ran into one of your girls downstairs," he said. His grin made me feel as empty inside as he was. "Quite the babe. I like your taste." I bit my lip to control myself. His grin turning into a leer, he asked, "Do you make it with any of your patients?"

Keeping my voice level, I asked, "Why do you think she was one of my patients?"

"Oh, I don't know." He lifted one eyebrow. "Maybe I've seen her before."

I didn't dare pursue this, and it was probably more my fear than for therapeutic reasons. "Why don't we get on with the session," I said, still keeping my voice level.

"Maybe I should listen to you about getting it on. Should we reverse roles?"

I gazed into his riveting eyes. He was enjoying this taunting expression of power. "Our roles as they are, are challenging enough."

"My, aren't you discreet," he said coyly. "It's like at the end of *Casablanca* when Humphrey Bogart tries to convince Paul Henried that he didn't really fuck the stuffing out of Ingrid Bergman."

Already exhausted, I let him go on, blabbing about the passion of Bogart and Bergman. The clock pendulum couldn't swing fast enough.

Icy gusts of wind and snow blew my hair straight back as I hiked to Bleecker Street. Deep inside, I had strong hopes that Rachel and I could work things out. But all I could feel was anxiety. Devon wasn't kidding: his hints about disguises and stalking were to be taken seriously. I was convinced of that. Now, no matter what happened between Rachel and myself, I was anxious for her as well as for my children.

I heard the crunch of footsteps behind me in the snow. He might be following me right now. There was nothing I could do about it: I wouldn't avoid Rachel any longer. Let him observe. Still, every few steps I paused to glance around, the cold wind and flying snow lashing one side of my face and then the other. I couldn't see anyone, but in this kind of weather that meant nothing.

Rachel sat at a table against one wall. She wore a blue dress with a multicolored floral print that accentuated her well-proportioned body.

Standing up she gave me a quick kiss. I tasted the fruity flavor of wine on her lips. "Thank you," I said, handing my coat to the maitre d' and sitting down across from her.

"I ordered a bottle," she said, pointing to the wine in the center of the table. "I think you need it."

"I do." I smiled.

"Let's order. I'm starved."

I couldn't concentrate, so when the waiter arrived I just seconded what Rachel ordered. Gratefully, I took a sip of the wine, the warmth flowing into my stomach.

"No work today?"

She shook her head.

"I felt this was more important."

"Yes, it is." I looked into her fawnlike eyes. "I am sorry. And that covers a lot of things."

Rachel put her hand on mine. "And it helps a lot. Okay, me first."

So she told me—not a confession, an explanation. Gary, the old boyfriend, had shown up unexpectedly at her door. "Don't you hate when people do that?" she asked. His company was relocating to Dallas. Just before he left town, he wanted to see Rachel one more time, in case there was a chance of rekindling their romance.

"Ever think about living in Dallas?" I asked.

Rachel admitted to being tempted momentarily. She and Gary had had a lot of problems, but one of them wasn't that he shut her out (a comment that made me reach for more wine).

"But even if things are falling apart with us, I'm not interested in being with Gary again, in Dallas or here. I've grown, and moved on." This was the present. She would rather determine her own future. "I told him I'd accompany him to the airport. We were leaving—not after a night of renewed passion or to go for an idle Sunday brunch, but to make sure he did leave town—when you showed up."

I believed her. Rachel had an honest, outspoken quality about her which had immediately and still attracted me. There was no doubt she was telling the truth. I felt a mixture of shame and guilt. First, because I had doubted her, when I was the one who had almost wrecked things between us. Second, because if I could so easily concoct an imaginary tale of rekindled romance and passion, couldn't I also be creating a false scenario of a patient who was a serial killer? By letting my imagination run wild, I was not only jeopardizing my relationship with Rachel, I was jeopardizing the standards of the profession that I respected and always wanted to honor.

Our food arrived. I looked down to see it was pasta

primavera which I liked. We dug in as though we hadn't eaten in weeks, the act of eating an obvious euphemism. When we were close to being done and slowing down, I told Rachel more about Devon. Of course, I still did not reveal details, that risked a break of confidentiality. I told her I had begun to feel that he might be committing violent acts yet my top priority was to help him, and that I had been for weeks obsessed with the dilemma of reconciling opposing concerns.

Sincerely, though without mentioning fear for her safety, I told her, "My immersion in this case has caused me to overlook important parts of my life, especially you."

"You need to trust me more, Marty," she said, finishing her wine. "If we are to go on."

"Are we?"

I nervously waited for her response. Finally, she looked at me and said, "I hope so. I really do."

We held hands like infatuated teenagers while the table was cleared. The waiter, not wanting to interrupt, didn't ask for our dessert order. He simply brought us espresso.

I was about to lean over and kiss Rachel when she asked, "This patient, was he the one I met in your building this morning?"

"Oh, uh, which one was that?" Suddenly my lunch was halfway back up my throat.

"Blond good-looking guy, big, but very strange eyes. He asked if I was one of your patients. I shrugged, but he kept asking. Finally I tried to walk away from him, but he cornered me, fixing those staring unblinking blue eyes on me. They made me shiver. Then he mentioned wanting to find an apartment on the Upper East Side, preferably near a subway station so he could conveniently get to work at a law firm. I didn't tell him where I lived, but I had the weirdest feeling he knew. It was creepy."

She sipped her espresso. "So. Was it him?"

"Rachel, I can't answer that."

I hated to risk breaking the mood between us, but I had to add, "And you shouldn't ask."

"Yes, you're right. But he was particularly odd. I've just wondered about him."

"Well, of course, if some people weren't odd, I'd be out of business." The attempt at humor sounded flat even to my ears, but I kept trying. "That guy could be watching us right now. He is especially interested in my personal life. And he likes disguises. Maybe that's him." I pointed at an older gentleman sitting alone by the window. "Or even her," indicating the middle of three attractive women sitting at an adjacent table. It didn't help that she looked remarkably like Callahan.

"Maybe we should leave separately," Rachel said, trying to help me. Whether or not she was trying to figure out if I was the strange one, I didn't want to ascertain.

"Okay."

"What?" she asked, shocked.

"Just kidding," I said quickly. I signaled for the check. "This guy. He's just another harmless patient. Let's not make what I do more dramatic than it is."

"Well, I do find it intriguing."

"That's it, we'll be a team and you can help me solve the mysteries of my patients. We'll be like the Nick and Nora Charles of psychology."

Rachel laughed, her eyes shining. "Nick and Nora? Since when are you such an old movie buff?"

I shrugged, maintaining a grin but knowing quite well where my remarks had come from. The check arrived and I immediately paid it, leaving the tip on the table. I took a sip of espresso. It was almost as cold as I felt inside.

"Should we leave through the kitchen?" I suggested.

"Let's not get carried away."

"Uh, okay. What are you doing with the rest of your day?"

She winked. "I had a few ideas."

I shook my head. "I can't. Too late to break appointments. How about later?"

"I'll try to wait up." She pretended to yawn.

I held her arm firmly as we left the restaurant, then escorted her down the street to the subway station. We stopped once to embrace, pressing ourselves against each other. Despite the brisk wind and whirling snow, I felt cleansing warmth spreading through my body. Rachel was a very special person and I admitted to myself for the first time, I wanted us to have a long future together. I just had to make sure we survived the present.

On the station platform I said, "I'll call you later."

"No, don't." She smiled. "Just show up."

We hugged one more time as the train entered the old station, rumbling and squealing so loud that even if we had anything more to say it couldn't be heard. Rachel stepped aboard, the doors closed, and she waved as the train pulled out of the station.

I leaned against the metal gate next to the turnstiles, feeling a blend of relief and loss. And dread. As I pressed back against the gate, its sharp spikes dug into my back and shoulders. Sharp objects. Used to hurt, to kill in the most vicious ways imaginable. Probably even a veteran homicide cop like Callahan hadn't imagined before the case of the Soda Pop Slasher what a mad maniac could do. Was doing. Would do.

I lurched, turning away from the metal gate. It was then in a frightening moment I thought I saw the flash of flaxen hair moving like a meteorite though the crowds.

Chapter 16

Deadly Similarities

Devon arrived at our thirty-first session right on time. On this occasion I had planned my strategy and was ready for him.

Even at the risk of his quitting therapy, or tapping into the reservoir of rage that could erupt as violence, I had to know: was he connected to the Soda Pop Slasher killings? Was he aiding and abetting someone who was torturing and killing young men and women? Even worse, was *he* the Soda Pop Slasher?

And because of fun or power or self-survival, was he a danger to those I loved? Or me?

I had decided that Devon had to be honest with me. If he was hiding a secret and violent life how could I help him? Perhaps worse, if he was enjoying the power games he played with me, it was certainly possible that our relationship was providing some sordid sort of assistance to violent behavior.

I had assumed the authoritarian parental role during

our therapy. Devon might not only be having fun by getting away with things behind my back, but he was also realizing the power he had over a parent by teasing and taunting about what he was (or could be) doing.

So I had worked out a scenario for the session. Or so I thought.

Devon's appearance was meticulous today. He wore a gray tweed business suit, perfectly matched by a pinstriped white dress shirt, black socks, and polished black shoes. Without a greeting he sat down in the chair and smiled expectantly like a cat waiting for the mouse to appear.

"Did you approach one of my other patients in the lobby before our last session?"

"'Approach' is too strong a word. Hey, I told you she was a babe. I appreciate the finer things in life."

"I'd rather not quibble about. . . ."

"Oh, all right. We spoke." He crossed his legs and the smile broadened. "Just trying to be friendly."

"Devon, you're well aware of the standard policy— and it's certainly my policy—of contact between patients outside of therapy." I returned his gaze. "Such contact is grounds for termination of therapy."

"I'm confused, Dr. Obler," he said, all innocence. "I respect your policy. But my question is, is she a patient?"

My heart froze for a moment. Was he toying with me? Did he know who Rachel was? How? "What are you implying?" I asked slowly.

"Maybe she's a patient, and maybe she isn't. Let's examine the evidence. Are you in the habit of hugging and kissing your patients?"

He was so full of himself that I hoped he didn't notice

the way my hands trembled before I clasped them on the desktop.

"You must have too much professional integrity for that. The ethical Dr. Obler fool around with *any* patient? That would be a surprise." He tilted his head and winked. "Do I assume she's your mistress? Too attractive to be a hooker."

I tried to breathe slowly and evenly. Okay, Devon had seen Rachel and me together. My first thought was it must have been in the subway station. Our parting on the platform had taken place after he had approached Rachel here in the building. Unless he was referring to months ago. Or, he was just playing games with me, games in which time and circumstances didn't matter as long as he could play and think he was winning.

"Have you been following me, Devon?"

"*Moi?* A startling question. It seems that trust has gone out the window."

"Have you? Is that what you're doing? Do you follow anyone else, my family, my friends, dammit?"

His smile was radiant.

I realized immediately that by letting fear and anger surface I'd made a big mistake. Having it be apparent that he'd rattled me was a three-pointer for Devon. His grin and raised eyebrow indicated he'd tallied the score. I would have to deal with the stalking at another time.

"I've been concerned about you ever since that call from Washington," I said as casually as I could. "We've never explored what that was all about."

"I thought what we were just talking about was infinitely more interesting."

"I'm the one who will decide the level of interest in

our sessions," I replied, noticing that his grin had narrowed. "See, you can score points, but I control the game. I can end it now. It's over, if you're not honest with me. Do you understand that, Devon?"

Now he was pouting. He lowered his head and murmured, "Yes, Dr. Obler."

"Good. So what exactly did happen down there?"

"Now that's not very interesting at all. I was pretending to be Jimmy Stewart, like in *Mr. Smith Goes to. . . .*"

"Devon."

"All right, Mr. Curious. Just a minor sexual engagement that got out of hand. Temporarily." He glared at me. "Is this really important or do you get your rocks off listening to patients describe their sexual lives?"

"Sexual behaviors indicate a lot. Exploring and understanding them is important if I'm to help you. So why don't you tell me what happened."

His cheeks were flushed. "I phoned you because I got a little concerned. Some S&M stuff, probably right up your alley. The prostitute got a bit hurt. It happens, you know. This isn't brain surgery."

"What happened?"

"I fucked the whore and instead of those cute animal noises they're supposed to make there was a little blood from our cutting up." Then he shouted, "Why are you making a federal case out of it?"

"That call was so similar to the one you made from the hospital after our very first session. You must remember that, Devon. Or have you forgotten?"

"Are you supposed to be helping me? Or is this a courtroom and you're fucking Perry Mason?" He was breathing hard, his entire face turning crimson. "I can't recall all my rendezvous with whomever. They get what they deserve, that's all."

"What do they deserve?"

"To be fucked."

Devon began laughing, emptying his lungs with loud, barking guffaws. He was close to losing control. I could press him harder and in hysteria he might reveal incriminating information, or like a bomb he might go off completely.

I really wanted to know if he was the Soda Pop Slasher. But what if I went too far? If Devon had no connection to the murders, was perhaps no more (though this was a lot) than a borderline psychopath immersed in sado-masochistic sex and I pushed him over the edge to total psychosis, then I had failed as a therapist, allowing my own needs to have priority over those of a patient. Forget losing my license. I would be contradicting the very reason why I had pursued psychology: to make people well and save them from self-inflicted misery.

The only thing about my dilemma which was clear was that it was a hell of a predicament. I decided to go right to the heart of the matter but in a direct, calm way.

"Devon, did you murder someone in Washington?"

It was my tone or his astonishing resiliency. His breathing slowed and the red splotches on his face vanished. "Do you think I did?" he asked, his voice steady.

"If I knew, I wouldn't ask."

I thought fast and with a pang of guilt realized that I was demanding honesty from Devon while concealing my encounter with Callahan.

"There was a report in the media about a young hooker brutally murdered in Washington during the time you were there on business," I said. "It was mentioned that sharp objects used to slash the victim were involved. Sounds similar, doesn't it, to the series of murders here in New York?"

Devon snorted. "Haven't paid much attention, actually. I'm still here, and that's all I care about."

"Well, I've paid close attention to you and what you've told me here. About picking up hookers. About glass bottles."

"I bet you like to fantasize about what I do. Probably because you won't, or can't." He grinned and folded his arms. "That stuff goes on all the time. Did you know one of Pomerantz's colleagues at the exalted university got off by having hookers piss and shit on him? Fun stuff."

"We're not talking about other people."

"We all have fantasies, and some of us live them out. Still, a lot of it remains fantasy. Surely you're aware that fantasies of murder and genital mutilation like the one in the Washington case are routine in red light districts all over the world."

"The media mentioned nothing about genital mutilation. How did you know about it?"

Our eyes locked. He didn't blink for a full minute. The pendulum swung slowly and easily, offering a series of soft clicks. Frozen rain dashed against the window.

"You said the D.C. thing was similar to the killings around here," Devon said slowly. "Everyone's reporting or hinting about those."

"I thought you hadn't paid much attention."

"Well, stuff like that. . . ."

Matching his soft, slow tone I asked, "Are you being honest with me, Devon?"

I hoped for a breakthrough. Instead, he flung one arm over the back of the chair, tossed back his blond hair, and gazed steadily at me.

"Are you a therapist or a cop?" he said. "Are you going to treat me or read me my rights?"

It was either a wild shot or a well-placed jab in this match: Devon had outlined my dilemma. Suddenly, I felt backed into a corner. Perhaps sensing my retreat, he moved in.

"I'm quite willing to continue this line of investigation. Guess I dropped out of the psychology program before taking the class in the uses of innuendo, suspicion, and accusation in treatment."

He grinned and sat up straight. "But as you said, let's not quibble. If we want to discuss imagination correlated to action, how about what may or may not be going on between you and your concubine. Meeting in your office—yeah, the desk is wide enough for a variety of positions. And at restaurants—ooops, too many things on that table, she'll receive many pokes. Smooching in the subway. C'mon, can't you afford a hotel room?

"But it's all circumstantial, isn't it? In a court of law, would this evidence suggest or prove that you were fucking her? Your Honor, I submit that it would not. We're making leaps. No, no, no, can't do that. Got to peek in a window, see you pumping away and then testify. Goodness, I wouldn't do that, not to my therapist."

Then he leaned forward, and his voice grew hard. "But I've got a therapist who, after months of my spilling out my guts to him on a weekly basis, is just at the point of tying me to terrible, vicious murders. Slice and Dice Devon, huh? Want honesty, Dr. Obler? Well, consider this: if you believe that I *am* the Soda Pop Slasher, why *haven't* you turned me over to the police or terminated therapy?"

He had me on the ropes. I didn't know if he was a psychopathic killer or emotionally ill. Whatever he was, I was bound by confidentiality and the ethics of my profession to help him. I wasn't doing that through accusations.

I tried one last feint, though it bore the burden of truth. "Whether you're guilty or not, I'll continue to work with you in therapy," I said. "The important thing is that we be honest with each other. I'm bound by my ethics to protect you, and even in a court of law I can't discuss what has transpired here."

"Poor, ineffectual man. I really do pity you."

"On the other hand, if you don't come clean with me, and we don't discuss the murders, I *can* go to the police. First, I'll end therapy. Then I'll turn you in."

For a moment his eyebrows shot up, then he began to laugh. "You're a fucking riot, Obler. You can think a lot of things about me, but I'm surprised you think I'm a goddamn idiot. What you have implied, hinted, accused, and conjectured is bullshit. I'm getting deeper into law now, remember? What you've said, or even what in your surprisingly and disappointingly tiny brain you suspect, would be laughed out of court, and your license suspended in the process. You'd be lucky to find a job as a nursery school counselor. Even the tabloid television shows wouldn't touch you."

"I'm not worried about myself."

"Of course you are." Devon leaned forward, placing his chin on folded hands. "Maybe the rest of your career is shit, and I'm all you've got to claw your way to respectability. Go ahead, pick up the phone. Call the cops. I dare you."

Suddenly I sensed that what he was enjoying most about this parrying was the possibility of my career and integrity being in tatters. The position of power and domination Devon had achieved in this session played right into his eager grasping hands. It didn't matter if he was a serial killer or not. He was getting off on this.

I could call the police. I was angry and frustrated enough to do it. And after meeting Callahan, I knew that she was anxious enough that she would put the cuffs on and follow up on details later. She would subpoena my records. There would be a search warrant to get into Devon's apartment, which might or might not lead to incriminating discoveries. I would be required to testify, and the legal issues would be resolved down the road, perhaps after an acquittal or conviction. Was that the right thing to do?

I needed time to think. This session had gone badly and I felt myself sinking deeper into a whirlpool. Yet I tried once more.

"I'm not trying to build a legal case against you," I said, attempting a smile. "But you can understand that there are quite a few coincidences and I don't want to be responsible for more deaths."

"Nor do I," Devon said. "That's why I'm here. But, golly," he gave an enigmatic smile, "I don't feel welcome at all."

"Let's begin again."

"Oh my, not much time."

"We could briefly go through your itinerary while in Washington."

"You really are set in your ways, old-timer." He stood up, smoothed his shirt and tugged his suit jacket down, and started to put on his long dark gray coat.

"We have a few minutes left."

"Dr. Obler, if we're going to talk about anything that truly engages my interest, then let's discuss your itinerary with your well-proportioned, brown-eyed main squeeze. Or is she one of several in your stable, you stallion?"

"Leave her out of this, you crazy bastard!"

In that moment, I'd lost my objectivity. The words escaped from my mouth before I knew it. We both immediately realized that Devon had won this round. He stared at me for a moment then started to laugh, his eyes squeezing shut as his whole body shuddered, the edges of his coat quivering. "Point to Devon Cardou," he said contemptuously. Silently he left closing the door behind him.

Chapter 17

Dark Abyss

Callahan had said she would wait until I was ready to talk but she must have changed her mind. It was like she was picking up a danger signal—just as I debated whether to grab the phone and call her, she suddenly called me. When I heard her direct, Bronx-accented voice, I let her leave a message. She didn't say what she wanted other than she had to see me as soon as possible.

I let a couple of days pass, thoughts ricocheting through my mind. On Friday there was a gentle late snow, not a major storm, more like a reminder that nature ruled yet could be a benevolent dictator. Huge flakes of snow fell softly and silently. The result for the weekend would be something like an old Alfred Steiglitz photo of the city I thought, watching it. For a short time at least, the look was surreal and timeless. Mark and Salena would be with me Saturday and Sunday. I planned to take them sledding in Central Park.

I was able to finish my work at the uptown clinic early and decided to walk all the way back to my office, where I could catch up on all my notes and miscellaneous tasks so the weekend would be free to concentrate on my children. As I began walking, the pearl gray sky above me fitted the idyllic winter scene. There was no wind. Commuters with heads down poured down subway steps or hurried toward Grand Central Station, their only interest in the weather to wonder if the snow would disrupt train service.

"Late final here! Get yer late final!" shouted street corner newspaper vendors. Every time I passed one I cringed a bit at his cry: "The Soda Pop Slasher strikes again! Read it here!" Finally I bought a paper.

THE SODA POP SLASHER STRIKES AGAIN
Body of Number Thirteen Continues the Jinx

The slaying of an exotic dancer, eighteen-year-old Stormy Sundae, was discovered at 7 a.m. in the morning. It was found on the roof of a tenement house by a young boy who kept pet pigeons there. Today, the police say this killing has been linked to the Soda Pop Slasher.

"Once again there are similarities too close to discount," Sergeant Paul Richard announced, "but we'll be making no further comment on them except to say we're pursuing every lead."

**The victim's parents, Frank and Alveda
Sunderheim, who live a few blocks from the
crime scene, last saw their daughter around
dinner time Friday night. After dinner she left
for the club where she performs.**

**Mrs. Sunderheim collapsed after identifying
her daughter's body at the Riverside Hospital
Morgue. Police are urgently searching for wit
nesses. If you know anything about the crime
please contact Sergeant Richards,
Fifth Precinct.**

I threw the paper in the nearest bin. The Knicks were
playing at the Garden that night, an unusual Friday home
game, this one against the Spurs, to make up for a game
that an ice storm had canceled two weeks earlier. A big
temptation was to go scalp a ticket and attend the game and
forget about the murders and everything else. Let the
aggressive play of Ewing and Oakley substitute for my
churning mind. Make a right here at Duffy Square and....

I pressed on, sorting out my thoughts. Would it be the
right thing to call Callahan, tell her everything, and let the
chips fall where they may? If my career suffered, so be it.

There would be professional sanctions. Of course, if I
had violated confidentiality by turning Devon over to the
cops and my motive was to solve or at least prevent more
murders, preliminarily I might get only a slap on the wrist.
However, the later ramifications would go beyond that. The
word would get around that I was a therapist who couldn't be
trusted, who would weigh a patient's mental health and his

own promise of confidentiality against other concerns, who might well be expected to bail out even if without solid proof he thought those concerns tipped the scales. Could I risk my integrity and develop a reputation that over time could ruin me professionally? One more thing: I simply believed that protecting confidentiality was the right thing to do.

However, my dilemma was more complex than that. Okay, Obler, you're a stand-up guy and a credit to the psychology profession. Is that going to help you sleep when another young man or woman is savagely killed? Won't you dwell on their excruciating pain and horror in their final moments? Are your honor and integrity and reputation going to soothe the anguish of future victims' families? Can you stand wondering if Devon is next going to go after your children, or Rachel, or you? What kind of life will it be, always looking over your shoulder?

Then there was another possibility: what if Devon *wasn't* the Soda Pop Slasher? In fact, what if he had absolutely no connection to the killings? He was someone who came (well, okay, he was sent) to me for help. Instead of providing that help, instead of making his mental health and future my main responsibility as a therapist, what if I had woven together shreds of information—offered in the sanctity of our sessions—as well as supposition, to form a disastrous "pattern" that labeled him a serial killer? In that case, I would not only corrupt my ethics by handing him over to the police, but, even if he was exonerated, I might damage his psyche beyond repair and perhaps push him over the edge to where he might truly become capable of murder. I would be screwed not only professionally but as a human being.

One more consideration: how much of my dilemma could be attributed to personal feelings, especially that I was affronted that I hadn't maintained control in therapy? Devon was a clever, intelligent, manipulative person, and too often he had had the best of me. Had that made me less than objective? Had my own self-pride been wounded so that I wanted him to be guilty? More than anything else, Devon enjoyed power games; presenting himself as a possible serial killer (with his intelligence, he could discover enough details about these awful deaths to be convincing) was the ultimate ploy. More and more, he was drawing closer to checkmate. If, deep down, I couldn't "win," did I want to break the rules and defeat him in another way, by breaking him psychologically or tossing him behind bars?

I brushed wet snow off my face. It was as though the heat of my thoughts instantly melted each flake at contact. The day had darkened, and when I looked up thousands of flakes suddenly appeared out of the pewter sky. They were caught and illuminated for a moment in the dull light of street lamps and Broadway shop windows before they wafted to the sidewalk and street to be dashed by trudging feet and rushing taxis and buses.

Was I being followed? After our last meeting, I had no doubt that Devon had been stalking me, and Rachel, for a while. And possibly, his remarks at the session led me to believe, he knew about and was following my children, if for no other reason than to enhance his power over me. Curiously though, I didn't even glance around to check. I felt a complete absence of feeling at this moment.

I hiked down the street to my office. Approaching the building, I envisioned how Devon had cornered Rachel, then through my mind's eye flashed the sight of the fear in my children's voices and eyes, and in my head I heard the screams of young people realizing too late that they were beyond help. I made my decision. I'd throw myself on the pyre, and hope that the phoenix that rose from it was a combination of safety, security, and relief.

I got on the elevator which finally reached my floor. I opened the office door and saw the red light of my answering machine blinking. I went over and pressed the on button. The first message was from Callahan, again requesting a meeting, more insistence in her tone. The second was from Rachel. Her voice sounded strange. "Marty, I need to see you right away. As soon as you hear this, please come over."

The third message was from her too. "Marty, please, come over. Right now." She paused for a few moments, and I heard ragged breathing. "You must come here. Marty, please. There is. . . ." There was an abrupt cutoff and then a beep.

I swiftly punched the numbers. After two rings, the machine picked up. Her voice was shaky. "Please leave a message. Marty, if this is you, please hurry."

I didn't wait for the elevator. I flew down the stairs and leaped out into the street. A taxi screeched and slid, stopping inches from me. "Holy shit, I thought you were a freakin' ghost!" the driver exclaimed.

I dove into the back seat and told him, "I'll give you a twenty-dollar tip if you get me to 77th and Third in ten minutes."

"Mac, don't you see it's freakin' snowing?" he said, his mouth working around the stub of a cigar.

"Make it thirty bucks."

"Hang on. Looks like freakin' July all of a sudden."

As we hurtled uptown, swirling snowflakes appearing out of the dark pasted themselves upon the windshield, I felt like I was falling into an abyss.

The answering buzz was short, barely giving me time to press the lobby door open. Again I avoided the elevator and took the steps three at a time. By the time I reached Rachel's floor my lungs were on fire.

Her door was half open. Lights were on within. Soaked with sweat and melted snow, I hesitated before going through the doorway, realizing that I might find a scene of unimaginable horror.

Flinging the door wide, I stepped into the apartment. The stereo was on. Had music been used to drown out the screams? Then, cowering near a small table that held the phone, I saw Rachel. Her hands were clasped and her head was down. She was alive. I felt immense relief.

Then I saw Devon. He was sitting in a large white chair near the window, holding a soda bottle, pressing it to his lips, smiling. Behind him huge flakes of snow like doves drove themselves against the glass.

"Welcome, Dr. Obler," he said, his voice light. "Sorry, Rachel, I win. It's been more than twenty minutes since the last message."

Rachel lifted her head and gazed at me. Terror shone in her large brown eyes, but otherwise she appeared unharmed. She wore a beige silk blouse and a long tan corduroy skirt and hiking boots. "I got home from work and found him here. He grabbed me from behind and forced me into the apartment.

"Marty, I want to call the police." Rachel asked, trying

to keep her voice calm.

I walked further into the living room. "That's not up to us." I turned to Devon. "Is it?"

"Of course it is. That's the whole purpose of this little visit. Options." He sat forward in the chair, tugging at his gray crew neck sweater, then flicking lint off his chino slacks. I looked down. His tall black boots were dry: he had waited a long time for her to come home.

And it was obvious he was enjoying this scene, whatever the outcome was.

"We need to talk, Dr. Obler."

"You know where my office is."

"She does too, huh?" he said, gesturing at Rachel, who remained frozen in place. "And you sure know this place. Especially the bedroom. Ow!" He squeezed his eyes shut for a moment. "The stories those sheets could tell."

"Stop him, Marty," Rachel whispered, eyes beseeching. "He's frightening me. He's. . . ."

"Disgusting?" Devon cracked his knuckles. "Hey, I've heard that before. And a lot worse. Doc, that's why we need to talk. Things are getting out of hand."

"You're damned right they are."

"Ooh. Righteous indignation. Sexy. Hey, truth time, she is high on the babe-o-meter, but deep down do you really want her alone? There are other experiences you might like."

"Truth?" I stepped closer. "I want to strangle you."

"Screaming headlines tomorrow. Forget your fucking career, we're talking decades of getting meals through a slot in some frozen upstate gulag." Devon sat back and crossed his long legs. "Think about your kids. Mark and Salena, right?" My God, how did he know my children's names? I'd been careful never to mention them. I glared at him. "Salena. Hell of a name. You must've been on prozac when you filled out the birth certificate. Instead of sending alimony, you'll be mailing clippings of your failed appeals."

He glared at me and said, "Are you that stupid? Or out of control?"

He shouldn't have used that word. I stepped closer, drops of water plopping rapidly on the wood floor. My fingers flexed. I could stop them, but I didn't want to.

"You'll have to decide, Devon. Look into my eyes."

He sank back in the chair. "Oh, Marty, let's not be so dramatic."

"It's Dr. Obler. That's how you will address me."

I hissed the words at him, focusing my anger and certainty. He blinked in reaction to the spit striking his face.

"Tell us what you want, Devon. Get it out. It might be the last thing you'll ever say. You crossed a line here tonight. I might cross one too."

"Marty, please. Don't."

I straightened and glanced at Rachel. Though her body shook, she gazed steadily. "Don't ruin everything for this . . . scum."

Devon chuckled. "Bet you two have some intense times. I'd offer a threesome if there weren't other things on my mind."

He laughed again, but I could tell that he had for a moment been genuinely frightened and now felt that he'd won some room to maneuver. He stood, scrabbling past me, and paced back and forth in front of the window, large hands clasped behind him. The shooting snowflakes appeared to be striking his broad shoulders.

"What do you have in mind?" I asked. "Do you intend to harm us?"

"Of course not. Random murder does not interest me. You should know that by now. Nothing deeply serious and deserved is random."

"Devon, are you the Soda Pop Slasher?"

"Dr. Obler, please. Reality check." He looked directly at Rachel and then back at me. "We are not in session here. This is a freebie, and it's mine. Such questions are not part of my game plan." He paused in his pacing. "Remember that night we played basketball? You said to me that evening, 'Win any way you can.' I learned from you. You should be flattered."

"I'm waiting for your move, Devon. Otherwise," I voiced the threat, true or not, "I'm going to call the police."

He resumed pacing. "Our therapy—and I use 'our' deliberately, because I'm convinced you need help too—has gone off in an unwholesome and potentially damaging direction. Do I need to seek treatment from a bastard? No way, Jose. Your line of questioning and accusations have cut me to the quick."

"Well, what do you want?" Rachel asked, exasperated.

He grinned, glanced at her and then me. "Gosh, I love alliteration even when it's imperfect. You are a gifted, gritty girl," Devon said, twirling his fingers in the air and then shooting them downward to indicate dunking a basket. "What words can I use to complement cunt?"

"Devon!" The rage and frustration caged within me broke out.

Backing away from me he interrupted his pacing for a

few seconds. He tried to get back on track, then, evidently frustrated, he strode past me and plopped down on the couch.

"Dr. Obler, if you can contain your violent tendencies for a while, I want to offer a bargain."

"What do you want?" I asked, facing him, my feet planted and knees flexed just in case I had to fight.

"First, I want you to believe what I'm about to say, because it is the absolute truth. Are you willing?"

"Yes. Go on."

"I do want to get . . . well, to put my life together so there is no more pain, just gain." He crossed his fingers and held them lightly under his chin as if he were negotiating a business deal. "I am really intrigued by the legal profession, and would like to be a lawyer. Not as exciting to the libido as psychology, perhaps, but it has its advantages. I continue to believe, despite your aberrant behavior, that *you* can help me. Obler, I want to put this whole nasty episode behind us."

"What nasty episode?"

"The accusations. Worse, the terrible things you've thought about me. They've been so apparent on your otherwise kindly visage."

He was right. "Okay, we're even. What do you want?" I asked again.

"Help."

Suddenly he was the vulnerable young man I had first met.

"I want to feel better," he said. "I want to be different. I want to change my life. Goddamn it."

His handsome face twisted, his body quaked, his hands reached out. It seemed to be a genuine cry of pain and fear, maybe fear of himself and what he was capable of, and what he may have done. The therapist part of me felt an immediate response. But I also was clearly aware that he had forced himself into Rachel's apartment and that Rachel was scared stiff. I wasn't too far behind, knowing the volcanic forces of violence that rumbled just below the surface.

"I want you to feel better, to be better, Devon."

His intense eyes shifted, trying to find deceit in mine. I met his gaze, and for once he blinked before I did.

"If I continue with you and don't call the cops," I said, "what's your offer?"

"My part of the bargain?" He stood and put on the coat thrown over the back of the couch. "I'll be on my best behavior."

"What else?"

"Quite the gamesman, aren't we?"

"Is this a game, Devon?" I asked softly.

"No. No, not really." His hands were trembling. He was having trouble buttoning his coat. "You think it is, but it's not."

"I don't know what to think right now except you have to decide to level with me or I can't treat you."

His head swiveled to the window, and he watched the large flakes crash and dissipate against the pane, the moisture joining the dripping flow downward. I tried to keep my gaze steady on him, knowing he felt it. My ethics, my doubts, my professional concerns, my fears, my judgment, all narrowed to this last offer of help.

"Don't go to the police, Dr. Obler," Devon pleaded, "and I will do whatever you want."

"Stay the hell away from Rachel and my family."

His eyebrows raised.

"Far away."

He nodded.

"You're my patient. I want to help you."

His face changed again, chameleon-like.

"Then we're on. Let the games begin."

He strode toward the door I had left open. After a sweeping bow, which concluded with Devon pushing a plain blue baseball cap down on his head, he closed the door letting it slam behind him.

"I'm sorry, Rachel," I said softly, opening my arms.

She fell into them. "Stop him, Marty," she murmured. I could hear her heart pounding.

"I don't know if I can."

"Stop him," she begged, her voice quivering. "Stop him any way you can."

I nodded and held her tightly to me. I too was frightened. But whatever I had agreed to, while I worked on a solution, I believed I had bought some time, for the woman I loved and the children who meant more to me than life itself.

That was enough . . . for now.

Chapter 18

Fear-Filled Dilemma

After the confrontation in Rachel's apartment, it was clear that whether or not Devon was the Soda Pop Slasher, he was dangerous. And, of course, no halfway intelligent investor would buy shares in my life. Many times my hand reached for the phone to call Callahan or walking on the wet streets I often was about to raise my hand to hail a cab to take me to One Police Plaza. It would be so easy!

Yet even though Rachel's plaintive plea, "Stop him, Marty," echoed in my mind, I couldn't seem to make either move toward the police. The code of ethics which to me was the very basis of my commitment to psychotherapy stopped me. Devon was a patient who desperately needed help. If I kept up my end of my deal with him, however coerced or ill-advised it was, perhaps he would fulfill his end, and he would heal.

In a way, I was the victim in this dilemma. To be true to myself I had to pull us both out. To do that our situation had to change. Devon's power play had worked, and it was reasonable to assume he would build on that advantage in one-on-one sessions. I didn't like nor did I think I was capable long-term of being a pawn in his sordid mind games. And my instinct warned: don't trust him.

To find an answer to benefit us both I had to shake things up, change the circumstances—and, I had to admit, find a way to regain the advantage.

Day and night I agonized about a solution. Despite the fact that I had previous experience with psychopaths having multiple transferences, I had never encountered a patient like Devon who could so easily shift from one emotional extreme to another without losing control of himself. He could in one moment beg for forgiveness (transferred father), switch gears to attack me for being irrational (transferred mother), and then curl up and retreat inside himself and plead for acceptance (transferred idealized parent figure). And, of course, he could be a monster, taunting me with details of violent deaths. In every role he had command of his emotions and was aware of his personality shifts—a capability it is impossible for non-psychopaths to learn.

In such cases there were many psychotherapists who resorted to drugs, lots of them, to curb and manage such deviant behavior and to put a leash on violent rage. I didn't believe drugs, whatever their potency, would work with Devon. First of all, I was certain he wouldn't agree to take them. Second, I doubted they would be effective enough. The force of his intelligence, resiliency and psychosis was too strong. I remembered clearly how through a seizure or some other powerful inner eruption Devon had shaken himself out of a hypnogogic state.

Devon had dealt the cards. I was going to make the

best hand out of them that I could. There was one type of therapy I felt might succeed. I decided to try group therapy.

"You want me to do what?" Devon asked during our next session at which he'd shown up calm as a lake, as though the incident at Rachel's had never happened.

I put the best face on it, explaining that if we really were going to live up to our agreement and I was to provide the help he said he wanted, it was time for other input. I wanted to see him interact. I implied a challenge, that successfully dealing with me had become easy and he was ready to take on an entire team.

"Why don't you call more shrinks in?" He grinned. "Maybe I'm a groundbreaking case."

I didn't doubt it. I leaned forward, placing my hands flat on the wooden desk. "I really don't think they could handle you, Devon. You're beyond that. If you still trust me, I think this is the way to go."

"Well, the prospect of. . . ."

Devon gazed to the side, one finger idly rubbing his cheek. "I haven't done this before, except as practice in the psychology program."

He looked at me and smiled. "By the way, I've definitely decided to go to law school. I registered for the LSATs. I'll get an astronomical score, zip through school; then I'll cut a swath through the legal ranks. I can see a brilliant career already. Hey, maybe I'll be President."

I shuddered. "Are you avoiding my suggestion, Devon? Perhaps, after all, you're not ready to. . . ."

He waved one hand. "Oh sure, let's do it. It would be interesting to take on a few of the knuckleheads you see between our sessions."

I nodded approvingly. There was one other reason I wanted to try group therapy, one that made me uncomfortable but was important: if Devon revealed something solidly incriminating, there would be a roomful of people to hear his disclosures.

I worked with several groups. The one I chose for Devon had in it an assortment of people varying in age, occupation, gender and sexual orientation. Their diversity might make it easier to elicit from Devon his own sexual feelings, violent or not.

Also, I thought that the personalities of some of the members resembled the personalities of Devon's family. Interacting with them would, if I handled my role astutely, provoke Devon's acting out as though they were his father, mother, brother, and others in his life. Psychologists called it multiple transference.

The first three group sessions with Devon were uneventful. Except for a few displays of charm and wit he just observed and listened, perhaps sizing up the competition or evaluating what, if any, threat the other members posed. When a few comments were directed his way, Devon deflected them or gave neutral responses. Other than a slightly bemused smile, he displayed no real involvement in the group process.

At the end of the third session when the group disbanded, Devon walked over to me, running artist-like fingers through his long blond hair. "Engaging, Dr. Obler," he said. "I'm not sure if I like this. On the other hand, although not much happens, the personalities are interesting enough to ward off boredom."

"I suppose I'm glad to hear that," I responded, "but group therapy isn't designed to be light entertainment."

"Surely *some* dramatic changes must occur." He raised one eyebrow. "Don't you mix things up to achieve critical mass and see what happens, at least hope *something* will?"

It was my turn to be coy. "I just might do that," I said, gathering my things and leaving.

I was anxious to get home. My relationship with Rachel was growing more serious. I had thrown practical considerations out the window: I had asked her to move in with me. This probably would have happened sooner or later anyway; however, after the jarring incident with Devon, I realized how much she had come to mean to me and even she accepted how vulnerable she was. We both felt better having the other one close.

So, ironically, the threat of Devon speeded up our relationship's pace and, I guess, did us a favor. I had begun to envision our future together. We only had to survive the present.

Another irony was that while Rachel and I believed Devon was a clear and present danger to us, the tension in the neighborhood was easing up. The Soda Pop Slasher had been out of the news for a while. I still walked Mark and Salena home but hadn't taken them back to my place recently. I had to figure the best way to break the news to them that Rachel and I were living together.

Then, a week or so later, they informed me that walking them home every day wasn't necessary. I felt a twinge of sadness at another one of my fatherly duties ending.

People had begun to think that the Slasher had either left the city or perhaps been killed himself in a murder attempt gone wrong. The media no longer carried daily reports of the investigation; they moved on to reporting other homicides, rapes, child abuse, and domestic battles.

Even the weather was better. Here we were, in late February, and there hadn't been a flake of snow or a temperature below twenty degrees in several weeks. Though days were still cold, a pale yellow sun appeared in the gray sky and did not set so early. A few newspapers even carried advertisements for spring clothing. Perhaps winter too had accepted a covenant.

My agreement with Devon seemed to be holding. Perhaps good would come of this devil's bargain. I had to handle the fact that, due perhaps to my silence, previous victims couldn't be avenged, but I would take on that guilt in favor of keeping the animal in his cage and preventing more savage deaths. Nevertheless, if I kept working at it, staying one step ahead and doing my professional best, perhaps that and the passage of time would soften his fangs and claws.

Well, it made sense, and I felt flickers of hope. Then, as Devon almost predicted, something dramatic happened.

The group therapy sessions were held in the basement of a church in the Chelsea section of Manhattan. Despite the religious setting, the acrid smells of cigarettes and coffee drifted through the air, probably because just about every day there was an Alcoholics Anonymous meeting there. Even on the coldest nights we kept the two small windows open.

In the fifth session Devon was finally confronted. At the beginning there were the usual questions tossed his way

that expressed mild curiosity, which he again deflected or
dismissed. He was in his movie buff mode, watching
and waiting.

But after just shrugging at the next question—the subject was sex—others joined in, asking him pointed questions
about what he did and with whom. Devon glanced around the
room trying to sense and feel his way, probably wondering if
he was about to be ambushed. I felt him look my way, but I
stared straight ahead.

"Well, I'm just a happy-go-lucky guy who enjoys
what he gets, male or female," Devon finally replied. "I'll
probably settle down before too long."

"I don't buy that." Peter, a fortyish man who led a
promiscuous life of sex addiction, periods of substance
abuse, and a craving for money and success, spoke with a
thunderous voice.

Devon smiled and crossed his arms. "Even among
my peers," he said with a trace of contempt, "it's not easy
to discuss or deal with sadomasochism. I happen to enjoy it
and have no regrets about it."

"You don't care if people feel pain?" Peter asked,
taken aback.

"No." Devon stifled a laugh. "I can honestly say I've
never felt guilty about anything I've done. If you participate
with me, you deserve what you get. Feeling anything about it
is a waste of time."

He was indeed being honest. I knew that what he had
just expressed was an important sign of a psychopath, but the
others did not. Disturbed by this admission though, they
began to close ranks against Devon.

"Why do you hate women?" piped up Alma, a petite

woman in her late thirties who had been divorced three times.

"Who says I do?" Devon shot back. "I am equally repulsed and attracted by either sex. Like George Bernard Shaw, if you ever heard of him," Devon said disdainfully, "I'm a misanthrope."

The room was silent. Devon looked at me, but now it was my turn to shrug.

"Are you afraid of us?" Alma prodded.

"Hell no," he replied with some irritation.

In that moment I knew that my purpose in putting Devon in group therapy was validated. The process of multiple transferences was beginning, and Devon was like a recalcitrant child, dealing once again with his hated mother and father attacking him.

I could see tension building in him, the way his blue eyes glared and the muscles in his broad shoulders tightened. It was possible that more tough questions would set off a chain reaction leading to exploding rage. However, acting out toward threatening parental transference figures was part of the process.

I was convinced that his capacity for violence stemmed from repressed anger all through childhood and adolescence for his parents. First the father, for being so domineering and hurting the mother, or what he perceived as violence and pain in sex. Then the mother, for apparently enjoying violence and pain time and time again and being too weak to resist the authoritarian father. Then Andre, the product of the violent heterosexual act and later sibling rivalry. Andre could be dominated and abused until later, when Devon transferred his rage toward others who had to submit and be abused and, I was coming to believe, may have committed murder in ways beyond barbaric.

If this group process worked, it could be the beginning of finding ways to manage Devon's psychopathy. He could vent his rage and related feelings under controlled conditions. Perhaps I could help him find nonviolent ways to express these deeply repressed emotions. By succeeding to teach a killer how to control his rage, I would protect society and serve my patient and profession.

At the time, my theory seemed promising.

"You're a flaming faggot and a disgrace to the rest of us sincerely trying to help ourselves!" Peter bellowed.

"There's nothing wrong with being a homosexual," John said, "and being proud of it."

I gave him an approving smile. It was the first time John had stood up for his own beliefs.

"Hell, it's not that," Peter backed down. "You're a coward," he said to Devon. "We sense you like to play control and power games. A fair fight and you would run for the hills like a bleating sheep."

"He's right," Alma said, and others echoed her.

Devon looked at me again as if expecting me to come to his rescue. I calmly returned his gaze but said nothing. Then his face turned red and his expressive hands became white-knuckled fists. Despite the open windows, the temperature in the room seemed to have risen ten degrees.

Devon jumped up, his body quivering. He grabbed the metal chair and turned to Peter who recoiled, suddenly aware that he had gone too far.

I couldn't allow this to go any further. "Devon," I began sternly, "you have a choice. We stop right here or we try something else." I didn't really want to stop here, so I added, "If you can take it."

He slowly put the chair down but remained standing. He forced a smile. "What do you have in mind, Doc?"

I explained what "psychodrama" was, a technique developed by Moreno in which individual group members assume the roles of various family members of the protagonist and recreate family dynamics on an ad hoc stage.

Devon laughed softly. "Do I need a ticket?"

"No. But you might not like the performance. Well, if so, there's the exit."

He flexed his arms and cracked his knuckles. "I'm not afraid of this flimsy crew."

It was clear to me by this point which group partici-pants should play major parts. Peter was designated to be Devon's father, Alma the mother, and John would substitute for Andre. I assumed the role of director.

We moved to "center stage," the space within the circle of folding chairs. The others stood and surrounded the space, an impromptu Greek chorus. The close air of the room crackled with a mixture of anticipation and fear. The others probably thought I could control this but I didn't know what to expect.

I explained that in this scene family members would be confronting Devon. They would blame him for being a narcissistic and self-centered person who took care only of his own needs and desires, spurning the family welfare. The father would threaten him physically. The mother and brother would cut him off emotionally. Devon was to react and respond the way he felt, verbally. No more picking up chairs. The chorus would articulate what they believed was not being expressed by family members.

For a while the scene went well. The dialogue, inevitably, was stilted as the "actors" tried to imagine themselves in the roles of people they had never met, and Devon, still angry, challenged them for being unloving and weak.

Then I felt the action sinking. It really wasn't exciting enough to engage the interest of someone as clever and demanding as Devon for any significant length of time. Once he glanced at me as if to say, *This is the best you can do?* Emotion drained from his voice and face as the droning psychodrama continued. Even the chorus sounded like they were improvising insights just to keep the play going.

Suddenly, Peter, perhaps wanting to spice things up or genuinely feeling his role, grabbed the front of Devon's navy blue crew neck sweater and dragged him down, pinning him on the floor and shouting into his face.

Alma and John joined in, holding down Devon's arms and legs. Members of the chorus stepped closer, thinking about adding to the writhing pile, but I motioned them back.

A strange and frightening thing happened. At first Devon was struggling, his face crimson, arms and legs thrashing. Then he stopped moving. The redness seeped out of his face. His blue eyes took on a glittering, hard look. Slowly he took a deep breath.

Gradually he got loose of his captors. The others were still trying to hold him down but their efforts were futile. They staggered back as Devon got to his feet, the force of his strength so powerful and intimidating that they were unable to resist. They stumbled backward and stared with genuine fear as, like shaking off flakes of snow, Devon tossed their hands away from him.

"Now it's my turn," Devon said, his voice surprisingly soft, almost sensuous.

He gazed at Peter, then at Alma. They backed away, thoroughly scared. A member of the chorus cried, "John, watch out, he's after blood!" That word triggered an instant reaction. Devon quickly shifted and went after John, who had stood his ground, throwing him to the floor.

The others looked to me. Time to end this, their expressions said.

"Oh my God," one woman whispered.

I didn't know if I could. Something extremely powerful had been unleashed, beyond anything I had expected.

Devon was on top of John who, slender and small, was totally overpowered. I had to stop them. Just as I put my hand out to exert some control, Devon shouted, "Give me a bottle! I'm going to fucking kill this little bastard!"

Then, realizing a room full of people were witnessing the event, Devon's own control mechanism took over.

He helped John up, even brushing off the back of his clothes. Then Devon grinned at the others. "Relax," he said, "I ain't so tough. Cagney, *Public Enemy*, 1931. Hell of a performance. This one was too."

Then he sat down, crossing his legs. None of us were ready for anything more. The group session ended.

Devon backed to the door, staring at me. I couldn't read the look. Then he offered a quick salute, turned and left.

Chapter 19

The Suspect

After office hours ended at six the next day, I was about to step out into the street to hail a cab on my way to meet Rachel for dinner, when a figure approached. I started, immediately thinking it was Devon. Then I realized it was a woman, Callahan. Her green eyes gazed up at me and red hair cascaded across her shoulders.

"Sorry if I startled you, Dr. Obler," she said, her voice more gentle than I remembered. "I have to talk to you."

"I know. I've gotten your messages."

"So why didn't you return them?" She smiled, squeezing freckles together. "That's okay. But I *really* have to talk to you."

"How about tomorrow?"

"Now."

The gentleness was gone. If she was just being pushy, I would have stalled her, but there was something else in her voice, and in her eyes. Anxiousness, maybe. No, more than that.

"I'd like to invite you to dinner." She leaned her head back. "I'm off-duty. This is an unofficial visit."

"I'm flattered, Detective Callahan. But I'm on my way to meet someone."

"A quick drink, then." Her green eyes narrowed, and the look on her face was intense. "I'm buying."

"Ten minutes."

"Let's do it."

On the corner of my block was a tavern that offered simple dishes and tall drinks, catering to a lunch and late night crowd. At this time of day it was nearly empty. Even though we were only having cocktails, the hostess seated us at a small wooden table next to a long window.

We took off our coats and draped them over the backs of our chairs. Callahan was wearing a dark blue dress that stopped above her knees, dark stockings, and black high heels. I doubted this outfit was standard issue in the department.

She smiled as she sat down, but I was nervous knowing that Rachel would be waiting.

"Thank you," she said. "Though, I have to say, in my business, I'm not used to having a request ignored."

"Was your call a request?" I smiled.

"They," she stressed the word, "were. And we might find this meeting mutually beneficial."

Callahan signaled the waitress and ordered a white wine. I did too. This was certainly not the stereotypical Bronx-Irish, beer-drinking cop. Maybe she was different when socializing. There were no rings on her slim fingers, but there was a perfect coat of red nail polish.

"I am sorry for not returning your calls," I said. Then, mentally crossing my fingers, I added, "I realized that I had overstepped by using a connection to get information from you. I didn't want to intrude again on your time."

"I wasn't very gracious, but I wouldn't call your visit an intrusion." Her green eyes gazed steadily at me. "And I realized there was probably more we should have discussed."

"Such as?"

Our drinks arrived. Callahan waited until the waitress walked away. She held her glass in her left hand and sipped from it with her pinkie extended. Her eyes held mine over the rim of the glass. If I were a more gullible guy I'd think she was flirting. But I remembered that she was a homicide detective. And that Rachel was waiting.

"Dr. Obler, since this is not an official get-together, but simply an after hours drink, nothing we say is on the record." She twirled the stem of the glass between her hands. "Okay?"

"Official or not, I'll try to be as honest as I can."

"Why do I get the impression you just left a door open?"

"Because you're a smart, experienced police detective, and you're able to combine your expertise with intuition."

"I wasn't asking for flattery."

"You asked for honesty. I just offered it."

"Your professional opinion, Dr. Obler?"

"I'm a smart, experienced psychologist. One of my skills is to objectively, and as accurately as possible, evaluate someone's personality and to try to go under the surface."

"Almost makes me feel naked."

Callahan continued to gaze at me. I felt uncomfortable. Imagining her naked was an attractive prospect, but I suspected that she was playing a role she wasn't too comfortable with either. Probably worked, though, with others. She had the tools.

"I have five more minutes, Detective."

She nodded, acknowledging that we were back to square one. "How hypothetical was the scenario you presented to me that day in my office?"

"There were some elements of truth."

"Can you give me a percentage?"

"No."

"Because you don't know yourself, or you don't want to?"

"I'd rather not answer that question either. But let me ask you one: what's happened to the Soda Pop Slasher? He's not in the news."

Callahan glanced around the tavern. There was loud talking and laughing at the bar, but only two other tables were occupied, both across the room.

"He's still out there. He may have killed again and we just haven't discovered the body, or bodies, yet. It wouldn't fit the typical serial killer pattern to hold off for such a long period." She lowered her voice further. "Unless something happened."

"Like what?"

"I was hoping that you could help me out with that."

I lifted my glass and sipped. My hand was steady. I'd figured out what was going on. Callahan was anxious because the Slasher case was open and nothing was happening. Even no more murders wasn't good news because each one heightened the odds that solid evidence could be found. She'd probably been trying to shake the tree. My turn now. I sympathized. This case had gone beyond protecting society. She was a cop who needed to nail the right suspect.

"I'm sorry. I can't."

"Because you don't want to, or. . . ."

"Because, Detective Callahan, I adhere to the code of ethics in my profession, which includes confidentiality and the mental health of my patients."

"Even the one who is a serial killer?"

Her eyes glared at me. I'd left myself open for that one. Experience and intuition: she knew. I kept my glass on the table. Anything more I said or implied would make things worse.

"I really have to go."

Her voice held a steel edge. "I will subpoena your records, Dr. Obler."

"You can try."

"I have connections too. Maybe to a judge who will sign a subpoena and maybe, if the judge is in a good mood, a search warrant."

She slid her glass aside and leaned forward. "We even might be able to persuade the judge that the need to catch a killer before he strikes again outweighs your precious ethics. We can show the judge photographs of what the Slasher has done, and will do, to another innocent person. Maybe next time it will be an old lady or man . . . or a child."

"That wouldn't fit his pattern."

"The original pattern has already changed. You know that. Can you say for sure what the Slasher will do next?"

The psychodrama episode of a few days before

remained fresh in my mind. I'd been able to exert enough
control over Devon to stop him from going further in his
attack on John, but how could I know what would happen
other times, other places?

So with complete honesty, I replied, "No."

Callahan sat back and folded her arms. Frigid air suddenly seeped through the window. I wondered where it had
come from. "But rather than go that route, I'd like to think an
ethical person who cares about human beings in this city will
cooperate in our efforts to catch a killer."

"We're in two different professions with two different
sets of priorities." I grabbed my coat. "I respect you,
Detective Callahan. You have an important job and do it
well, one I admit I couldn't do. I sincerely hope that the
Slasher is stopped before he murders again. But thinking I'm
going to hand the Slasher to you is wasting your time." I
tossed a ten-dollar bill on the table. "My treat, since this was
unofficial." I stood up.

"Let me ask you one more thing." Her voice and eyes
had softened.

"Yes?"

"Do you believe me when I say that the Soda Pop
Slasher is still out there?"

I phrased my words carefully. "I believe you think
that, yes."

"Then you might be interested to know that we've
made an arrest in the case."

Shocked, I sat back down. "When?"

"Early this morning. There's been no statement yet.
You're the first outside of Homicide to know. And, of course,
Legal Aid."

Her eyes searched my face. I wanted another sip of wine but didn't trust either hand, both of which were trembling. I kept them in the pockets of my coat.

"Who is it?"

"A man named Sven Jorgansen. In his late thirties."

If she was waiting to see relief or guilt on my face, she didn't get it. I didn't know how I felt.

"Only known address is Tompkins Square Park," Callahan continued. "Been homeless for years, when he hasn't been behind bars. Long arrest record: assaults, sex crimes, harassment. Uniforms got him during an assault on a teenage girl in an alleyway around two o'clock this morning. Trying to rape the kid. He had a box cutter."

"What makes you think he's the Slasher?"

"He confessed. Said he did 'em all. Very graphic descriptions. And he has no alibis." Callahan finished her wine. "I can tell you, there's joy throughout the police and political levels, all the way to City Hall. Big press conference scheduled for noon tomorrow."

I slumped back in my chair for a moment, then I stood up. "I have to congratulate you and the Department. The gold of your badge will shine even brighter now."

She glanced down, then remembered that she wasn't wearing a badge. Then she gazed straight ahead. "Dr. Obler, he's not the Soda Pop Slasher."

I buttoned my coat. "What makes you think so?"

"Because he's a wetbrain derelict who would confess to murdering the President of the United States if asked, and if that's what we wanted him to say." Her emerald eyes rose to meet mine. "The real Slasher is still out there, Obler. I want him." She added softly, "I need help. And I don't have much time."

I realized how difficult this was for her—to ask for help from a man she didn't like, a man who she felt was harboring a serial killer. At that moment, I didn't like myself very much either. The blood of an innocent man could be on my hands. Inside my coat pockets my hands clenched into fists.

"You say you have enough juice to get patient records subpoenaed and a therapist's office searched. Do you have enough to get a press conference postponed?"

"Maybe. If I had something solid to offer." She looked up at me, her head tilted. "What do *you* have to offer?"

I hesitated, then all of the reasons I had refused to divulge information before flashed through my mind. I shook my head. "Nothing. Good luck, Detective."

As I walked away, Callahan called out to me, loud enough that even the folks at the bar looked over. "A man's in jail who didn't do these murders, Obler! I know it—and so do you!"

I kept walking. "Obler, how can you live with yourself?" she called.

Sometimes, it wasn't easy.

Chapter 20

More Games

The police press conference on the Soda Pop Slasher had been a smash. I'd watched highlights of it on the television news, and newspaper headlines had screamed that the Soda Pop Slasher had been nabbed—red-handed, so to speak. Sven Jorgansen had looked confused, lost, and very guilty. He also, I realized with a start, resembled Devon. He had smiled once into the flashbulbs and strobe lights of cameras, a wide grin of momentary pleasure and even pride. It was apparent to me that some part of his disoriented mind was enjoying the most attention he'd ever been given in his sorry, sordid life.

"I apologize for what I've done," he muttered once, microphones practically pressed into his mouth, surrounded by the smiling upper brass of the New York City Police Department (excluding, I noticed, Callahan). "I didn't mean to hurt nobody. Stuff happens, you know?"

Two days later there had been a group therapy session in which Devon participated. Well, not participated exactly.

He showed up, for which I was relieved considering what had happened the previous time. However, he spent the session as he had the earlier ones, with a bemused expression, volunteering nothing, avoiding questions. Except for a few mild suggestions that he join in, the other group members had left him alone. The psychodrama was still clear in their minds, and with Devon they now walked on eggshells.

He lingered after the session for a minute, as if waiting in case I wanted to talk to him. I had the impression that he missed our one-on-one encounters; some of the thrill of therapy was gone. He could play power games with the group, but these games were not of the same caliber as those he had played while gaining a big advantage over me. I couldn't look at him, my own thoughts and feelings in turmoil, and out of the corner of my eye, as I spoke to John, I saw Devon shrug and leave.

The surprising mild spell continued through early March. Though still chilly at night, during the day the temperatures exceeded sixty degrees. The sun glowed a deepening amber, except for a few times when the sky was overcast.

People talked about the "greenhouse effect." Some joked about the melting of the polar ice caps and how waterfront apartments would be on the thirtieth floor of buildings. A few spoke eagerly of the heads of sprouting crocuses about ready to bloom.

My thoughts turned to Rachel. Living together had been working out well. Rachel and I were drawing closer together, a very special intimacy. We both suspected that we would get married, but neither of us was quite ready to articulate that eventuality yet. We spent all of our free time together, and believed it wasn't because of the specter of Devon—but due to our deepening bond. Nevertheless, we were cautious about where we went and when.

The only downside: in my small apartment it had become difficult to get a few minutes alone to think. One evening at twilight, I took advantage of the weather and decided to go upstairs to the roof to gaze at the pink and orange sky. I left a note for Rachel, who wasn't home from work yet.

The building had only eight floors, so there wasn't a panoramic view, but I was surrounded by city streets slowly filling with lights. Not to feel frozen by the winter wind was a welcome change. I'd brought an old blanket and spread it across the tarred and graveled roof, then sat cross-legged. My muscles would probably rebel in a while. I hadn't kept up with playing hoops and I felt like I'd lost any semblance of an athlete's muscle tone.

One of the things I needed to consider was what to do about Mark and Salena. Only when by myself had I seen them lately, taking them for hamburgers and to parks and bookstores on weekends. I'd made excuses not to have them stay with me for weekends.

I loved being with them. They were wonderful children; maybe that was a little bit thanks to me, but most of the credit went to Stella, a fine mother. Whatever our conflicts, and any lingering unhappy feelings she had toward me, they never intruded on the children's life. Except, of course, that their parents lived apart.

Now I lived with Rachel. Mark and Salena hadn't met her yet, and procrastinating wasn't smart. I certainly would have advised a patient to act differently. The spring vacation from school was approaching. I knew Stella would agree if I asked that the children spend it with me. She might even enjoy the break. But, I told myself, the apartment had gotten even smaller with Rachel there. Damn, I thought, knowing that was only a small part of the reason.

As I shifted position, I peered over the ledge of the roof and saw that there were thousands more lights glittering throughout Greenwich Village. Interspersed, though, were gaps of darkness, consisting of alleyways and shut-up buildings. Those small black realms made me think of Devon again. Was he indeed living up to the agreement? Would he indefinitely, or was he just biding his time, using the protection of my adherence to confidentiality to develop a different modus operandi that would make him, if he was the Soda Pop Slasher, even harder to catch?

Maybe, I thought, I should switch Devon out of group therapy because. . . . The metal door to the roof opened, casting a shaft of dim yellow light. Rachel stepped out, looked around, and spotted me.

She held two plates and a bottle. Handing me a plate, she said, "I stopped off, got a pizza, and a ninety-three Merlot."

"Is that supposed to be very good?"

"Beats me. Hoped you would think so." She sat beside me. "You haven't been in the mood to eat, drink and be merry, but I thought I'd try it anyway."

"You're terrific." I kissed her. Wine was fragrant on her lips. "I'm sorry for being so moody lately."

"Is it Devon?"

"Yes. No. I mean, not altogether."

I shared my thoughts about Mark and Salena. "I'll go

visit my parents in Pennsylvania for that week," Rachel said.

I resisted, shaking my head. "The situation has to be faced. But I'm grateful for the option in case I chicken out."

After we spent a couple of minutes eating, passing the wine back and forth and gazing at the sky—which was now a hazy dark gray with a half dozen stars punctuating the darkness—I changed my position again, bones cracking in a disconcerting, out of condition way.

"And it is Devon," I began.

"And?"

"I'm not sure he's sticking to our agreement."

"But, Marty, no one else has been murdered."

"As far as we know."

"You think he's still doing it?"

A stiff breeze jarred us, a reminder that spring hadn't yet come. "Actually, I really don't think so. I think Devon feels a strange sense of honor about living up to his end of the bargain if I live up to mine."

"Well, at least he feels something."

It was as if the breeze contained light along with air. "What did you say?"

"If you're correct, it indicates that deep down he has some feelings, and maybe honor is just one of them."

"Or, he's fascinated by making himself feel this way, and he'll carry it out as long as he wants or has to. Like an actor staying in character," I mused.

"Either way, it's working."

I nodded, feeling more reassured. "Perhaps I can work with it," I said.

Rachel took a drink from the bottle and passed it over. "What are you getting at?"

"What's been on my mind most is should I keep confidentiality now that another man has been arrested. That's what has changed, Rachel. There's a variable none of us counted on, certainly not when the deal was struck. Do I keep standing between Devon and the police and allow an innocent man to rot in prison or, the way things are now, possibly face execution?"

"Marty, this guy is far from innocent."

"Oh, I know. Without question he should be in jail, or at least get the help he needs to reduce his danger to others. But he's not the Soda Pop Slasher."

"You're sure of that?" she asked.

"I'm not sure, but the odds favor Devon."

"Why?"

"He's not smart or crafty enough. I'm sure, and Callahan is too."

"Maybe you two should get together and be the Nick and Nora Charles of the nineties."

I glanced at her. Rachel grinned. I had told her everything about the detective, including how attractive she was.

"I have always been a sucker for red hair."

"I can grow and color mine. Buy a badge too."

"You're perfect." I kissed her lightly. "But if Devon *does* have positive feelings, or as part of playing power games is willing to go far enough to pretend he has feelings, there's a chance."

"For what?"

I had to think about this more, so I just said, "The arrest of this Jorgansen guy might be the best thing that's happened."

"The best thing that's happened tonight hasn't happened yet," she said gently.

"Then I better not have any more wine." I took her hand and pressed my lips to it.

We sat silently, gazing at the darkening sky, delighted with every star that emerged from the haze.

The next afternoon at three, Devon arrived at my office a bit out of breath but as punctual as before. It was a dark gray business suit day. He looked very handsome and imposing. I could imagine his effect on a jury.

I had called him that morning at the law firm and suggested a private session. He accepted quickly. Now he was perched in the chair, his breathing slower, looking at me with those hypnotic blue eyes.

That morning's newspaper was on my desk. I pretended to idly leaf through it. "How's it going in the legal world?" I asked casually.

"Terrific. One of the partners has made me his assistant. Fat raise too. Man, the lives these guys lead. The billing. The intriguing cases. The. . . ."

"Power," I finished.

"Yes, that too." He shifted in the chair and smoothed the legs of his pants. "We could have discussed this over the phone."

"I'll reimburse you for the cab fare."

"You're getting cute on me, Obler."

"What's my name?"

He lowered his head. "Dr. Obler."

"Better. Now, Devon, do you read the papers every day?"

"I thought I told you. I can't be bothered with all that

stuff. Well, maybe once in a while."

I kept my eyes on the newspaper. "Yesterday they announced the alleged," purposefully I strung out the word, "arrest of the Soda Pop Slasher. The defendant's attorney says he's going to plead insanity."

"Poor Sven. They should call him the Kindergarten Killer to conform with his sixty IQ."

Okay, he had been following the chain of events. "The police don't really think he did it."

"You must be reading the paper upside down." Devon grimaced. "The heat seems pretty excited over this one."

"All right, but there are a few of them who don't buy it," I said, though as far as I knew there was only one smart, persistent detective. "What do you think about Jorgansen's arrest?"

"Gets me off the hook, doesn't it?" He leaned back and grinned. "Thank Zeus I never admitted anything to you, especially after all the preposterous pressure you put on me. Tell me, would you have turned me in?"

I met his eyes. "No."

"See, I knew you were a stand-up guy, a true pro. Though I have to admit you upset me. Even lost a few winks of sleep over it. But I don't hold grudges. You've done wonders with me. There should be an Academy Award for shrinks. We can move on, and be pals." He saw the look in my eyes. "Well, patient and therapist again. Let's jettison those fag fools and repressed pussies in the group."

I returned to looking at the newspaper. "You said, 'Poor Sven.' Do you really have any sympathy for him?"

"Sure. His life is worth shit now. He'll be convicted, or plead guilty like he should, and spend the rest of his worthless years being gang fucked if he's not fried. And I bet at no time along the way will poor Sven have any understanding of what happened to him."

"You've summed it up pretty accurately."

Devon's chest swelled. He was on a roll. "Of course. When I'm sitting at that asshole partner's desk, I'll. . . ."

I broke in. "He's not the Soda Pop Slasher."

"What?"

I locked eyes with him and asked softly, "Is he?"

"I'm not a prosecutor yet." He clasped his hands nervously. "You're sounding like one again."

"This man is going to have an existence of endless misery."

"Come on, his life sucked anyway. And he wanted to fuck and hurt kids. Not that I blame him for that."

"But it's *his* life."

"Yeah, and *his* problem. He got caught. Tough shit."

I closed the newspaper. A box on the cover reported that the Knicks had traded for a backup guard. I used that. "Devon, I think there should be a trade."

"Of what?"

"You for Sven. I believe he's not the Soda Pop Slasher. You are. But he'll pay for another's crimes."

Devon shrugged. "Not my problem, Doc."

"Think about it. He is a poor man. He has nothing. No power, no money, nothing. Maybe like you felt when you were a child. Somebody might have helped you. No one did. You had to make it on your own, with your strength and intelligence. Sven doesn't have those qualities. He's like a child who desperately needs help. Your help."

"Ah, he's no kid."

Something told me I was reaching him. This was a direction I had never taken with Devon in therapy. However, the game, and the rules, had changed.

"He still is, in a lot of ways," I continued. "An innocent kid who did do some bad things, but he's in way over his head. I'm sure he's in a lot of pain now. And it's going to get worse. Don't you feel that?"

"No."

Almost whispering, I repeated, "Don't you feel that?"

His eyes darted around the room, focusing for a few seconds on the swinging pendulum, then on the window dotted with condensation, then on his own expressive hands, clasped and trembling, and finally on me.

"Yes."

"He has no one, Devon. He's all alone."

"Yes."

"You've said you never felt guilt, or remorse. I don't believe that. You're an intelligent, intuitive young man, you know what deep pain is like. The pain that empties your soul, that burns your brain, that makes you think no one cares or feels anything about *you*. My God, I couldn't live like that."

Now his whole body shuddered. "It's . . . hard."

"And you shouldn't live like that." I kept my voice soft and low, and my hands pressed against the desk. "Unburden yourself. Tell me. Be honest with me. I will do everything I can for you if you go to the police. Save that poor, desolate man who is without hope. You know what it's like to be without hope, don't you?"

He wouldn't look at me. "It's very, very hard," he said, his voice quaking.

"So let's be completely honest with each other." I felt like I was only inches away. "You killed those young men and women, didn't you? I can understand why. You couldn't help yourself. The pain inflicted on you wasn't fair. I can help you. I will help you. If you can't help yourself, let me."

"I can't help myself."

I met his blue eyes, which were shining brightly—and this should have tipped me off. "Of course not. But I can."

"Oh, Doc, I wish you would!" he cried, suddenly on the verge of laughter.

I felt everything draining out of me. "What do you mean?"

"I mean it's really, *really* hard!" He was close to giggling. "Whoa, I can't help myself. Mr. Cardou here is ready to blow his stack!"

Then I knew what he was talking about. And that I'd been led down another false path, right into one more power play. "Devon, you're not listening."

"Ooh, I listened. This was better than a peep show. You should charge for this." He bent over, laughing. His face was red and his eyes wet when he straightened up. "Actually, you do. It was worth every penny. May I suggest for next week we try a group grope? I'll pay double."

Frustrated and careless, I said, "Maybe you'd rather have a bottle."

He stood up and leaned over the desk, giving me the unblinking stare. "You're getting cute on me again, Obler. And you were trying to break our bargain, weren't you?"

Pressed back against the chair, I replied, "Devon, I had to try. . . ."

"Yeah, sure you did. And it didn't work. Feel something? A little. I do. Contempt."

I felt his spit hit my face like a corrosive substance.

"You've got to do better, Obler. Much better. I played my game. So I feinted and now I'm going to the hoop. Win any way you can, right?" He raised a fist. "Score!"

"Devon, winning won't help you."

He backed away, laughing. "Hey, it won't hurt either. In fact, it feels pretty fucking good." He gave me a conspirator's look. "Now I have to deal with what you did to me here. Hope I don't hurt anybody."

"We have an agreement."

He stopped laughing, and his lips curled. "You tried to break it. I have to see if I have it in me to forgive you."

"You sick bastard!" I shouted, leaping up and confronting him at the door. "What will it take for you to stop?"

For a few moments our faces were inches away. I looked deep into those eyes and could sense, just for an instant, the enormous reservoir of pain and violence inside. I had to get away from it. I took a couple of steps back. He tugged at his suit jacket, smoothing it, and carefully straightened the knot of his gray tie.

"I don't think I can be stopped," he said calmly.

He opened the door and stepped out. "But I'll throw you a bone, Marty, a reward for effort."

Just before Devon closed the door he said, "I do believe if anybody can do it, baby, it's you."

Chapter 21

Stalked

Stella was almost hysterical on the phone. "Someone," she choked out, "approached the kids. I think it's him."

She didn't have to explain whom she meant. We both knew—the Soda Pop Slasher.

"Where are they?"

"Right here, thank God."

"Are they all right?"

"Just scared. They need you, Martin."

"I'll be right over. I'm leaving now."

Pinning a note on my office door, I dove down the stairs two at a time and ran the blocks to Stella's apartment and pounded on the door, hardly able to catch my breath. Stella, red-eyed, let me in. Mark and Salena sat huddled together on the couch.

"Hey guys," I said and motioned I wanted to sit down between them. I plopped on the couch putting one arm around each. "Everything okay?"

They nodded solemnly.

"Can you tell me what happened?"

"We really don't know what happened," Mark said.

I looked over at Stella perplexed.

"Marty, they're scared out of their wits!" Stella exclaimed. "I'm surprised they can speak at all. And you want them to relive the incident?"

"I'm not sure that it was an 'incident.'" I turned back to the children. Salena shifted uncomfortably and looked past me; I suspected she wished she hadn't had to call me. I said to Mark, "One more time, kiddo?"

He scratched the tip of his nose and then the top of his head. "Well, we were just standing around outside, right by the front door, watching the snow," he said, pleased to be designated as the spokesman. "We wanted to see if there was going to be enough by morning to make a snowman."

Stella broke in. "I called to them to come in when it started to get dark."

"Stella, please." I wanted to add that she shouldn't have let them be out by themselves, but that wouldn't have helped. Though some of the tension had abated because the Soda Pop Slasher had been discovered, the neighborhood was still clutchy. And, of course, with a pang of guilt, I had to admit that their father wasn't around. "Go on."

"So Salena wanted to walk down the street to the shop where Cory's mom works and she started walking. I ran to catch up with her to stop her but she ran on."

"Did not," Salena muttered.

"Did too. Anyway." Mark sat up straight and folded his arms, waiting, and glad to have gotten in the last word. "So I caught up to her just as she was about to turn the corner, and a tall man stood there, and he said, 'Hi, kids.'"

"What else did he say?"

"He said, 'You're Dr. Obler's kids, right? Tell him I said hello.' Then he patted me on the head and patted Salena's arm. Then he walked away. We ran back and came up here to tell Mom."

"Did he say his name?"

"Nope."

"What did he look like?"

Mark shrugged. "He was big. It was getting dark." Mark glanced at his mother. "I mean, he had on a jacket with the hood up, and green sunglasses. They looked like the kind pilots wear. I was still trying to figure out what he said when he turned away."

"It's him," Stella said.

"Who, Mommy?" Salena asked, rescued temporarily from the descent into boredom.

Stella gave me an angry glance. "If it's not, it could be someone your father knows . . . professionally."

"Hey, who wants to watch television?" I asked, diverting the kids' attention.

I switched on the set, and the children were immediately involved in what looked like a juvenile detective series but was an episode of "Carmen Sandiego." I motioned Stella aside.

"Really, if they are scared at all, you're making it worse," I told her. "And let's not fight. That would be more upsetting than a man greeting them on the street."

She took a deep breath and let it out. "You're right, Marty. And it was stupid of me to leave them outside." She smiled. "I do tend to overreact sometimes."

"Because you're a great mother, and this

neighborhood *has* had its troubles." I started to put my coat back on. "Call the police if that will reassure you. But I think that might upset the children more."

"You don't think it was anything, this man?"

I shrugged, biting my tongue. Then I said, "Probably not. But I would just . . . I mean, it's up to you."

"I know. I'll be more careful. Stay for dinner?"

"I really have to finish up at the office."

This time Stella shrugged, and it was a familiar gesture from the many times in the past I had made work a higher priority.

I kissed Mark and Salena goodbye—they allowed for the momentary distraction. Then they returned their attention to the tube and I left. Once outside, I walked up to the corner, looking around carefully. There were hundreds of footprints in the inch or so of snow. No evidence here, certainly nothing that indicated Devon.

Nevertheless, what I couldn't say to Stella was that I too believed it had been him. I trudged toward my apartment instead of the office, my head bent against the rain-bearing wind. Why had he confronted my children? Would he really have hurt them, or what had his "hello" meant?

I trudged back to my apartment. I was about to walk up the steps to my building when someone fell on me: Rachel. She was crying in long huffing sobs.

"Marty! It was him!" she cried. She wrapped her arms around me. "Let's go in. Hurry!"

Glancing behind, I half-carried her into the building. There was a small lobby with a cushioned bench against the front window across from the elevator. Rachel pulled me down onto it with her. Her face, twisted with fear, was red and wet. Tears brimmed over her large brown eyes.

"Rachel, what is it? Who?"

"That guy . . . in my apartment. Devon. He came after me." She took a deep breath, trying to steady her voice. "He *stalked* me."

I suddenly felt more in turmoil than the wind outside, which was making the window vibrate. "Tell me."

She did. Rachel had left work over an hour before and gotten on the subway. Just before the doors closed, another person squeezed into the crowded car. At first, she hadn't noticed him, just felt a body pressed up against her at rush hour on a subway train. She wasn't surprised. On the trains just before and after the business day there is an almost accepted intimacy of bodies all hurtling through the dark to different destinations and lives.

But then—call it instinct or some kind of subliminal signal he was sending—Rachel turned around. She saw part of his profile under his hood and recognized him. "It was Devon."

"I tried to move away, but there was no room. I scanned the people nearby, wondering if he tried to do anything who would help me. All the surrounding faces wore the same expressions: bored, hot, waiting, don't bother me. I felt completely vulnerable."

I nodded understandingly. "Go on."

"When the train stopped at Times Square, the doors opened on the other side and I joined the flow of people pouring onto the platform. As soon as there was some space I walked fast, almost skipping, and jumped onto an escalator. I was afraid to glance behind but I had to, once. Devon was just stepping onto the escalator. His hands looked so large gripping the moving banisters."

She stopped for a moment to catch her breath, then went on. "Stepping off the escalator, I glanced back once more. Devon raised his head and, with one eyebrow raised, grinned at me."

"What did you do next?"

"I ran to the platform for the #7 train, then to another set of stairs and down again. Without looking back this time, I kept running. Then I went down more stairs to the shuttle."

This was, she realized too late, a mistake. The shuttle to Grand Central Station waits until capacity is reached before setting off. "I found a seat and hunched down between two people, an attractively dressed black woman and a large disheveled older white man. I kept my head down, knees squeezed together, arms clutching my elbows, sneaking glances at the open door, asking myself won't this goddamn train ever move?

"Finally, the doors closed. I looked the length of the car. No Devon. The train shuddered out of the station. Then I saw him. He was standing with his back against the window of the next car and then Devon turned around. His blue eyes gazed steadily at me."

The shuttle stopped at Fifth Avenue. "I stood up but couldn't get out; the rush of people pressing in was over-whelming. I pushed my way toward the other compartment. People cursed at me as in my hurry to get away I stepped on their feet and elbowed them in the ribs. I kept apologizing but I was crying.

"At Grand Central I leapt out and began running again. This time I took the stairs. Looking back from the top, I saw Devon pushing people aside as he tried to keep up. I ran to another subway line. At the stairs to the N and R trains was a uniformed policeman. He looked younger than me. He barely shaved.

"'There's a man following me,' I told him. But all he said was 'Oh?' He gave me a disinterested, tell-me-another-one look and said, 'Where?'"

Rachel turned around and pointed. There was no sign of Devon. She described him anyway. "He's been after me, one train then another," she said, almost pleading for the policeman's attention as his eyes skipped across people going down the stairs. "Can you come with me? Look for him?

"And he says, 'Sorry, lady. I'm stationed here. Why don't you go ahead and I'll wait for him here.' As if I were a dummy, Marty."

Seeing that was all she was going to get from him, Rachel thanked him anyway and ran down the stairs. "By now I was sweating, my clothing was all twisted, my shoes were falling off, my stomach was lurching, and I was starting to feel lightheaded. I worried I might faint on the platform. Fortunately, there was a train waiting and just as I pulled myself aboard the doors closed."

"Rachel, what can I say?"

She nodded but rushed on. "It moved out of the station. Just before it left, picking up speed, the flashing lights pinpointed Devon. He stood at the end of the platform and, when he spotted me, he grinned again and twirled his fingers at me."

Because a large crowd got off at 14th Street Rachel did too: she felt some safety in numbers. As she took the stairs up two at a time, she noticed another train entering the station. She was suddenly afraid that he would follow her back to my apartment so, on the street, the wind blowing rain drops into her eyes, she ran down one street then another, not caring about direction, just hoping she could make Devon more confused than she was.

"And when I arrived at our building I waited a few yards away, pressed against the metal grille of the closed stationery store, watching and waiting, not sure who would show up first. Luckily, you did."

"Let's go upstairs," I suggested.

Her eyes roamed wildly. "He could be out there, Marty. He'll see where we live."

Now was not the time to remind her that if he wanted to Devon could find out easily enough anyway, or he already had. "It's okay. You need a hot shower and a cold drink."

As I led her to the elevator Rachel sighed, "He wants us, Marty. He's coming after us."

Again I didn't want to tell her, and it was hard enough to face it that having just seen my children, "us" had taken on a bigger meaning.

The elevator doors opened. We stepped in. During the few seconds before the doors closed, I stared out, half expecting to see a large hooded figure standing in the falling rain, grinning at us.

Chapter 22

Another Long Night

I put Rachel to bed almost the same way that I had
Mark or Salena when they were sick, with warm milk, comforting words, reassurance that all would be better in the
morning, blanket tucked under her chin, and a light left on.

I wished I had a magic wand to make Rachel and the
children's fears go away, but the strongest feeling I had was
guilt. I had tried to do my best and live up to a code of conduct I believed in, but in doing so I had put people I loved in
jeopardy. And, certainly in Rachel's case, but probably in
Mark and Salena's also, put terror in their hearts.

That had to change. I was throwing down the gauntlet.

Flicking the television on, I made a cup of coffee and
sat in a chair by the window. Fierce raindrops were crashing
against the pane, dashing into the wall and hardier ones
bouncing off to fall to the dark street below. I didn't watch
the television, but it felt like there was another presence in
the room. This wasn't a good night to be alone.

My mind's eye skirted about sorting out the chain of

events. Devon had stalked Rachel, but she had managed to get away or he had been content to let her go, knowing that his message, whatever it was, would be delivered. Then, by design or sudden inspiration, he had headed down to my children's neighborhood, familiar hunting grounds, and presented himself to Mark and Salena. Special delivery, Dr. Obler. I twisted in the chair, racked by a combination of fear and relief. There was no telling what his intentions were for Rachel. However, there was no doubt that on that dark evening, he could have done something to my children. My God, how close they had come. What would happen next time?

That was the key—had Devon planned to harm anyone close to me, or was sending a message sufficient? If I didn't grasp its meaning, would there be a next time? Probably. Then, how far would he go?

After our last session it was clear to me I might very well throw ethics and other considerations aside and offer him up to the police, breaking our devil's bargain. It made sense then that the message he was sending now was, keep the agreement or you will lose more than your life—meaning my children and Rachel.

He was telling me to repair things between us, to live up to the agreement. Though it sounded crazy it was, probably, a short-term solution. As I sat sipping coffee and staring out at a kaleidoscope of snow, I knew it, at least, offered some protection.

Then my ears pricked up. The ten o'clock news was on and the anchorman, jittering in his seat and speaking solemnly, was reporting a new murder.

"The body was found this morning in an apartment on University Place," he said. "Police have not released the identity. They say she was a woman in her thirties who apparently was killed during violent sex."

The screen showed a body bag being carried out on a stretcher to a city medical examiner's ambulance. "The victim was stabbed and slashed repeatedly though, police say, a weapon other than a knife was used," the anchorman continued. "Police have asked that anyone with information about the incident, which took place at around 2 A.M., call them," and he gave the phone number.

Yes, there were differences. Maybe more than I knew, yet at the same time there could be similarities I didn't know about. My fear was that it was Devon. And if he was the killer, he was expanding his pattern to older people. No one was safe—including the people I loved.

But the remnant of objective psychologist in me said I had to know more. I went to the phone and punched in some numbers. "I'm here," said a sleepy voice.

"Todd. The new murder. What do you know?"

"More important is the murder they'll be reporting tomorrow for waking me up."

"What are you doing asleep so early?"

"It's, what . . . Max, eighteen-year-old twins, consider the possibilities. And you call."

"You're in bed with eighteen-year-old twins?"

"I wish. Remember Tony Roberts in *Annie Hall*?"

The last thing I needed right now was another movie buff. "Todd, you lazy Brooklyn bastard, there's been another Soda Pop Slasher murder."

After I described what I'd heard on the news, Todd said, "Could also be some asshole who listens to mental fuck-ups all day and can't relax. Anyway, that Slasher stuff is dead news, forgive the pun. We don't care anymore, other fish to fry."

Then his voice cleared, and I pictured him sitting up on the side of the bed. And the way he lowered his voice, he probably wasn't alone. "You really think it's the Slasher?" he whispered. "How do you know?"

"Well, the report had some information that. . . ."

"Marty, how do *you* know?"

God, I wanted to tell someone, to push this weight off my chest. Instead, after a pause, I said, "Todd, all kidding aside, and I'm aware of the business you're in, but can I count on you as a friend?"

"Yes."

"Then don't ask me that."

"Oh, okay." The disappointment was evident. I pictured him struggling, Brooklyn days and male bonding versus the chance at a scoop. Finally, he said, "What do you need?"

"More information. I have to know more. If you don't have the details, where can I get them?"

After a few seconds he said, "The dailies will know before I do. I have a friend."

"Is she there? Put her on."

"Well, not yet, though I'd love to. What you do. . . ." His voice lowered more. "I'll call Bridget Leary. Crime beat, a totally tough fox. I've done her a lot of favors. I want to. . . ."

"Todd, talk to me."

"Sorry. Whatever it is, she'll know. Loves bodies. Alas, not mine. Yet."

"Thanks."

"Well, now that you got me up, which is more than I can say for. . . ."

"Playoff tix for the Knicks. I owe you."

For the next hour I switched stations, my fingers as active with the remote as if I were playing one of Mark's video games. But the reports were all the same. Another random murder. No one was making a connection to the Slasher yet.

But in my churning guts, I knew. We were connected in an uncomfortably perverted way. This was another message. The animal was stepping out of his cage because I hadn't closed the door. I would think about my responsibility to the community later. For now, I had to think about those who meant most to me and of course others who would come into the crosshairs of his apparently uncontrollable rage.

Survival was an animal's top priority. So he would kill those who presented the most danger—me first, or perhaps, knowing his enjoyment of power and pain, my children and Rachel—and then he would be free to kill again, for who knows how long.

I stood up and paced restlessly around the room. Forget coffee. I wanted a drink. More than one. I wanted to hit the street, go to the nearest bar and down enough scotches to produce oblivion. Sure, that's all I had to do to compound my guilt, leave Rachel alone while he was out there.

That was an idea, though. Even in this thunderstorm, which looked like it was a hurricane, Devon might well be prowling or nearby, waiting. A message he hadn't delivered was one directly to me. That was still to come.

I could give him the opportunity. Go downstairs, hit
the street, walk around, didn't matter where. If he wanted
me, I would make it easy for him. And just maybe, as he was
saying a soft hello, or grinning as he silently slipped out of a
doorway, or offering one more taunt with eyebrow raised and
a hand raking through wet blond hair—maybe I could be at
his throat, getting a grip even his strength couldn't break, and
I wouldn't let go until the motherfucker was dead at my feet.

I stopped pacing and pressed my forehead against the
moist glass of the window, almost feeling hundreds of raindrops striking. That's what I wanted, to kill Devon. To stop
him for good before he killed again, especially the people
I loved.

Who would blame me? I would rid the city of its most
violent form of vermin. From what I knew about Callahan,
even if she despised me she would come down on my side.
Self-defense might work. And I'd be out from under. I could
even think of a few patients, and colleagues, who would
have more respect for me because I stopped listening, and
acted. The prospect of squeezing the life out of Devon was
delicious.

But then I felt an overwhelming sense of failure. If I
too was reduced to an animal then I had gone against everything I believed in. There had to be another way. Come on,
Marty, you've got half a brain, use it.

I returned to the chair and flicked the remote again.
Talk shows, syndicated sitcoms, updated weather reports, old
movies, some so obscure maybe even Devon hadn't seen
them. The images began to blur. I fell into a dreamless sleep.

When the phone rang, I thought it was Devon,
another call from another place, begging for my help, then

beginning to laugh.

Opening my eyes I felt disoriented not seeing my ceiling or feeling Rachel next to me. Then I realized I was still in the chair. The clock against the wall read a few minutes after eight. My arm ached as I reached for the phone.

"Dr. Obler?" A female voice, both scratchy and sultry. "Bridget Leary."

"Who?"

"Todd asked me to call you. I'm a crime reporter for one of the city's dailies. Now what do you want to know about yesterday's murder?"

"Did Todd tell you why I wanted to know?"

"No. I'll ask that myself. He just asked me to do a favor for an old friend."

"You're very kind."

"No, I'm not. Now he owes me. I like that. Anyway, I'm not kind. I'm a reporter."

I immediately liked her. And if her voice indicated anything, I could understand Todd's frustration. I tried to be as honest as I could.

"I'm a psychologist, and I have a special interest in the Soda Pop Slasher case."

"Thought that was closed out."

"Maybe it is and I'm wasting my time." I rubbed my eyes, then saw Rachel go into the bathroom. Lowering my voice, I said, "The murder yesterday on University Place. How was the woman killed? What happened?"

"I'd like it if you owed me too."

"How many chits do you want?"

She laughed, a full-throated sound. "Okay, this is for Todd. Victim's name is Charise O'Day, whore extraordinaire.

Sorry, you don't use such terms in your profession. Let's say
very sexually challenged. Should have been an S&M poster
girl. Rather notorious in the Village. Way she got about,
odds were one day, or night, she'd hook up with the
wrong pickup."

"You think it was a pickup?"

"Cops do. A liaison that went loopy big time. Maybe
she didn't do what she was supposed to, or tried to do too
much. The killer paid her back, full price."

"Did you cover the Slasher case?"

"I was part of a team assigned to it. Not that numbers
did us any good. Or the heat." She paused, and I heard a
lighter being flicked. "But you're thinking she's just another
kind of victim. A new one. And you want to know what
did her."

"I do." I waited, then added, "Please, Ms. Leary."

"Jeez, I love when men beg. Even Todd is getting to
me." I heard her exhale a stream of smoke. "You ready?"

"Yes."

"Lips of the vagina were cut off but that wasn't what
killed her. Had a bottle stuffed up her ass, broke up inside
and cut her to ribbons. Charise tried to get away. She was
dead and didn't know it, and the more she moved the more
her insides got sliced to shreds. Ate her up. Blood was like a
new paint job."

"Did you see it?"

There was another exhalation of smoke. "Yes."

"I'm sorry."

"My job. What about yours?"

"What?"

"Mr. Psychologist, what do you have to do with the

Soda Pop Slasher?"

"Was it him?"

"That's four questions we've asked in a row. How about an explanation?"

"That's five. I can keep counting."

Bridget laughed again. "All right. The cops don't want to admit it's the Slasher. One, they've announced they've got him. Two, pattern is different: this is an older woman. Three, their experts say it's a copycat, happens all the time with serial killings, especially after the main guy is caught. It's like a salute, kill a couple more to honor the king. Know him, Doc?"

I wasn't going to answer that one, especially to a good reporter. "The man arrested is a molester," I said.

"Not the same thing and you know it."

"There's a lot more I don't know about this case. That's why I asked for information."

"Sure. Now it's my turn."

"What did you say?"

"I said. . . ."

"The connection—something's wrong." I rubbed my thumb across the off button. "Can't hear you."

"Don't you pull that crap on me."

"What? Call me back."

I hung up. Three seconds later the phone rang. I let it ring. Rachel came out of the bathroom, wrapping my robe around her.

"Was it him?" she asked, brown eyes large that, so soon after waking, should be squinting.

"I called the weather line."

"And you talked to it?" Rachel's sense of humor

couldn't be downed.

Smiling, I started to get up from the chair. "I'll make coffee."

"I'd rather you held me."

"I'd rather that too." I shifted over and she eased down beside me. We held each other and stared out the window. A few raindrops still drifted down, but the sun had emerged between clouds. I hoped that was a good omen.

I refused Callahan's offer of coffee and sat in the chair across from her desk. I'd answered her request Tuesday and met her on the street, where she once again begged for the Slasher's name. Now she'd answered mine and I was at her office. The piles of folders on the desk appeared to be higher than the first time I'd been there. And there were darker circles under her green eyes.

"Well, at least you called ahead," she said. "Why do you want to see me? I thought you'd said it all, which was nothing."

"No." I looked at her steadily. "There's politics in my profession too," I said. "You should have been at the press conference to share credit in solving the Slasher case but you weren't."

"I didn't want to be there. We both know it's not solved."

"That's why I'm here."

"You're too late," she said angrily. Her face was flushed, making the freckles more prominent. "Where were you when Jorgansen was being put through the ringer?"

"He's a goddamn pervert too, deserves to be looking at bars. Every month he's in, some child is safe. I can live with that. But you can't sleep because the Soda Pop Slasher is still out there. And you'll get the call next time he strikes."

"Yes," she said softly.

"Like yesterday."

She turned away and gazed out the small window behind her chair. The sky had cleared and afternoon sunlight streamed in, more intense because of the reflection off the glistening streets. I listened to keyboards clicking and phones ringing along the corridor. The heat was set too high in the building; maybe that's why her face stayed red. But I knew that wasn't true. The heat came from within.

Callahan turned back. "Yes. They're calling it a copy-cat killing."

"But you aren't."

She almost smiled. "No."

"And do they believe it?"

"They want to." There was no trace of a smile now. "Don't enjoy fucking with me, Obler."

"I don't. Not for a second."

"Then don't fuck with me anyway. You can change what's going on, and I mean all the way, so talk to me. Otherwise, go back to your safe, secure, ethical practice."

I lowered my head, almost as if I'd been hit in the stomach. Safe? Secure? No, that didn't describe the way I felt about my children or Rachel or myself. Ethical? Then I wouldn't be here, wondering if I could bring myself to reveal what could destroy my patient and profession.

I said, "What happened yesterday, I think that was the Slasher's work."

She nodded. "I do too."

"But there were differences. An older victim being the main one. This could be the beginning of a whole new phase of murders. He has transferred his hatred and power over others to older victims who represent, in a way, his father."

She leaned forward. "You know this?"

"I . . . suspect it."

Callahan shook her head and reached for a cigarette, tapping it against the desktop and staring at it longingly. "That's not enough. Can you give him to me?"

We locked eyes. This was the moment when I could change everything. In some ways, desperately wanting something from each other, she and I were more intimate than anything I had experienced before. The glittering eyes bore into mine.

Finally, I said, "Let me see the brass."

She suddenly stood up, thrusting the chair out from under her. Her legs, protruding from a short light tan skirt, were shaking, as was the finger that pointed to the door.

"I'll take you down the hall."

I went towards it, feeling confused and not the least bit justified. That deep core of idealism within me throbbed, but it offered no comfort or direction right now. We walked down the corridor to her superior's office. The door was open. A thin, but imposing man sat behind a massive mahogany desk.

"Lt. Joe Villaney," Callahan said, "This is Dr. Martin Obler; he wants to tell you something about the Slasher case."

"Yes?" he drew out the word.

I took a deep breath. "Sven Jorgansen didn't commit the crimes."

"No," he replied in a flat monotone.

"No. I'm almost certain one of my patients did."

His eyebrows shot up. "Then why didn't you come forward before?"

"I didn't want to disclose his name."

"And now you do?"

"No—yes," I said my voice shaking.

Abruptly he rose to his feet. "Well Dr. Obler, I don't want you to waste your time," he paused then went on, "or mine. We have the murderer."

"But" I said.

"There *are* no more buts. The case is closed. I'm sure you, and I know Callahan," he glared at her, "have more important things to do; so I won't hold you up any longer. I do thank you for coming Dr. Obler."

Trying to keep my voice even, I replied from the depth of my being, "Can't anyone help me?"

"You're on your own," he said flatly.

With a gentle push, I was out in the corridor. The door firmly closed behind me. There was nothing more to do. I had to handle Devon myself.

Rachel was feeling better, but she was still vulnerable and knew it. Fear would never go away—and would no doubt have a debilitating effect on our relationship—as long as the animal hunted. And there were other victims out there: the next one might already be in the Slasher's sights.

Every free moment I had I cracked the books with a fervor I hadn't had since graduate days. The university library had as much or more material related to psychopathology than any place in the country. I checked out every book I could carry and explained to the overwhelmed librarian I was preparing an important paper. Whenever my eyes blurred or crossed I rubbed them furiously, and made a mental note to visit an optometrist when this was all over.

I was looking for precedents—ironically, in the same
way that Devon did at his law job. First, there was material
on personality disorders and then psychopaths to review.
Then there was material on serial killers. And material on
the managed care of psychopathic serial killers.

I read textbooks, case histories, papers delivered at
symposiums, transcripts of panel discussions, even the
donated notes of professors at the university. (Another
irony was coming across some notes jotted by
Pomerantz, who had been too happy to hand the ball off
to me.) I stared at papers, microfilm and microfiche, and sent
out requests through the Internet. Some of the responses
were useful. Others were from individuals whom I suspected
one day would give Devon a run for his money.

My plan was to exhaust every possible avenue available
in the field, weed out the failures, and examine thoroughly the
claims of success, until I could narrow down the methods that
I felt had potential with Devon. I became so immersed that I
believed I would either find the answer or become a psychopath myself.

There was *A Clockwork Orange* approach, which had
been publicized in Kubrick's film where bad behavior and
impulses were painfully punished by machines. Devon, of
course, would never subject himself to such treatment. There
were a wide variety of drug therapies. Ditto. More recently,
the treatment of chemical castration was gaining favor. There
were two problems with this: again, Devon would resist, and
the chemical attacked the libido. Sex was an important part
of Devon's behavior, even though the root of his psychopathy went well beyond that.

A very interesting theory was that if the subject can

be given a very real and certain threat of punishment, he is able to restrain himself from engaging in behavior that will result in that punishment. But the jury was still out on this one because enough research hadn't been done and, understandably, there were few professionals in the field willing to go on record as being successful punishers; this was contradictory to the goals of therapy. Plus, there was plenty of evidence that the threat of life in prison, even capital punishment, doesn't deter some people from committing new crimes.

There was something to this, though. One of the harshest consequences of being in prison was losing control to those who ran the prison. And Devon was very much into power and control.

Between my research and my sessions with Devon, I used everything I learned to free him of his homicidal urges. When I came home exhausted, Rachel tiptoed around me, concerned and a bit scared. I was bent to the task to such an extent that I could hardly talk and my eyes stared hard wherever directed. I felt like a basketball player preparing for a playoff game. This playoff was life or death.

One night, after I fell into bed, Rachel asked, "How long can you keep this up?"

Though already half asleep I replied, "To what are you referring, my love?"

She hit me with a pillow. "I'm talking about your search. I look at you, and I think you've hit a wall."

"You might be right."

I replaced the pillow under her head and drew the covers up over her. Rachel had been shivering at night ever since the subway incident.

"But I've got to keep going," I said. "It's the only way I know. Not very dramatic or sexy, but it's the best I can do."

"Then that's the best that can be done." And, thinking I was about to fall asleep, she kissed me and turned over, switching off the light.

I desperately wanted to sleep, of course, but couldn't. With a pillow folded in half under my head I stared at the ceiling, slightly illuminated by light from the street fighting with the shadows for space.

I could not cure Devon or manage him as things were, but perhaps I could redirect him. If the object of his fixation could be shifted, perhaps to a goal that didn't involve violence or murder, then Devon could live a semi-normal life, perhaps. There was someone I wanted to discuss my theory with, my old professor, Lydia Forsythe.

No doubt it was my mind allowing for a way out of the dilemma. At least it relaxed me enough for sleep. And it was the soundest sleep I'd had in a long time.

I got up feeling better, Rachel was still asleep, this time on her back. She looked so lovely, her lips parted, a sprig of dark hair across one eye. I got up slowly and quietly padded into the kitchen. Light was visible out the window. The days were getting longer.

I opened the door to my apartment looking for the newspaper. But it was still too early: the paper wasn't there yet. What I did find was a broken glass soda bottle. Maybe it was my imagination, but the pieces glittered.

Chapter 23

Narrow Opening

I made three reservations on three different airlines and was taking the third one, a flight that left from LaGuardia at 7 A.M. Perhaps I was overdoing it, but I didn't want to leave anything to chance.

Feeling like characters in a Cold War spy story, Rachel and I switched cabs twice on the way to Grand Central Station, then took the #7 train to Penn Station, then walked briskly to the Port Authority Terminal, glancing over our shoulders the whole way. Rachel was spending the night with her parents; her bus left at 9 P.M. We had a short but sweet parting. She kissed me, her eyes wet, lips quivering.

"Be careful," she whispered. "Please."

"I will."

"Call me?"

"Yes."

She accepted that. We both knew that our future depended on what happened between Devon and me. Rachel got on the bus. I stood by the terminal doorway, surrounded by clouds of exhaust fumes, and watched carefully everyone else who got on. Then as the bus pulled out there was a quick glimpse of her at one window, waving.

I took a cab back to my apartment building and went directly upstairs and threw on all the lights. If Devon was watching he might wonder why I was alone, maybe assume with all the lights I was expecting Rachel shortly. If he had any inkling that Rachel had left it was too late. The Greyhound's first stop wasn't until Wilkes Barre.

Every ten minutes I switched off another light, until just one was left on and the television set, the sound turned a little higher than normal.

Now it was my turn for a disguise, and I was lucky again that it was a cold, clear but moonless night. I grabbed from the back of my closet an oversized sweatshirt that I never wore because it was too big. After putting it on I stuffed the inside with bath towels. Then I tugged on a Nets cap that a well-intentioned but apparently inattentive student had given me. Devon was smart enough to notice such a detail. When I left the apartment I looked a bit taller but mostly a lot heavier, and otherwise my features were covered.

I had arranged for a cab to be outside the building at midnight. It idled out front as I emerged. I limped and shuffled to it like an old man. No one else could be seen on the street. The driver, a young Hispanic man, stared at me, then somewhat nervously muttered, "You for airport?"

"Fast," I said, my voice somewhat muffled. "How long does it usually take?"

He shrugged. "Forty minutes."

"Make it in less than thirty and you get an extra fifty."

He shifted and took off. I looked out the back window until turning the corner on two wheels sent me sprawling.

He earned the fifty dollars. I lurched into the terminal, my stomach queasy from the ride and sweating from the extra clothing. I probably looked like a large terrorist but no one gave me a second glance. I tossed the towels into the garbage and sat in the waiting area of an airline I wasn't taking.

At 1 A.M. the first flight to Charlotte left. With the cap pulled low over my face I dozed off and on. At 4 A.M. the second flight left. I couldn't risk falling into a deep sleep so I bought a cup of coffee from a machine—as I'd hoped it was like sludge, filled with caffeine. I walked to the airline waiting room, standing just outside of it against a wall, I could observe who came in and out.

By 6:55 my legs and shoulders ached, the inside of my mouth tasted like an oily rag, and my eyes burned. Hoping I was the last passenger I hurried up to the counter and checked in. "Any luggage?" the young male attendant asked.

"No. Just me. Day trip."

"Good, because you've got only a minute. That way," he said, pointing down a carpeted corridor.

I hustled down it, getting dizzy from spinning around twice to look behind. Only moments after I stepped into the plane, the door closed. The next flight wouldn't leave until 10 A.M. I went up and down the aisle scanning the faces, no doubt a nuisance, until a stewardess gently but firmly directed me to a seat.

I wasn't fond of flying, so it helped that this flight left close to on time and it was a smooth trip. The day before I had sent a fax and received a reply, so Dr. Lydia Forsythe should be waiting for me.

Though already exhausted, I couldn't sleep. I sat on the side of the plane facing the sun, and it was a bright, clear day. But mostly I stayed awake thinking about what I was about to do . . . if Lydia agreed it stood a chance.

Retired for five years, Dr. Forsythe was still a legend at the university, where she had taught for over thirty years. She had been a nationally recognized expert in the field of psychopathology. It was often remarked in articles about her that she was one of the first and was probably the foremost female in this field. All of her colleagues and students realized she was indeed one of the best whatever the gender. I had been one of her students and then she had been a supervisor in some of my post-graduate work.

Even at seventy-five her keen intelligence, work habits, energy, accomplishments, and instinct had been the envy of colleagues anywhere and the university faculty. Then, abruptly, saying that she had "done my bit, now it's your turn," she had retired and moved south. But it didn't seem like she had given up on campus life completely because her house was just minutes from the University of North Carolina.

At her retirement party she stated that she wanted "to see a concert or basketball game from time to time, and not think about nuts." Lydia was salty, direct, fun-loving, and independent. She'd never married, yet because of so many students it was like she had thousands of children.

Some of them had been favorite sons and daughters— like me. We had kept in touch, by phone, fax, and e-mail. I didn't know if I'd ever see her again. Now I was, in circumstances I never would have imagined.

Stepping down from the plane onto the tarmac of the small, sunlit airfield I spotted her, waving a handkerchief by the gate. Lydia looked exactly the same: rail-thin, tall, well-lined face, long grey hair, wearing a flower-print dress thrown on a minute before leaving home, brown sandals wrapped around thick white socks, and a wide-brimmed straw hat. She had always reminded me of an actress from years ago, and suddenly I thought of her name: Jo Van Fleet. Adding to the similarity was her craggy smoker's voice.

"Martin, what a nice surprise!" she barked as I approached. "What did they do up there, kick you out?"

"Not yet. Soon."

We embraced. Her bones felt fragile yet inner strength emanated from her. Her piercing, hazel eyes danced when she looked at me. "I'm so glad you're visiting." Then her smile faded. "But I sense this is business, huh."

"You're as wise as ever, Lydia."

Her laugh evolved into a cough. When she regained her breath she said, "I remember a skinny little nervous student who could barely address me as Dr. Forsythe."

"If I'm more confident and forward now, that's thanks to you."

"C'mon, my porch beckons."

She drove a red station wagon that was at least a decade old, though the odometer read less than 30,000 miles. We left the airport and turned onto a highway that curved around the university campus. The tall brick and stone buildings appeared to be very old. I could see some students lying on benches, basking in the sun.

Spring showed in abundance here; it was the kind of day New Yorkers were dreaming about. The sun appeared large in a pure blue sky and mild air streamed into our open windows. After we turned off the highway and took increasingly narrow roads I saw some green leaves protruding from branches and on bushes small clumps of white and yellow flowers. It was like I'd suddenly hurtled forward in time. I wished that this were true, and everything had been resolved.

During the drive we talked about trivial things, former students and changes to the campus, retirements of former colleagues, and a bit about my career, which she had been following in the professional journals and through contact with professors. While we talked she smoked three cigarettes, casually flicking each butt out the window.

"Is it my imagination, or do I remember that you were told to stop smoking?" I said. "Something about heart disease, as I recall."

"Yep, still got it. And I'm seventy-five. Go figure."

"Well, that's just it . . ."

"You come down to lecture me, I'll let you off here, let the raccoons eat you." She laughed, then lit another unfiltered cigarette. "I could die tomorrow. Or now, while I'm driving, take you with me. Or live to be a hundred. Every day is a blessing, Martin, and I live it with anticipation."

I didn't want to point it out, but it was kind of amusing the new, slightly southern lilt in her voice. Lydia had gone southern on us for sure. It seemed comforting in a way, but maybe I was thinking about myself and leaving troubles behind.

Lydia's house was much older than she was, maybe twice as much, a two-story building painted white with green shutters and a screened-in porch across one side. There was a sloping-down green lawn in front and woods bordered the other sides. The trees were half-filled with green leaves. When I got out of the car I removed my coat but still felt warm.

"You sit down there, and I'll get us a cool drink," she said, pointing to the porch. "Maybe a sandwich too, for all your troubles."

"What troubles?"

"Oh, you're here to see how *I'm* doing, is that it?" She laughed, her eyes twinkling, and went into the house.

I sat in a cushioned, white wicker chair on the porch. Flies buzzed against the screen. Birds chirped in nearby trees. This was a different world. I could see myself throwing everything else aside and moving down here with Rachel. No, that wouldn't work, I'd miss my children too much. And I had plenty of unfinished business. Still, it was nice to imagine sitting on a porch, looking out at green grass and reawakening woods beyond, sipping a mint julep and letting a much more disturbing world go by—one that included serial killers.

Lydia emerged holding a tray, and on it were tall glasses already lined with condensation. She pushed one into my hand, and I sniffed it. "Mint julep?" I said. "Lydia, it's not even noon."

"Let's forget the 'not even' part."

She sat in the chair next to me and we clinked glasses. "To being good to others and ourselves," she said.

The cold strong drink and the mint coursed down, then flowed up and around. After one sip I set it down, knowing that after the night I'd been through it wouldn't take much to have me slumped down and snoring.

"So, Lydia, how are you doing?" I asked.

Her eyes fixed on me as she lit a cigarette. "I'm flattered you thought of me, Martin," she rasped. "But you're not
here to pass the time of day."

"I did want to see you."

"Accepted. Now, out with it. You look like the dog ate
your dissertation. What's wrong?"

"A patient is at stake here. Can we go back to being
grad student and supervisor? That's the only way that I can
ethically . . ."

"You always were a stickler for ethics. But here we can
do whatever we want." Then she laughed, smoke billowing
above her head. "Does it really matter? What you tell me I'll
take to my grave." She pointed off to one side. "It's waiting
there for me. I'd appreciate carrying some luggage into it."

So I told her. I had thought of trying my plan on Lydia
because of who she was and how smart she was and the
strong feeling in our former relationship, but also because
now she was hundreds of miles away and I hoped to feel
some distance. . . and safety. Also, after carrying the burden
of confidentiality for months, I could conceivably talk to her
as a supervisor.

Of course, I had to start at the beginning about
Devon, and I did. Her only comment was early on, a quick
"Pomerantz is still the cowardly asshole I remember," otherwise she listened, lighting cigarettes and taking short sips of
her drink and gazing at me intently.

When I finished it was my turn to gaze at her, hoping
for a pearl of wisdom, but instead she said, "I never got you
that sandwich."

"At the moment, Lydia, I'm not particularly hungry."

"Or thirsty, it seems. Give me yours."

I handed her the wet glass. "I think I have a way to resolve this."

"That's surprising."

"Why, because you don't think I can?"

She laughed, then applied her lighter to another cigarette. "Don't play the ego-bruised student with me. I understand what you're up against. Even if the police had listened, I don't think you would have gone ahead. Confidentiality is sacred. The health of your patient is your top priority. And," she smiled, showing short yellow teeth, "even a psychopath should have someone to trust."

"So there is no way out?"

She ground the half-smoked cigarette under one brown sandal. "I didn't say that. Or I'm getting senile and don't remember that I did."

"Lydia, help me."

It was a sincere request, and she put a small, wrinkled hand on my arm. "What's your idea, Martin?"

I prefaced discussing it by telling her the research, which of course she knew of, I had done. But as I pulled some threads together her gaze grew sharper as though imagining the journey through undiscovered country that I was suggesting.

"Using fear," I said, "that I will turn him in because I choose to to save lives. Survival, that only because of me can he escape a fate of abuse and possibly death in a prison system that will target him—if the cops don't do him first. Power, in that he will be totally without it if I turn him over and by changing he can keep and redirect it. And the opportunist in him has to see there is another way to go that offers rewards with reduced risk."

I went on to elaborate on these tactics and how I

intended to employ them. I summed up by saying, "One thing won't work by itself, but I want to. . ."

"Do you think it will work?"

"I don't know."

Her eyes stared into mine. "Do you, Martin?"

"I think so, but . . ." Then I told her of his stalking Rachel.

She nodded and lit another cigarette. "Even so, you have no other choice."

"I don't?" I replied, wishing I still had the drink, which Lydia had almost finished.

"Of course not," she said, smoke streaming past my face. She held the cigarette vertical. "If you had turned the maniac over to the cops, even for the very best reasons, you would have gone against everything that you believe in and what is the ideal in our field, the health and welfare of a patient we are sworn to help, from Freud to today."

She held up her glass. "And if you keep trying to work with him to unlock the door to his dementia all the while that you pursue this Holy Grail, more people die." She put down the glass and dragged on the cigarette. "Martin, do you know why I retired?"

"Because you're old and senile, have heart disease, smoke too much, and prefer to sip mint juleps on your southern porch?"

"Aside from that."

"You couldn't stand students like me anymore?"

"That's true too. But the biggest reason was I sincerely believed, and I still believe, that I couldn't keep up with the sickest-fuck cases that were coming down the pike. These monsters do things that I couldn't objectively deal with any-more. Yes, maybe it's me. But I also think that we *do* have a new generation of psychopath and they are killing faster than we can keep up. I saw the signs, and I bailed out. I did mine, now it's up to somebody else." She blew out smoke. "Like you."

"But here I am asking you for guidance."

"Keep on, Martin. You have to. No other options are practical or ethical. When I started out they were still using shock therapy, burn the brain. We know that ultimately doesn't work or turns people into tomatoes. You've come up with a different kind of shock therapy."

Lydia drained the rest of her drink, dropped the cigarette on the porch floor and squashed it, and gazed at me. "Take a chance on a final encounter, Martin. Do it or your career is finished."

"I'm not thinking about my career . . ."

"If you're successful you'll be heralded from one coast to the other, one continent to . . ."

"Damn it, Dr. Forsythe, I don't give a flying fuck about that now, I just don't want anyone else to die!"

For a few moments we locked eyes, and I was as angry as I've ever been, feeling cornered and betrayed and misun-derstood. It was startling when Lydia threw her head back and laughed, which eventually turned into a coughing fit.

"Dr. Forsythe, eh?" she wheezed. "You reverted, Martin. I won, didn't I?"

"What do you mean?"

The wrinkles of her face deepened, as did her hold on my arm. "That's what he wants, this Devon, to win. He's got you; he can do what he wants indefinitely, and he knows that." She lit another cigarette and waved away the smoke. "Martin, to do what you have to do, you can't remain trapped in a monster's cage."

"But I have to be in there with him."

"Yes, but at the crucial moment, step out and close the door. And lock it behind you."

I sat back in the chair, rubbing my face, which was wet with sweat. "I don't know if I can do that."

"Yes, you can. *You* can. I saw it long ago it's in you. What I don't know is something else."

I wasn't sure if I wanted to hear her answer, but I had to ask. "What else?"

"You have to risk everything and mean it." She leaned forward, and a sudden breeze blew smoke away from her set, wrinkled face. "Be as determined and ferocious as the monster. Don't meet him halfway. That's not enough. Flick the whip and force him back into the cage. Make him *want* to stay there."

Remembering my dream, I wondered, "What if I create a different monster?"

"How so?"

"He veers off one path onto another. I've created another killing field, it's just in a different area."

"I'll get you another drink."

"What?"

She had started to stand up, and yanking on the hand that had held my arm, I tugged her back down. She looked at me and slowly shook her head.

"Martin, you know you cannot control that. You *know* that. Do the best you can with what you have."

She stood up and stretched, the dress clinging to her thin body, smoke seemed to come from the top of her grey head. "Leave now," she said.

"It's nice here."

"It is. But you've got to go back. I see it in your eyes . . . unfinished business, right?"

"Yes."

She drove me back to the airport, no more erratically after two drinks than when we had come. There was a flight to New York leaving in a half-hour.

"I won't wait to say goodbye," Lydia said. "I don't have that much time to spare."

I held her, the bones feeling even more brittle. "I think you're right," I said.

"Not me."

"Okay, maybe I am, and I've got to try it."

"I know you will." Then she closed her eyes for a few seconds, and when she opened them she said, "Stay here, Martin, if you want. Bring Renee, Rhonda . . ."

"Rachel."

"Whoever. Don't go back. Let it go. You did what you could. Just be here away from the monster."

Feeling the warm sun on my shoulders and smelling the soft breeze the scent of newborn leaves and flowers, and knowing that my old teacher's offer was real, I was sorely tempted. How nice it would be to turn my back on city and especially Devon.

But I knew that if he wanted to he could find me here. He would be able to roam at will. And if it wasn't him, it would be someone else, or others, who would be loose to prey, that new generation of psychopathic killers. Maybe I did have the key to the cage . . . I would never know that if I didn't go back.

And ultimately, whatever compromises I could accept, I couldn't accept one with myself.

"Thank you," I said, hugging her again. "But I'm on my way."

"I pray it's a safe one."

The flight was announced over the terminal speaker. We stepped away from each other. We looked into each other's eyes and knew it could be the last time we would see each other—her with her health problems as well as age and me with the goal I had set.

As I stepped into the plane, that narrow doorway represented the little chance I had. I didn't look back.

Chapter 24

Another
Sudden Death

I picked Rachel up at the Port Authority. Our reunion was blissful and I was able to stop thinking of Devon that night, until the next morning. After seeing Rachel off to work—she was now taking cabs to and from the office—I stayed in the apartment to read the newspapers' first editions.

The murder of Charise O'Day was not the most prominent news: after all, it was days old. Hers was just one more killing, and of a prostitute at that, another social misfit. Bigger stories had supplanted it: a child kidnapped in Queens, a teachers union demonstration in upper Manhattan, and a feud between the mayor and the governor over welfare cuts. In the three dailies there were small articles; two had little information.

Bridget Leary's article was more detailed; still, she seemed to be holding back something.

Downtown Murder Puzzles Police
by Bridget Leary

The death of Charise O'Day, 38, early Tuesday
morning remains a mystery to police and to
neighbors on University Place.

Residents were shocked by the violent murder
and concerned that police do not have a suspect.
O'Day was stabbed about two dozen times at
approximately 2:00 A.M. The two-bedroom apartment was awash in blood, impressing even the most
taciturn of cops.

"This woman was cut up real bad," said Detective
Jack Hutton, who is leading the investigation.
"Whoever did this was very, very angry. Something
went wrong, and Ms. O'Day didn't stand
a chance."

Police say that at present they will focus on
evidence in the apartment where the murder took
place and on questioning frightened neighbors, in
addition to friends and acquaintances of the victim.
O'Day was well-known in the community, and one
police source speculated that the victim may have
quarreled with a former lover.

The man, whom police are seeking for
questioning, is not a suspect at this time, Detective
Hutton said. He emphasized that this murder is not
connected to the Soda Pop Slasher homicides. Sven
Jorgansen, who has been charged with those serial
killings, remains in police custody, awaiting a
hearing on his ability to stand trial.

It didn't surprise me, after having tried to talk to the police, nor did it surprise Callahan, that the officials were quick to discount the Soda Pop Slasher connection. At the least it would be embarrassing to admit that perhaps the wrong man was behind bars. Another angle was that if the public believed the Slasher was still out there, had resumed killing, and his pattern was widening, panic would return at an unprecedented level.

I didn't have such reservations. I believed I knew who had killed O'Day. And, as Callahan had said, I was on my own. *Good luck, Obler. What are you going to do about it?*

Before he killed again.

I suggested going out to a festive dinner and Rachel very much wanted to go. "I've got to get my mind off this Devon business," she said. "We can't stay cooped up all the time like prisoners."

"You feel up to it?"

"Yes, I do." She smiled.

I was glad she agreed. Rachel's feeling ready to do more than just be in an office and the apartment was a good sign that she was recovering from the stalking experience. We still had to be careful, we realized, but this seemed like a safe enough exercise—I would take a cab to the restaurant that was two blocks from Rachel's office.

I didn't tell Rachel that I had made two calls. One was to Stella, offering to pay for her and the children to go to Disneyworld for the spring school break. It was the truth that I could now afford such a trip, a luxury that we could only dream about during our first years together. I was less than candid when I said the trip was a good idea to get a dose of

warm weather, good for the kids' health, that they deserved
a big treat after doing so well in school, etc.

Stella knew me well enough to sense what I was
really asking: get out of town for a while. She agreed. After
she told Mark and Selena, they called me back to say thanks,
and express disappointment that I couldn't go along. I was
genuinely disappointed too. The second call was to Devon.
Actually, two calls, one to his office and one to his apartment—keeping my voice neutral and a bit light that I had to
cancel all my appointments because of the pressure of having
to finish a paper I was to deliver at a conference in Chicago.
There was no response from him. The next day, when we
were to meet, I stayed away from my office. I needed to continue studying the recent literature on psychopaths.

And I wasn't ready to encounter Devon yet. One reason was, after his recent stalking, I couldn't trust what I
might say. Another reason was fear. There was no telling
how far he might go, and I didn't want to be alone with him.

That evening I took Rachel to a chic French restaurant
near my office. Rachel looked lovely in a black dress with
white cuffs and was especially animated, relieved at having a
taste of normal life again. I knew the maitre d' Rene who
gave us special attention, and the food was very good.
Wine flowed, and I tried to be jovial. We talked about our
hopes for spring trips we might take. Under other circumstances, it would have been a lovely evening.

But, as always, unfortunately, I couldn't stop thinking
about Devon. Finally, I excused myself. I needed to walk
around outside. "I'm feeling claustrophobic," I explained.

"Sure," Rachel said. "This place is safe enough. Look

at all the people."

I walked to the front door.

"Is anything wrong, Dr. Obler?"

I shook my head and told the maitre d' that I just wanted a breath of fresh air. I stepped outside. The breeze was gentle and, the sky clear, the street was softly lit, creating shadows. I sat on a short brick ledge a few doors down, watching the shapes.

Immediately, I felt like I was being observed, but I didn't care. Let him watch. Devon might be thinking how pressured could I be if I was out to dinner? Fine, let him wonder. I relished the thought of confusing him a bit. What I couldn't figure out was how to stop him.

It was obvious that the therapy I had used with him had failed. Devon remained a man without a conscience, who used people viciously and without remorse to serve his own ends. The only thing that mattered to Devon was himself. And murder. And getting away with it.

And, I had to admit, along the way winning a power struggle with his therapist who by following a straight and ethical path may have enabled Devon to act out his psychopathic dysfunctions. Callahan didn't want to speak to me anymore. Case closed. You're on your own.

So nothing had worked, or at least not in a long-lasting way. It was too simple to say that he was born evil. Previously, I hadn't believed anyone was, including total aberrations and mass murderers like Hitler, Stalin, Idi Amin, and Muammar el-Qadaffi, and recent serial killers like John Wayne Gacy, Ted Bundy, and Jeffrey Dahmer. I had believed that in every case something or a combination of factors had produced a twisted individual who, without the constructive intervention that psychology can provide, progressively became more demented and violent. To me, evil was not a condition at birth, even though we routinely accepted the expression that someone was "born bad."

Devon might well be different, for three reasons. He probably began his life in a family that early on set the stage for his eventual psychotic behavior. Subsequently, there were negative and confusing sexual encounters during childhood. Finally, with his intelligence and physical strength and lack of conscience (but with the ability to manufacture emotions), he gradually both reacted and adapted to an increasingly violent and desensitized society.

Especially in this last crime, he could represent the next generation of psychopaths. He had evolved. Or mutated. That could be one reason why O'Day was murdered, and no one was safe. He was an amorphous killer with an innate ability to keep adapting and changing, to alter his pattern. Devon had broken the bounds of a pattern and now, to some extent, he could create and control new patterns. Perhaps, eventually, he would get to a mental state where there were no boundaries at all. He might be a mind-shifting and, in a sense, a shape-shifting psychopath. A thinking killing machine.

Depressed, I got off the ledge and slowly walked back to the restaurant. Inside, I made my way back to the table, but when I got there it was empty.

I looked around and didn't see Rachel; so I sat down thinking she had gone to the ladies room.

But as the minutes passed I felt more and more anxious when she didn't appear. Finally, I called over the maitre d'. "Rene, do you know what's happened to my lady friend?"

"I'm sorry, Dr. Obler. The strangest thing occurred. A good-looking man with striking blond hair came by while you were gone." Rene looked puzzled. "They seemed to know each other. He only said a few words to the lady and they got up to leave. I asked her if everything was alright and she just nodded."

Rene scratched his head. "Oh, I almost forgot. As they walked away, he called to me, 'Dr. Obler will know what we're about.' A very bizarre comment, don't you think?"

I was in shock. I didn't trust myself to speak.

Chapter 25

Kidnapped

Rachel was gone. Never had I felt so alone. I was past blaming Devon. He was a crazy psychopath. There was only one person responsible. I blamed myself, but there was no time for such recriminations now. I had to get her back before. . . . Oh my God, I couldn't let myself think of that. No, I'd get her before he touched her, laid a finger on her precious head. But how?

Callahan? The police had closed the book. The only way to get Callahan's help was to give her the name she'd tried so hard to extract from me. I had tried to give it to her superiors, and they hadn't listened. I knew Devon's condition better than Callahan did. If the police made one false move or Devon got any inkling they were on to him, he would kill Rachel and probably himself.

I had waited too long to exercise the police option. Now there was no choice. I had to find him myself. I raced to my office building, bounded up the stairs and flung open the door. Maybe he was. . . . It was an idle hope. The office was deserted.

I flipped on some lights and threw open the file cabinet in which my records were kept. Pulling out the important notes, I photocopied the pages. I knew where I was going to put them. Finally I grasped Devon's file and rushed to my desk. With shaking hands, I searched the huge folder for his new address. "Damn," I cried out after scouring the pages, "I forgot to write it down." The only one there was his old dorm address at the university and his new telephone number. He'd always asked for and paid his bills in person. I didn't have the canceled checks because his bank automatically returned them to him, and I couldn't remember the name of the bank on which they were drawn. Another dead end. My mind rummaged for ideas.

The law firm he worked at—he had said their name in one of our sessions. I began slowly reading through all my copious notes. Twice the phone rang. It was other patients, but I couldn't take the time to find out what fears were frightening them this night. Hours passed. It was taking an eternity and my anxiety was growing. Then I found the name. I realized they would be closed now. I looked out the window. The darkness was no longer a black shroud. The edges of the sky were gray. My watch read 5:30 A.M. Morning had arrived.

Morning. The word pealed like a tolling bell, and that's when I remembered. Stella and the children were leaving for Florida at seven. Devon. I knew how his mind worked. He would grab them too. Then he would have all the cards and Stella, the children, Rachel, and I would all be at his mercy. I phoned Stella. No answer.

Running downstairs, I searched for a cab on the

deserted streets, running first down one block and then another. Finally I saw one parked on the side of the road, his "Off Duty" light blinking. I ran over. "Please. This is an emergency. I'm a doctor." *Half truth.*

"Where to, Doc?"

"Kennedy Airport."

"You've got it," he promised. He whammed down the flag on the meter and took off. He knew how to fly. He didn't want chitchat. Neither did I. When we got to Kennedy, I handed him a fifty. "There's two more just like this one if you wait."

"Wish I could, Doc, but I have a union meeting. We're voting whether to strike. Anyway, at this hour there are plenty of cabs impatient for a passenger; you won't have any trouble getting one."

I hoped he was right. I rushed into the terminal, checked the departure board, and saw that their plane was scheduled to leave on time. I waited anxiously near the gate.

It was still too early to phone Devon's law office and I knew when I did I would still have to be very careful not to arouse suspicion. If I was right, Devon wouldn't skip work today. The job figured in his future plans; it meant too much to him. He would stash Rachel somewhere. I tried to figure out the place.

The loudspeaker announced the departure of Stella and the children's flight. A large crowd of passengers moved toward the gate. Stella and the children were among them.

Then, my heart almost stopping, I saw Devon sauntering into the line. Just as he was about to make his move I yelled, "Mark! Selena! This way!" I ran to them and scooped the kids up in my arms.

"Martin," Stella said, her face pleased. "This is a surprise. I didn't expect to see you here."

"Daddy." "Daddy," Mark and Selena squealed. "Come with us."

Suddenly from somewhere nearby I heard familiar laughter escalating into inhuman howling. I knew who it was.

"What's that?" Stella asked, shuddering.

"Just some nut," I said, shepherding her and the children to the baggage claim, explaining that there had been a sudden change of plans They were disappointed, but saw how upset I was.

Outside, I saw that the cabbie who had brought me had been correct. There was no line of people waiting and plenty of cabs were available at this time of the morning. I easily got one. On the way to their apartment, I cautioned Stella, "Keep the kids home with you today. Don't go out and don't let them out of your sight."

"What's wrong?" Stella asked, thoroughly frightened.

"Please don't ask any more questions. Just do as I say and everything will be all right."

Telling the cab to wait when we got to their building, I hustled them upstairs. "Stella, put the chains on all the doors and don't let anyone in. If anyone you don't recognize comes, call the police."

Handing the doorman a twenty and promising him more, I asked him to watch their apartment. Then I told the cab driver, "Take me to the North American Bank on 11th Street." I rushed in and deposited my papers in the vault. I marked the envelope: to be given to the police on my death. They might not have chosen to see them before, but if something happened to me I knew they would. Then I got back in the cab and directed the driver to my office. The grandfather clock was chiming 9 A.M. when I entered.

Devon's office might be open now. I called using Dr. Pomerantz's name.

"Yes, Mr. Cardou is in," the receptionist said, "but he'll be in conference most of the day and he has to go upstate on a family emergency late this afternoon. Can someone else help you?"

"No, it isn't important. I'll call back in a day or two."

I went back to my file. Devon's family. He saw them rarely. I scanned the original information Pomerantz had given me. No, I only had his parents' home number and Mrs. Cardou might not help me. His father's business number, that's what I needed. I called Pomerantz's office. Luckily the file had not yet been moved to storage. The secretary gave me Devon's father's name and office number.

I dialed it and the secretary put me right through. "This is Dr. Obler." I explained who I was. "I need to get in touch with Devon and I was told by the secretary at his law office that he's headed upstate on a family emergency."

"Family emergency!" I heard the chortling at the other end of the phone line. "Well, Devon may have some of the old man's blood after all. He called me late last night to find out where we keep the hide-a-key at our cottage upstate. I told him the electricity was off, but he said he didn't care. He's got some hot number he wants to be alone with."

Rage like bitter bile filled me. I choked it down. "I really need to get these papers to him, Mr. Cardou. Could you tell me where the cottage is located?"

"Well," he explained, "it's in Rhinebeck, but I don't think any courier service will deliver to the address."

"Don't worry. I'll send a grad student. They do anything one of their committee heads tells them to." I paused.

"Mr. Cardou, these papers are about a scholarship for Devon. I'd like it to be a surprise."

"It will be our secret," he promised.

As soon as the call was over, I left the office, not even taking my coat. A block down, I rented a car, got a map, and set out for Rhinebeck.

Never had I driven so fast. I had to get there, get Rachel, and leave before Devon returned. Frightening images and thoughts juxtaposed in my mind over and over as the car sped along. A little more than two hours later I saw the small white hotel in Rhinebeck which held the murder mystery encounters on the weekends. I had toyed with the idea and discussed with Rachel that it might be fun to go to one; now the irony accosted me.

Following Devon's father's precise directions, I was soon at the gray stone cottage. Leaving my car hidden behind some bushes, I quietly tiptoed around the house through the trees searching for another car, making sure Devon hadn't changed his mind and left his office early. No, there was no sign of him. A sigh of relief escaped my throat. I didn't allow myself to dwell on the fact he might already have accomplished his objective.

Quietly, I approached the front door. It was locked. Making my way to the side of the house, I used a stick to jimmy open a window and climbed inside. It was dark and musty. At first, I saw nothing. No footprints in the carpet. No sign anyone had recently been here. My heart fell. Perhaps he'd taken Rachel somewhere else. Walking to the bedroom I slowly opened the door.

Then I saw her. She was lying on the bed bound by chains which were knotted and gagged, her head strapped sideways away from me. I looked in that direction.

There on the night table laying on a white towel was a large glass soda bottle, and as I approached I could see the jagged pieces of another spread out neatly and precisely like surgical instruments.

As I edged closer, I saw Rachel's eyes were shut tight. Not wanting to frighten her, I moved to within a few inches of the bed. "It's Martin, Rachel. Don't be afraid. I'm here. Everything will be all right. I'm going to remove the gag and undo the chains. Please don't speak, darling, until we're in the car."

Her eyelids opened and closed twice to indicate she understood. Then silent tears began falling.

As quickly as I could, I undid the chains and got the gag off her. Then I helped her up.

"We have to get out of here quickly," I whispered. She nodded and, my heart pounding, my chest tight with the effort not to hyperventilate, we left the bedroom. I couldn't chance the doors so I led her out of the cottage through the same window I'd come in.

It was not until we were safely in the car that I could breathe normally. And it was not until we were back on the highway that Rachel spoke.

"Martin, he was going to kill me," she said, her voice hoarse. "He's an absolutely crazy animal."

I nodded. "He'll have to turn himself in or I'll kill him myself."

"No!" She put her hand, still bearing red welts from the bonds, on my shoulder. "If you do, he'll have succeeded in destroying you. Everything you've worked so hard to achieve. He told me that's what he wants, to ruin you, our future. You'll be known as the psychologist who turned a patient in, despite his vows. No one would want you to treat them. They'd be afraid. A doctor they can't trust. He laughed that eerie way as he explained to me that he had you whichever way you turned. No, I won't let you. There has to be another way."

I shook my head. "I thought so once but now...."

"There has to be," she repeated. "Tell me."

I nodded and explained to her the theory I'd formed with the help of Lydia and my reading. "I think it might work but he's become too dangerous to try."

"You have to," she said decisively.

There was a rest area on the road. I pulled over and put my arm around her.

"Even if I were willing, How can I expose you or the children to him after today?"

"The children," she said, her eyes filled with fear again. "When he made me leave the restaurant he said he had them and was going to kill them if I made any trouble. I was afraid to scream or struggle."

"Don't worry. They're safe," I assured her.

"Thank God," Rachel murmured.

"But, whatever I do, I can't let everyone I love suffer. Devon started a war last night. I will finish it."

Chapter 26

Confrontation

He would arrive in a few minutes. I sat at the large wooden desk in my office, the chair tilted back, my feet up on the desk. I was far from being as relaxed as this pose implied. I was seething. I had left a message on Devon's tape warning him to meet me here or suffer the consequences. There was an eerie silence in my office, broken only by the slow yet incessant swinging of the tall clock's pendulum. Out the window dun colored clouds lumbered across the sky, blotting out what remained of the morning light. Forecasters said a rain storm was moving in.

"Be as determined and ferocious as the monster," Lydia had said. I was about to find out if I could be as determined and ferocious, even if it cost me my life. The time had come to put all my research into practice, to be harsh and unyielding with Devon, to lay it on the line, to scare the hell out of him and hope it would force a change.

The bell rang. Slowly, I swung my legs down and under the desk, placing both my hands on top of it. Then I buzzed Devon in.

He sat down across the desk from me, placing one leg over the other, brushing back his blond hair, which appeared shorter. "I missed you," he said. "I spent yesterday wondering how you found her." He appeared quite pleased with himself. Then he looked over at me. "You having a bad day, Doc?" He grinned. I pressed my hands hard into the desk top. I thought I might strangle him.

"You've followed me, made me feel threatened," I told him. "I could probably live with that, this is a profession with risks. But when you stalked and kidnapped Rachel you crossed the final line. See, I love her, Devon. That's an emotion you will never experience, and so you don't realize how protective that makes me feel, how much I want to kill you."

"Hey, listen, keep your shirt on." His fingers twitched, and when I said "kill" he blinked rapidly. "Just fooling around, Marty, okay? That cottage escapade? Bet it never occurred to you that it was like a scene from Hitchcock's film *Spellbound*."

"You crazy fuck, this isn't a movie. And what scene did you think you were playing when you stalked my children, frightening them, threatening them?" I lowered my voice to barely a whisper. "Would you really kill Rachel, Devon? Would you kill my children?"

"You're having a bad morning."

"Would you kill me, Devon?"

"No. If I did that. . . ."

Speaking evenly, I said, "You're going to have to."

"What?" His eyes were wide and his shoulders trembled. He started to rise. "You *are* having a bad day, Doc.

Maybe I should come back next week."

"Stay where you are," I ordered. "The only way you can leave here is to kill me right now, right here."

The clock pendulum swung back and forth, but this time its rhythmic ticking didn't mirror my heart, which I thought had stopped beating. Devon shifted in the chair, looking around the room, fingers forming fists.

"What, is this place wired? Somebody listening?" he asked, his voice suddenly high and nervous. "Or do you have cops right outside? I go for you, they burst in, gotcha."

"It's just you and me here, Devon. And one way or the other, this is it. You or me."

"Look, calm down, all right? So I was a bad boy. I'll stop. Okay?"

"Stop what?"

"You know, bothering your lady friend. Them."

"That's not enough, Devon."

I was playing the power card. Devon wasn't in control anymore. I was. And the prospect of killing me, the transferred father figure, was making him short-circuit. I leaned forward and gazed steadily into his eyes. They continued to blink, momentarily covering large pupils. His entire body started to shake and beads of sweat formed on his forehead.

"Should I get you a bottle, Devon?"

"Hey, okay, cut the crap. What is it you really want? Let's work something out."

"I want you to suffer. Can't feel anything, you fucked-up psycho? You'll feel lots of pain, humiliation, and fear. That's what's going to happen."

"Oh, it is, huh?" He tried bravado, but it was weak. "And how is that?"

"I'm going to the police. With all my notes. And I'll tell them everything. Bye-bye, Devon. Like movies? How about *The Maltese Falcon*: you're taking the fall. And you earned it, you weak piece of shit. And if you think you can stop me by killing me think again. I've made duplicates of all my notes, been to the bank and put them in my safety deposit box to be given to the police on my death."

He made one more attempt, though the shaking and sweating had increased. "Really." He stood up. "Well, if you live you're going to hell with me, Obler. I know something about your profession, remember? They'll pull your license. You'll be a pariah. Colleagues won't even piss on you if you're on fire. Worried about your bitch mistress and your homely kids, sure. How are you going to support them when you'll be lucky to get a job scraping up piles of horseshit in Central Park?"

He had made a hit. But I was in all the way now. I charged around the desk and stood facing him, grabbing his collar with both hands, bringing his head down low, my eyes boring into his. "I'll tell the newspaper, Devon, juicy tidbits from our sessions. Your short, humiliating life. Frightened so much by your father you pissed in your pants. The mother you couldn't stand, who loves you anyway, you can't escape that. The little brother you probably abused, who survived and no doubt has more genuine courage than you'll ever have. Your leather and sketches and chains. Adds up to very little for such a smart, talented, strong guy, doesn't it?"

"You're way out of line."

"I'm going all the way. Try this scenario, you pathetic bastard. If you're lucky, the cops will kill you. It happens sometimes, you know. Especially with animals like you.

They figure it saves the court time and money, and eliminates the chance you'll get off on a technicality. Resisting arrest, caught in the act, self-defense . . . one's as good as the other. A bullet in the head. Maybe somewhere else, let you die slowly, in agony."

He recoiled, chin quivering.

"That might be doing you a favor," I continued, my voice strangely calm, even to me. "See, the time's going to come when some victim, bigger or smarter than you or just lucky castrates you or shoves a bottle up your ass and breaks it off. You'll be whimpering, experiencing pain you never thought possible, watching your guts spill out in a river of blood. Am I making you hard now, Devon? Are you enjoying this?"

"N-no," he stammered, cowering. "Stop."

"You must want more, you always want more, don't you? *I'm* going to stop you, Devon. Maybe *you* will be unlucky and they'll lock you away; but we've got the death penalty in this state now. Either they'll inject you with a burning substance you'll feel every moment of dying or you'll be strapped in and fried like a hamburger. Sparks will shoot out of your ears. You'll feel the most helpless, exquisite pain."

"Please. . . ."

"And even if you don't die, fuckers like you don't last long in captivity. Gacy and Dahmer, totally twisted like you, were killed in prison. The chair for Bundy. You'll be just one more lifeless lump of dung thrown on the prison heap. They will murder *you*, Devon."

"I don't want to die!" he cried, fists pounding his thighs.

"Hey, maybe you don't. Capital punishment would be too easy. See, I'll testify on your behalf. I'll even cry and beg for your life. So you can spend the rest of it in prison. What kind of survival is that, huh?"

He fell back and I pushed him into the chair, whining and writhing. Then I backed up a few inches. Suddenly I saw something change in his eyes—from fear to a look of conniving. He had to save himself. This was the moment. A wave of rain suddenly battered the window. The pendulum kept swinging. I could be dead in a few seconds. Devon started to lean forward. To make this work, Lydia was right, I had to be as determined and ferocious as the monster.

"Yes, you'd better kill me now," I said, almost seductively. "We both know you can. What's one more? Because if you don't kill me, I might kill you."

I bent toward him, and he cringed. "In prison there will be no survival, only pain and humiliation. Seemingly forever. You're a strong young man, you'll live a long time. You'll count the hours, the days, the years, and they won't end. In prison they'll know what you did and what you like . . . and especially what you don't like. They'll cut you up, over and over. Bigger and stronger monsters, some maybe even more sick than you are. And you'll never, ever, get out. Welcome to your new life, Devon."

He was whimpering and shuddering, his arms wrapped around his chest, feet repeatedly scraping the floor. I had reduced him to a frightened, helpless animal—and I felt ill inside. But if I were to succeed, I had to go further. I had to turn him, to redirect his pressures and rage, get him to follow another path. He would not be a homicidal psychopath anymore, but still a dangerous psychopath with safer outlets

for his aggression. I had to turn the monster, have him travel
a different road and if I was lucky, not let him know I was
leading us both back into the cage. After we were both
inside, then I had to quickly step out before it was too late.

"There's a way out, Devon."

"W-what is it?" he sobbed.

"You have to stop killing."

I couldn't tell if he shook his head or the motion was
another involuntary shudder.

"Yes, Devon, because like all animals you must survive. Am I right?"

After a moment, his head nodded up and down.

"That's your top priority. Hold on to that. Now! Think
about that. Tell me: I want to survive."

"I-I want to survive."

"Say I'm the lowest form of disgusting life but I have
a right to survive."

He repeated the phrase, his voice shaking.

"You have a *right* to survive, Devon. Do you accept
that?"

"Yes."

"Do you believe that?"

With a spark of strength in his voice, he responded,
"Yes. Yes, I do."

"Good. You have one chance."

"What is it?"

I stared hard at him. He swallowed and said, "Please
tell me what it is, Dr. Obler."

"Be smart, Devon. I don't care how high your IQ is
and how brilliant you think you are, because you've been
pretty fucking stupid. When you kill you risk being killed or

getting caught. That's not smart. You like power, don't you?"

"What do you mean?"

"The games you play, the games we've played. Cheap victories, Devon. Any asshole can play them. And eventually they lose. You'll lose too."

He wiped his nose. "I'm not a loser."

"Of course not. I saw that the first time we met. But what you've done, the way you tried to manipulate me . . . so disappointing, Devon. You can do better."

"Yes." He sat up. "Yes, I can."

Hoping I could trust my legs, I walked around behind my desk. When I sat down, I was grateful for the stability of the chair.

"What do you want to be, Devon?"

He looked at me then away several times, worried this was a trick. "A lawyer," he finally said.

"Not a killer?"

"No."

"Then what else?"

"I-I'm not sure."

"But not a killer?"

"No."

"You know what will happen to you if you kill?"

He let out a long, slow breath. "Yes."

"You don't want to kill any more."

"No."

"You know what will happen to you."

"Yes."

"Tell me."

"Yes."

"Tell me, Devon."

"No, no, no!" He slipped out of the chair onto his knees, his hands clawing at the desk. "I don't want to kill!" he cried. "I want to live! I have to!"

"Shut up and sit down."

"Help me, Dr. Obler."

"Then do what I say."

The ill feeling inside me intensified. I choked it back. Devon slumped in the chair. His face was covered with red blotches and his lower lip trembled. At any other time I would have felt sorry for him. But this was for keeps.

Almost kindly, I said, "Devon, you must realize now that you have let your violent urges and impulses rule your behavior. Your life has not been your own. First your parents hurt, scared and intimidated you, filling you with rage and contempt. You had no control, you only reacted."

He nodded, leaning forward as if eager to hear more—probably anything was better than my dominating cruelty.

"Then your peers insulted you, filled with jealousy and their own twisted contempt. You reacted to that with aberrant, potentially harmful behavior."

"Yes. Yes, I did. But I. . . ."

"This isn't a conversation, Devon. Shut up unless I ask you something. You are listening to me because I am about to save your wretched life."

"Please."

"And then you crossed a line no one should cross. But you weren't powerful, you were lost. Now you're a weak, feeble little man, still searching. It's so humiliating that you have no control over your impulses, that you think you can't help what you do."

I held his eyes, and they didn't blink. "But you can,"

I said.

"How?"

The question hung in the air. Rain washed against the window, and the sky behind it was as dark as night. This was where I went the distance. I swallowed hard.

"You do what you want."

"But I thought you said. . . ."

"You want to go to law school?"

"Yes."

"You want to be rich and powerful?"

"I think so."

I gazed into his eyes again. "There's a whole new world out there, Devon."

"There is?"

"Don't hunt for scraps, when you can have the whole meal."

"It's there?"

"Do it, Devon."

"It is there."

"For you, Devon."

"Yes, it is."

I wanted to avert my eyes, but I wouldn't let myself. I had to see this through. Devon wasn't looking at me but out the window, and perhaps beyond—through the windswept rain and the swirling dark gray clouds to something else, his undiscovered country, a new and inviting hunting ground.

With my last bit of energy, and resolve, I said, "With a law degree, some experience and your family connections, you can go very far, Devon. Do you see the opportunity?"

"I think so," he said softly, twisting several strands of blond hair.

"Better see it now, Devon, because the alternative is death."

"I do."

"Unlike death, opportunity is a wonderful word, wonderful concept. It's exciting, isn't it?"

"Yes."

"Go for it."

"I think I will."

"You must if you want to survive."

"Yes."

"Keep searching. Seek and ye shall find."

Suddenly his head snapped back, his eyes glaring. "Don't quote the Bible to me."

"All right. But we understand each other now."

"Perfectly."

He stood up, flung out his arms and spread his legs, stretching. The gesture was indeed as if he had found a new source of power and was drawing on it. Once more I was astonished by his resiliency. He simply would not be consumed. Every fire was an opportunity to rise anew from the ashes. I had, I hoped, provided the biggest, most intense flame, and perhaps what would come of it would be a new and different person. Maybe not less dangerous, but for now less lethal.

Finally, Devon looked at me and smiled. "You're right, Dr. Obler."

"About?"

"Everything."

"That remains to be seen." I paused. *"This* is our final session, Devon."

"But. . ." he began.

My stomach lurched again. Part of my plan was to reinforce his new direction, at least for a while longer. I wanted to make sure the lock on the cage remained secure. For a moment, I hesitated, afraid to step out. But I held fast.

"Our last," I said definitively. "Of that I'm quite certain."

"Yes," he said hesitantly. He stood up behind the wooden chair and braced his legs against it.

"You need to go off in a different direction now, to move on."

His face grim, he nodded. "I see."

Trying to keep a sigh out of my voice, I said, "Yes, you have to. You must."

"I must, Dr. Obler."

"Be careful, Devon."

"Thank you."

He gazed at me for a few moments with an expression that was almost genuine gratitude, but I didn't trust it or him. He thrust his arms into his raincoat. The wind outside was still fierce, but it held more air than water. He started for the door.

"Devon," I said, my throat very dry.

"Yes, doctor?" He was at the door.

I walked over to him. He opened the door. But as he tried to step out I held the door firm. Both our hands were on it and for a moment we struggled and our eyes locked. Then he took his hand away.

We were only inches apart. Once more I wondered what I could really do. Could I surprise him right now, and maybe kill him? Part of me still wanted to, thinking about the fear my children and Rachel had experienced. In a way, it would be easier than letting him go. Could I do this instead?

I leaned over and whispered in his ear, "I'm in you and all around you. As long as I live—and you'd better hope that's a long time—remember those papers in my safe deposit box. The exposure and ruin and humiliation they represent. Remember I'll be checking, listening. I am the guardian of the gate, Devon, and I'm watching. . . ."

He blinked. I stepped back out of the cage. And hoped I was locking it behind me.

I released the door. He hurried out. I listened. Devon didn't take the elevator. I heard his footsteps pounding down the stairs, sounding as though he was being chased.

Epilogue

Time has passed, and my career has continued upward. Since my last meeting with Devon, I have become a well-respected psychologist, widely published and a full professor at a leading college. Ironically, the case that would have had the widest impact on the psychology community is the one I could not reveal.

Rachel and I have married. Soon after, Rachel and I adopted a child and we moved out of the city. Our new home is in a suburban community which has pastoral qualities that, growing up in the Brownsville section of Brooklyn, I only dreamed about. When Lydia came, our joy was tinged with sadness, because her namesake had died six months before. Selena and Mark, who have warmed to Rachel, were, at first, curious and hesitant about their new sibling. Then they became her protectors and as she grew, strong friends.

Our life continued, filled with possibilities and the joys as well as the disappointments of a happy family.

Although I didn't obsess about Devon, I discreetly
followed his progress. He did indeed score very high on the
law boards and enrolled in law school in a nearby state,
graduating two years later with honors. I scoured newspapers, television and radio reports for announcements of
crimes that bore his stamp. There were a few murders with
marginal similarities, but in this city that was inevitable, and
the subtle checking I did indicated others were responsible.

Sven Jorgansen, the man who had been accused of the
Soda Pop Slasher crimes, ended up with a good lawyer, with
visions of a high-profile case. The lawyer announced he'd
go for insanity. Of course, the D.A. knew he'd get it.
Jorgansen walked.

One night Kitty Callahan called me at home and we
met. I felt I owed her that. As we sat in a Houston Street coffee shop, the windows frosted just as they had that time we
had met for a drink. She was still tough, attractive, aggressive, seductive, and smart—but the same urgency wasn't
there. She was going through the motions, one last time.

"We never caught him, you know," she said, her
emerald eyes darting around the shop, occasionally lighting
on me. "I think he's still out there."

"He hasn't killed again."

"How do you know?"

I shrugged. "Let's not kid each other. At this late date
we both know I have a special interest in keeping watch.
None of the new crimes of which I've read have matched his
M.O."

She thrust her chin out, then lowered her head,
pushing a stray red curl back, and spoke more to her coffee
cup than to me. "I can't stand that the Soda Pop Slasher

got away with it. I'm beg . . . I'm asking you to tell me."

My heart ached, for her personally and for all the dedicated in-the-trenches cops she represented. But I gritted my teeth and said, "They wouldn't listen then and I can't now."

I stood up. She raised her head and her eyes gazed at me. I had to turn away. "No one else is going to be hurt," I said. "Protection of society—isn't that your job? You did it. You're doing it."

"And did you do yours?"

For a long time after that her question reverberated in my mind. But in my heart of hearts I truly believe that I have done my job. Even if it was in a way neither I nor anyone else could ever have anticipated. I am alone with my decision and my actions.

I continued to follow Devon's progress. After law school, he was hired by a law firm that was bigger and more prominent than the one that had employed him as a clerk. And once on a television newscast I spotted him standing behind a congressional candidate who was making a speech. He had gained some weight and his blond hair was cut very short. The suit he wore was better cut than the candidate's. I almost saw strings going from him to the speaker at the podium.

He was on his way. More than anyone else, I could imagine the impact of his redirected energy, intelligence— and impulses.

Psychopaths cannot tolerate deferring gratification or controlling their rage and hatred. They exude such powerful energy in finding outlets for these needs that other people who are on a lower energy level find them extremely attractive. We often put them in positions of power because of this attraction. These people, who are ruthless and self-serving live out our repressed striving for domination and control.

Devon had the potential, and given certain circumstances and luck, he could indeed be on a par with Hitler, Stalin, Hussein or any other totalitarian figure one could name. All had a remarkable instinct for self-preservation at other people's expense. Their psychopathic vision of personal survival was all that mattered. Other people were merely instruments serving this goal.

Those psychopaths who enter the political arena strive mightily for power and once they have it they devote much of their energy preserving it. When they sense that they are losing power or control is jeopardized, they will annihilate anything or anyone who threatens them It was possible I had channeled Devon's energy in this direction. But not only might I have created a different monster, I would have tossed out the psychologist as healer and replaced him with the psychologist as manipulator.

Time passed. Rachel and I stopped speaking of Devon and, after a while, the intensity of my focus faded, although I still kept track of him.

Then, one night, just a few weeks ago, when I had been up late with Lydia who had the flu and had just gotten her off to sleep while trying not to wake an exhausted Rachel, the phone rang.

Rushing over, I grabbed it.

"Marty, how you doing?"

It was him. An instantly familiar voice. No mistaking

it. Even after all this time, it was as recognizable as my own. Even more so, considering how often I had heard it in my head. The only slight difference was his tone, more brisk and powerfully confident.

"Devon."

"You remember me. Flattering. And reassuring, Doc."

Suddenly I was thrust back to our sessions, the power games, the quick moves to gain advantage. I wasn't about to fall into that trap again, after all this time. "What do you want, Devon?" I asked grimly.

"You're supposed to ask, 'How did you find me? How did you get my number?' Flatter *me*, okay?"

"Consider it done," I said curtly.

"Well, I just wanted to express my best wishes to your family. Actually, both of them. I understand Stella and the kids moved back to Brooklyn. Hey, sometimes you can go home again. How nice. And your life in New Jersey, that's nice too?"

So, the little bastard had been keeping track of me too. I swallowed hard. "It is, thank you."

"Up till now, huh?"

"No, Devon, it still is. And it will be." I took a deep breath. "And yours?"

"It's terrific. You were so fucking right, Obler. It's a whole new world."

"Does it include killing?"

"Oh, you cut me to the quick."

"Nice choice of words."

He chuckled. "Tell me, Doc. Does it drive you crazy that you'll never really know what I did, and to whom?"

"I think about it, yes. Why are you calling?"

"Just wanted to make sure you're all right."

Then I understood. It came to me quickly and clearly: I was a loose end for Devon. He lived in the fast lane, and I was a liability. The bigger he got, the more vulnerable he was. I had lost sight of that, and a lot more, as I let the responsibility fade.

"What do you really want, Devon?"

"Maybe your license, Doc. I have a lot of friends now, powerful ones. More powerful than me. Of course, that's just a matter of time and opportunity." He started to laugh. "I never properly thanked you for what you did, you cruel fuck. Most impressive."

He continued laughing, the sound escalating in a way that was painfully familiar. "But now there's much more I can do, Obler. You'll never know what hit you. I like that. A lot."

"Have you forgotten the papers I keep in the bank?" I asked.

His laughter stopped abruptly. "Oh, relax, Marty. I'm just kidding. No one else could've done what you did. Maybe I'll even steer a few nut job cases your way. You'd be surprised how sick some of these people are here."

"No, I wouldn't." I bit my lip hard. "Devon, why did you call? Bored?"

"A little. And to warn you."

Instantly I thought of Rachel and my children.

"About what?"

"Got you there, eh, Doc? Really though, you know what made the difference? What you did . . . yeah, sure, you got to me. Turned me down another street. I like it. But I keep thinking about those other streets with real dark places.

What made the difference, Marty, was knowing you were watching me. And, oh my dear Doctor, I don't think you're doing that any more."

His voice lowered to a growl. "That makes me fucking angry. I don't like being ignored. Or bored. I might not be able to control myself."

"Devon!"

"In fact, I'm feeling so pissed now that. . . ."

I broke in. "Come off it," I said, a steel edge in my voice.

With some annoyance, he replied, "I'm not used to being interrupted either."

"You must remember something and never forget it."

"What?" he broke in, obviously startled. "What's that?" he asked, his voice cracking.

"I *am* here. Always. Always. I am with *you*. We cannot exist without the other, Devon. *Never* forget that."

For a few seconds there was only low, heavy breathing on the line. I was, in a strange way, sincerely grateful to him for this call. I had begun to drift away, remembering Devon, who he was and what he had done, but gradually forgetting that the cage I had put him in had a door—and he knew where it was.

The sound on the phone changed. Devon began to laugh again, quickly reaching a crescendo now, then changing into an awful, gut-wrenching howl. Suddenly there was a click and silence.

After I hung up, I sat there thinking about that call and what it meant through the night. Then just as the light broke, I knew.

I *was* still guardian of the gate. And I had to remain there. My watch was not over.